Regions, Institutions, and Agrarian Change in European History

*Economics, Cognition, and Society*

This series provides a forum for theoretical and empirical investigations of social phenomena. It promotes works that focus on the interactions among cognitive processes, individual behavior, and social outcomes. It is especially open to interdisciplinary books that are genuinely integrative.

Titles in the Series

Ulrich Witt, Editor. *Explaining Process and Change: Approaches to Evolutionary Economics*

Young Back Choi. *Paradigms and Conventions: Uncertainty, Decision Making, and Entrepreneurship*

Geoffrey M. Hodgson. *Economics and Evolution: Bringing Life Back into Economics*

Richard W. England, Editor. *Evolutionary Concepts in Contemporary Economics*

W. Brian Arthur. *Increasing Returns and Path Dependence in the Economy*

Janet Tai Landa. *Trust, Ethnicity, and Identity: Beyond the New Institutional Economics of Ethnic Trading Networks, Contract Law, and Gift-Exchange*

Mark Irving Lichbach. *The Rebel's Dilemma*

Karl-Dieter Opp, Peter Voss, and Christiane Gern. *Origins of a Spontaneous Revolution: East Germany, 1989*

Mark Irving Lichbach. *The Cooperator's Dilemma*

Richard A. Easterlin. *Growth Triumphant: The Twenty-first Century in Historical Perspective*

Daniel B. Klein, Editor. *Reputation: Studies in the Voluntary Elicitation of Good Conduct*

Eirik G. Furubotn and Rudolf Richter. *Institutions and Economic Theory: The Contribution of the New Institutional Economics*

Lee J. Alston, Gary D. Libecap, and Bernardo Mueller. *Titles, Conflict, and Land Use: The Development of Property Rights and Land Reform on the Brazilian Amazon Frontier*

Rosemary L. Hopcroft. *Regions, Institutions, and Agrarian Change in European History*

# Regions, Institutions, and Agrarian Change in European History

Rosemary L. Hopcroft

Ann Arbor

THE UNIVERSITY OF MICHIGAN PRESS

2002   2001   2000   1999      4   3   2   1

*A CIP catalog record for this book is available from the British Library.*

Library of Congress Cataloging-in-Publication Data

Hopcroft, Rosemary L. (Rosemary Lynn), 1962–
    Regions, institutions, and agrarian change in European history
/ Rosemary L. Hopcroft.
      p.   cm. — (Economics, cognition, and society)
    Includes bibliographical references and index.
    ISBN 0-472-11023-3 (acid-free paper)
    1. Land reform—Europe—History.   2. Agriculture—Economic
aspects—Europe—History.   3. Europe—Rural conditions.   4. Land
tenure—Europe—History.   I. Title.   II. Series.
HD1333.E85   H66   1999
338.1'094—dc21                                                         99-6089
                                                    CIP

*For Joe, Mark, and Sophie*

# Contents

List of Illustrations ix

Preface xi

1. Introduction: Issues, Theory, and Methods 1

2. Explaining Regional Differences in Economic
   Organization across Europe 15

3. The New Institutional Economics, Field
   Systems, and Economic Change 46

4. Rural Institutions and Agrarian Change
   in England 58

5. Rural Institutions and Agrarian Change in
   the Netherlands 90

6. Rural Institutions and Agrarian Change
   in France 124

7. Rural Institutions and Agrarian Change
   in the German Lands 157

8. Rural Institutions and Agrarian Change
   in Sweden 196

9. Conclusion: Rural Institutions and Agrarian
   Change in the Preindustrial West 230

Notes 241

Bibliography 249

Index 269

# Illustrations

**Figures**

1. Factors hypothesized to influence agrarian change      10
2. Communal open field system, depicted
   without common      19
3. Less-communal open field system, depicted
   without common      23
4. *Strassendorf* (street village), depicted without
   arable fields and common      23


**Maps**

1. Field systems in preindustrial Europe      21
2. The counties of England      60
3. Field systems in England      63
4. Rates of growth of lay wealth in England, 1334–1515      74
5. Farms of 5 to 100 acres, as a percentage of all farms
   over 5 acres, 1851      80
6. Wheat yields in England, 1800      84
7. The Netherlands      93
8. Field systems in the Netherlands      94
9. The French provinces      126
10. Field systems in France      128
11. Wheat yields in France, 1840      147
12. Average farm sizes in France, 1862      149
13. The German lands, c. 1550      159
14. Field systems in the German lands      168
15. Sweden      197
16. Field systems in Sweden      201


**Photographs**

1. Ridge and Furrow at Wimpole Hall and Park,
   Cambridgeshire      18

# Preface

This book discusses the relationship between field systems and agrarian change in European history. The focus on small-scale studies of agrarian and social change in particular locales has often precluded more general studies, which tend to be regarded by historians as "superficial or unwieldy" (Ziegler 1969). Thus, the general relationship between field systems and agrarian change across preindustrial Europe, which this book discusses, hitherto has been overlooked. Yet this relationship has both theoretical and historical significance. First, it illustrates the role of local institutions in shaping economic change, as field systems were a product of local institutions. It thus demonstrates the usefulness of the new institutional economic approach to history—with the addition of a more sociological focus—a stress on the importance of *local* institutions in shaping the process of economic change. Second, agrarian change has long been an important independent variable in comparative historical studies of the rise of the West, and this work examines the local institutional causes of that change.

The principal theme of the book is the contrast between the more communal, "open field" systems and the less-communal (including enclosed) field systems and the differential effects of these systems on agrarian change (defined as structural changes in tenurial relations and farm layout as well as changes in agricultural productivity). Regional variation in field systems existed across western Europe since the early Middle Ages. My central argument is that outcomes of agrarian change in the various countries may only be explained by considering local field systems (treated here as a product of local institutions) *in conjunction* with state institutions and other factors such as access to markets. Following Homans (1987, 1988 [1962]; see also Hopcroft 1994, 1995) an important subargument in the text is that local field systems were primarily a result of social or institutional differences between regions and not primarily the result of ecological (or some other) difference between regions.

The theoretical framework is that of the new institutional economics (Coase 1960; North and Thomas 1973; North 1990). Previous applications of the theory have focused on the role of state-made institutions in shaping economic change. This study builds on prior work by arguing that, while state institutions shape developmental outcomes, local institutions and the field systems they produced also shaped development in important ways. Communal field systems slowed change in some regions by increasing transaction costs. Significantly, this was not because of communal rights per se but because enforcement of those rights was more difficult than in other systems. For these reasons less-communal field systems proved more flexible and more conducive to long-term change. Communal field systems proved more resistant to change and could pose a barrier to agricultural improvement. These regional field systems proved amazingly enduring and influenced regional patterns of change for hundreds of years. This argument blends well with extensions of the new institutional economics into concerns with the cultural bases of institutional forms (see Greif 1994), as the field systems discussed here were closely associated with regional variations in local cultures.

The work lies within the comparative historical tradition in sociology established by authors such as Barrington Moore (1966), Theda Skocpol (1979), and Jack Goldstone (1991). That is, it seeks to develop macrosociological theory through cross-national comparisons of the phenomenon of interest. In Moore's case it was the development of democracy; in Skocpol's the outcome of major social revolutions; and in Goldstone's the relationship between demographic change and social unrest. Furthermore, this work fits in directly with the substantive concerns of these authors. For all of them agrarian issues were of paramount importance. Successful rural development and the transition to commercial agriculture was a crucial factor in smoothing the way to democracy in Moore's book and for blunting agrarian unrest in the works by Skocpol and Goldstone. My work examines local institutional causes of what was for these authors an important independent variable: agrarian change.

My own dedication to this topic alone would not have produced this book. I would like to thank the Graduate School of the University of Washington, the London School of Economics, and the University of North Carolina at Charlotte for financial assistance along the way. The support and interest of a variety of people have sustained the project—most important, my former dissertation director, Pierre van den Berghe, but also many others, including Bruce Campbell, Jack Goldstone, Edgar Kiser, Maryanne Kowaleski, Margaret Levi, Victor Nee, Gi-wook Shin, and Robert Stacey. They have all commented on parts or all of the manuscript at various points in time and otherwise supported the research endeavor. Daniel Chirot, Samuel Clark, Jan de Vries, Harald Gustafsson, Philip Hoffman, Ulf Jonsson, Richard Lachmann, John Markoff, Douglass North, Thomas Robisheaux, and Charles Tilly generously read and commented on the final manuscript, and the work has profited greatly from their feedback. I owe tremendous thanks to all of you. To Professors Gustafsson, Jonsson, and Robisheaux I owe particular thanks for helping remedy the anglocentric bias of early drafts and correcting my more grievous errors concerning Sweden and Germany. Any remaining mistakes, of course, are my responsibility alone.

I would also like to thank Rebecca Dobbs for her wonderful work on many of the maps. Special thanks are due to the secretary of my department, Susan Masse, who in small ways did a great deal to help my research efforts. Most important, it would never have been written without the enduring intellectual and social support of my husband, Joe, who also translated most of the Swedish and German sources.

*Grateful acknowledgment is made to the following for permission to reprint previously published materials.*

*Journal of Economic History* for portions of chapter 2. The University of California Press for the epigraph to chapter 2 from *French Rural History: An Essay on Its Basic Characteristics,* by Marc Bloch. Copyright © 1966 by the Regents of the University of California. Reprinted by permission. Althone Press for the epigraph to chapter 3 from *Land and Family in Pisticci,* by John H. R. Davis (London: Althone, 1973). Part of chapter 4 previously appeared as "The Social Origins of Agrarian Change in Late Medieval England," *American Journal of Sociology* 99(6): 1559–95. Copyright © 1994 by the University of Chicago. All rights reserved. Cambridge University Press for the epigraphs to chapter 5 from *An Historical Geography of France,* by Xavier de Planhol with Paul Claval (Cambridge: Cambridge University Press, 1994); *Plain Lives in a Golden Age,* by A. T. Van Deursen (Cambridge: Cambridge University Press, 1991). Reprinted by permission. Leipman AG for the epigraph to chapter 7 from *Über den Prozeß der Zivilisation,* by Norbert Elias (Franfurt am Main: Suhrkamp, 1990). Copyright © 1939, 1969, 1976 by Norbert Elias. Reprinted by permission of the Norbert Elias Foundation. Random House for the epigraph to chapter 8 from *A History of Swedish People,* by Vilhelm Moberg, translated by Paul Britten Austin. Translation copyright © 1971, 1972 by Paul Britten Austin. Foreword © 1972 by Gunnar Myrdal. Reprinted by permission of Pantheon Books, a division of Random House. Transaction Publishers for excerpts from "The Rural Sociology of Medieval England," in *Sentiments and Activities,* by G. C. Homan. Copyright © 1988 by Transaction Publishers. St. Martin's Press and Routledge for an excerpt from *Agricultural Fluctuations in Europe from the Thirteenth to the Twentieth Centuries,* by Wilhelm Abel. Frank Cass for the poem from *The Agricul-*

*tural Revolution in Norfolk,* by Naomi Riches. BBC Worldwide Limited for the excerpt from *The Vision of Piers Plowman,* by William Langland. Copyright © 1981 Terence Tiller.

*Every effort has been made to trace the ownership of all copyrighted material in this book and to obtain permission for its use.*

CHAPTER 1

# Introduction: Issues, Theory, and Methods

Analytic and microscopic scholarship is abortive without
the complementary work of the synthetic scholar who
builds minute details into comprehensive structures.
　　　　　—Albion Small, "The Era of Sociology"

Understanding agrarian change in preindustrial Europe is fundamental
for an understanding of the "rise of the West." By the mid-seventeenth
century, if not before, a turning point in agrarian conditions occurred that
was to culminate in the "agricultural revolution" in England (Munro 1994,
181; Overton 1996, 8), thought by many to be a necessary prelude for the
transformation to an industrial economy (Moore 1966; Jones 1968, 1988;
Wrigley 1985, 1988; Beckett 1990, 67). Most countries witnessed some sort
of agricultural revolution in the eighteenth century or sometime thereafter,
and the year 1700 marks the end of the "Malthusian" era of regular subsistence crises in Europe (Brady, Oberman, and Tracy 1994, xviii). Why
did this change occur? Why was a small country such as England the first
to witness an agricultural revolution? Previous macrosociological comparative studies examining this issue have focused on factors operating at a
protonational or transnational level of analysis: the role of class relations
within the protonation (Moore 1966; Anderson 1974; Brenner 1987;
O'Brien 1996); position of the country within the global economy (Wallerstein 1974); state institutions and policies (North and Thomas 1973); and,
more generally, factors distinguishing European civilization from those of
the east (Jones 1987; Chirot 1985). Regional factors operating within each
protonational setting have been lost within these larger-scale concerns,
dismissed as inconsequential details within the larger canvas.[1]

In this book I argue that a focus on such factors cannot fully explain
agrarian change in preindustrial Europe. I show how agrarian outcomes in
each country depended in part on the process of change at the regional
level, which was in turn shaped by the nature of local institutions. These
local institutions and the field systems they produced were not solely a
response to local material conditions such as ecology, technology, demography, or market access. Nor were they unique to each protonational setting but were found in similar forms across Europe. As a result, similar

regional patterns of change can be found in all countries. This patterning means that the regional differences cannot be dismissed as idiosyncratic regional particularities and can (and should) be theorized. To note, however, that regional institutions shaped outcomes in important ways is not to disregard the effects of factors operating at a higher level of analysis. The point is that to explain outcomes fully the role of these factors must be considered in conjunction with local factors. Accordingly, the lead of England in the agricultural revolution may be explained by a favorable combination of factors at the transnational, protonational, and local levels.

In preindustrial Europe local institutions produced distinctive forms of economic organization in different regions. These differences have formed the familiar backdrop of rural life in Europe for centuries. In many places they exist to this day and are frequently associated with regional differences in class relations, inheritance customs, religious practices, languages and dialects, housing styles, settlement patterns, and landscapes. Their association with landscapes and settlement patterns has given them their most commonly used names: *field systems* in English, *paysages agraires* in French, *Feldformen* in German, *odlingssystem* in Swedish. As noted, they were found in similar forms across protonational boundaries.

These regional differences in economic organization have been the subject of an extensive literature, although they have never been examined explicitly as a result of "institutional" differences between regions, nor have their effects on long-term economic change ever been systematically analyzed. Literature on the subject dates back several hundred years. Travelers often wrote about the contrast between regions of enclosed fields and scattered habitations (enclosed field systems) and regions of open fields and compact villages (open field systems) in particular. For example, the Englishman Arthur Young, traveling in the late eighteenth century, noted the transition from open fields to enclosures in northern France as follows (1794):

> Between Bouchaine and Valenciennes, end the open fields, which have travelled with me, more or less, all the way from Orleans. After Valenciennes, the country is inclosed; here also is a line of division in another respect. The farms in the open country are generally large; but in the rich, deep, low vale of Flanders, they are small, and much in the hands of little proprietors. (1794, 1:321)

A hundred years later (1891) Hardy somewhat more poetically described a similar transition in southern England:

> The traveller from the coast, who, after plodding northward for a score of miles over calcareous downs and corn-lands, suddenly

reaches the verge of one of these escarpments, is surprised and delighted to behold, extended like a map beneath him, a country differing absolutely from that which he has passed through. Behind him the hills are open, the sun blazes down upon fields so large as to give an unenclosed character to the landscape, the lands are white, the hedges low and plashed, the atmosphere colourless. Here in the valley, the world seems to be constructed upon a smaller and more delicate scale; the fields are mere paddocks, so reduced that from this height their hedgerows appear a network of dark green threads overspreading the paler green of the grass. (1960, 19)

Similarly, in Germany open field regions struck travelers with their appearance of wide-open spaciousness. In 1773 Johann Friedrich Mayer described the Hohenlohe region of southwest Germany:

The whole region is completely open, where the sun shines directly, the winds blow unhindered and never does one miss fresh air; the wind never blows too strong because in the south from east to west the plain is protected by a chain of hills. (Qtd. in Robisheaux 1989, 18)

Open field regions in France received a similar reaction as early as the fourteenth century:

Once he entered into the Beauce,
The wind played havoc with him,
For he was unprotected there

Since the Beauce is wide and rude
So that it affords no shelter
Nowhere to take refuge
In forest, hedge, or bush.
    (J. Maillart, 1316, in *Roman du comte d'Anjou;*
      cited in de Planhol and Claval 1994, 201)

In the late nineteenth century regional differences in field systems attracted the attention of a variety of scholars. For example, Marx differentiated the open field, or what he referred to as the "Teutonic," system of agriculture from other systems. Marx thought that common property, a defining characteristic of open field regions, "was an old Teutonic institution which lived on under cover of feudalism" (1906, 796). Shortly thereafter, the German scholar August Meitzen (1895) wrote one of the first works that, among other things, served to explain the regional differences in field systems. Meitzen thought that the economic and social differences between regions could be traced back to the different ethnic groups that settled in the different areas. Like Marx, he thought the open field system was established in various regions by Germanic groups, hence was a Teutonic system. Max Weber, a student of Meitzen's, focused on certain aspects of regional agrarian organization and labor relations (in eastern Germany) in the 1890s in some of his first scholarly work (Roth 1978, xlvii). Across the channel, somewhat contemporaneously, Gray drew from Meitzen's work in his own analysis of regional differences in rural structures in England in his work *English Field Systems* (Gray 1915). In this work Gray distinguished the highly communal (open field) system of central England from what he called the "Celtic" system in the southwest and the "Kentish" system in the east (enclosed systems). Like Meitzen, he traced these economic and social differences back to the different groups that had settled in the different regions.

Interest in the regional differences in field systems continued into the twentieth century. For example, in Germany, regional differences in field systems were described by Barthel Huppertz (1939), who described regional differences in landscapes, settlement patterns, farm sizes, and local customs and noted the association of the different field systems with different inheritance customs. Similarly, regional differences in field systems in France were central to Marc Bloch's *Les caractères originaux de l'histoire rurale française* (published in English as *French Rural History*). In this work Bloch categorized the types of field systems existing in late medieval and early modern France and noted the association of the different field systems with different types of society and culture (see Bloch 1966a). Open field areas of the north of France, he noted, were characterized by both communal agriculture and a communitarian ethic, while the enclosed and irregular field areas in the south and west were characterized by more privatized agriculture and a spirit of individualism. As his title makes clear, for Bloch these different forms of economic organization were key to understanding French rural history. Similarly, Homans (1941) discussed the differences in field systems across England in the late medieval period, although most of the work was devoted to describing the open field, or "champion," system of midland England. Homans also documented the association of different field systems with differences in local cultures and inheritance customs.

Bloch (1966a), Homans (1987, 1988), and others (e.g., Rösener 1992) further suggested that regional economic structures had implications for long-term economic change in the various regions. For example, Bloch discussed how certain aspects of agrarian change such as enclosure, the shift toward more individualistic agricultural practices, and commercialization of agriculture occurred in less-communal regions in France before others. Homans also hinted that regional differences in field systems had important implications for subsequent agrarian change in England (1987a, 1988), as did Gray (1915, 402).

Despite this, there has been no previous attempt systematically and comparatively to examine the effects of these different local field systems on regional patterns of economic change. Part of the reason for the neglect of regional differences is simply one of evidence: the details of village and rural life have been poorly documented all over Europe (Roth 1978, xlii; Robisheaux 1989, 7). Lords, princes, state bureaucracies, town councils, and urban merchants kept the records upon which most historiography is based, and they only rarely document rural affairs fully. This was particularly true of less-communal regions, which were often regions where there was a large free peasantry and control by lords, princes, towns, and the state was weak and few official records were kept.[2] Further, many of the records that were kept have since been lost or destroyed during wars and revolts. In some regions we will never know what the agricultural systems and/or local social systems were like, let alone what regional patterns in rural development were. This is a problem with which the current study has had to grapple.[3]

Furthermore, despite widespread acknowledgment of regional differences in economic and social systems, they have never been analyzed as a result of institutional differences between regions. Instead, especially in the past four decades, regional differences in social and economic organization have been ascribed to ecological differences between regions or to differences between arable and pastoral regions (Thirsk 1967; Clay 1984, 64). Yet, as I discuss fully in chapter 2, although ecology was clearly an important factor shaping regional landscapes, it cannot account fully for regional differences in field systems (see also Overton 1996, 61; Magnusson 1996, 56). The particularities of economic and social organization characteristic of different field systems do not follow directly from local agricultural specialty, climate, terrain, and soil type. Instead, they are a result of institutional characteristics of regions: results of social, not material, conditions. Nor can regional differences in agrarian change be accounted for solely or primarily by ecological conditions in the various regions, although the local ecology certainly influenced the change that occurred. In short, as is apparent in later chapters, ecological conditions cannot explain differences between regions.

Bloch (1966a) gave a technological explanation of regional differences in field systems in France (see chap. 2). Yet, as I argue in the next chapter, technology cannot account adequately for regional differences in social structures. Basic agricultural techniques and tools were much the same all over preindustrial Europe. Nor can technological differences account for regional differences in agricultural productivity. This is because the techniques for improving agricultural productivity (deep plowing, fertilizing with lime or manure, growing of legumes and nitrogen-fixing crops) changed very little between the fourteenth and the eighteenth centuries, and farmers were familiar with them everywhere (even if they did not use them extensively). It was only with the advent of new fertilizers in the nineteenth century and new agricultural machinery in the later nineteenth century that agricultural technology really began to change. Thus, at least before the nineteenth century, improvements in agricultural productivity resulted entirely from the intensification and/or improvement of traditional methods and were not the result of labor-saving innovations, mechanical gadgetry, or modern methods. This was true even in England, the most advanced agricultural country (Overton 1996, 121). This is not to say that, within the confines of the basic techniques described here, there was not innovation, for example, in the type of plow, whether the plow was drawn with the horse or the ox, type of fertilizer (there were a variety of naturally occurring types), type of leguminous crops, etc., that served to improve productivity. All of these innovations, however, required additional human effort and expenditure. As we shall see, this kind of innovation and improvement was more common in less-communal regions than in the communal regions of preindustrial Europe.

Differences in field systems have often been attributed to demographic factors and/or the presence of market incentives (e.g., Thirsk 1967; North and Thomas 1973; also see chap. 2). Yet neither demographic pressures nor access to markets can entirely explain the regional differences in rural organization. Field systems were not simply results of these factors (see chap. 2). It is true that both communal and less-communal field systems were changed and agricultural productivity was improved in response to both demographic pressure and market incentives. Yet, as we will see in later chapters, despite population pressure and market incentives, in all countries fundamental change in communal systems did not occur spontaneously in response to demographic and/or market pressures and had to be forced through by political means. In England this occurred via the parliamentary enclosures; in Germany and Sweden there was similar enclosure legislation in the eighteenth century; and in France communal agricultural systems were only fully dismantled in the aftermath of World War II.

Nor was the regional pattern of economic development solely a result of market incentives and demographic pressures in different regions, although these are the factors that have been traditionally used to explain regional differences in economic performance (e.g., Boserup 1965; Le Roy

Ladurie and Goy 1982; Overton 1996, 207; Postan 1973; Tilly 1994, 22; van der Wee 1993, 8). In the most dynamic economic regions of early modern Europe market access and population growth certainly promoted economic development. While it is true, however, that both access to markets and demographic pressure in these regions created incentives for the effort and expenditure required to improve agricultural productivity, it is also true that response to these factors was facilitated by the less-communal field systems characteristic of these regions. This can be discerned by examining regions where there existed both communal and less-communal field systems, a high population density, and access to markets, such as existed in northern France, southern Germany, and parts of southern England in the early modern period. Despite demographic pressure and easy access to major urban markets, the communal regions were far less dynamic economically than neighboring less-communal regions.

Further, neither population growth nor urbanization can be considered factors entirely independent of local field systems. Both of these factors were dependent on the easy availability of foodstuffs, which was made more likely by a growth in agricultural productivity, which in turn was made more likely by less-communal field systems. Thus, I argue that it is no accident that some of the most urbanized and densely populated regions of preindustrial Europe came to be located in or very close to regions of less-communal field systems, for example, in south eastern England and the Netherlands. In countries and regions where agricultural productivity was lower, such as in most of France and Sweden, the development of an urban system was similarly less vigorous. In most of Germany, where there is evidence that agricultural productivity declined over the seventeenth century (see chap. 7), there is likewise evidence that urban potential or the urban system also declined during this time (see de Vries 1984, 160–63, 167).[4] The exception was northwest Germany, where both agricultural productivity and the urban system were maintained over this period.

For all these reasons, and for the reason that these factors have been given a center role in most previous studies of agrarian change in European history, in this book I do not focus on the role of population pressure and market access in agrarian change. Instead, I focus on an equally important, but neglected, component of regional differences in agrarian change and economic performance: the nature of local institutions. I argue that in some regions local institutions that provided clear and exclusive property rights in land and facilitated individual economic freedom produced enclosed field systems and less-communal open field systems. These enclosed and less-communal field systems encouraged development and change by reducing the costs involved in production and exchange. In other regions local institutions that provided uncertain property rights in land and inhibited individual economic freedom produced communal open field systems. These communal field systems slowed development by increasing the costs of production and exchange.

The effects of field systems on economic change may be theorized using new institutional theory, which contends that economic change is shaped by institutional conditions. According to new institutional theory, institutions are social rules, which may be formal rules: for example, constitutions, contract law, the specification and protection of property rights, and so on (Coase 1960; Barzel 1989; North 1982, 23); or informal rules: norms, mores, customs (North 1990b, 192; Knight 1992). Institutions shape economic outcomes by influencing the costs, choices, and incentives for individuals (Coase 1960; North 1991). Particularly important are social costs, or transaction costs, which are defined as the costs of defining and enforcing property rights, of measuring the valuable attributes of what is being exchanged, and of monitoring the exchange process itself (Coase 1960; Williamson 1975; North 1981; 1990a, 27; 1990b, 184 [see chap. 3]). Institutions that serve to lower social costs (transaction costs) for producers and traders promote development; institutions that maintain high transaction costs for producers and traders inhibit development. In an early application of this theory to economic history North and Thomas (1973) drew particular attention to the role of the state in providing legal and financial institutions that reduce economic uncertainty and transaction costs and, hence, promote development.

Here we may treat regional field systems as results of local institutions, that is, local customs and rules about the use, ownership, and inheritance of land and informal normative rules. Communal institutions created both communal field systems and increased transaction costs. These higher costs reduced incentives to invest in land and increase production. Other costs associated with the communal system limited incentives for cultivators to innovate and increase production. For example, village regulations made it costly, if not impossible, to change cropping practices. Less-communal institutions created both less-communal field systems and reduced transaction costs. Lower transaction costs meant there were greater incentives to invest in land and increase production. Other costs were often lower in less-communal regions also, which meant cultivators were both more willing and more able to innovate and to increase production. For example, there were few village regulations limiting choice of crops and crop rotations. For these reasons agricultural development and agrarian change were more common in regions of less-communal field systems than in regions of communal field systems.

The use of this new institutional theoretical approach does not exclude the possibility that material factors such as ecology, population density, patterns of urbanization, and market access or political factors such as local class relations and state institutions and policies also had important effects on regional development outcomes. The effects of such factors are quite consistent with the theory, as these factors also shape costs and possibilities for farmers, as discussed in chapter 3. Chapter 3 elaborates the new institutional theory and its application to rural development. Nevertheless, a summary of the factors hypothesized to influence regional development according to the theory is given in figure 1. Regional development outcomes are shown as a product of local institutions, local class relations, market access, and state institutions and policies. Specifically, development is hypothesized to be most likely in regions characterized by less-communal local institutions, weak overlordship, easy market access, and state institutions and policies that decrease transaction and other costs for economic actors. Population and urbanization influence development through their effects on markets. That is, both a high population density and extensive urbanization create a greater demand for agricultural commodities and thus improve market access for economic actors. Ecology is shown as also having a causal influence on market access, and it is also correlated with local institutions. For example, a remote ecological setting decreases market access, while an ecological setting near rivers or other waterways increases market access. Ecology is correlated with local institutions because communal institutions tended to be found in the best agricultural regions of Europe. This figure omits feedback effects, for example, positive effects of rural development on urbanization and population density, or effects of development on state policies and institutions and on local institutions themselves.

To sum up, despite a long literature documenting similar regional variation in rural economic organization across national boundaries within Europe, there has been no systematic, macrosociological examination of its effect on long-term economic change. Nor have regional differences in field systems been treated as a result of institutional differences between regions; rather, they have been traced to ecological and material conditions and then, for the most part, ignored.[5] This book makes two main points. First, the variations in field systems were not simply a reflection of regional variations in ecology (i.e., soil type, topology, climate), agricultural specialization or technology, market access, demography, or other material factors. Fundamentally, they were a result of institutional differences between regions. Second, field systems varied in similar ways across regions in Europe and had somewhat similar consequences for agrarian change. Economic behaviors that we today associate with capitalism flourished first in certain rural regions of Europe, which were characterized by a system of agriculture and economic life quite

Fig. 1. Factors hypothesized to influence agrarian change

distinctive from that found in many other regions. These regions were characterized by little communal control over agriculture, considerable peasant proprietorship, and weak overlordship. Where other conditions (most important being access to markets—urban and otherwise—as well as political and legal conditions) were also favorable, as in parts of southern England and the Netherlands, these local conditions gave rise to rapid economic development and agrarian change. The implication of this study is that "modernity" has rural origins, not just the urban origins often noted in studies of the rise of the West (Chirot 1989, 4).

This book covers the time period from the crises of the fourteenth century to about 1700. This includes a great deal of economic history: the late medieval depression, the fifteenth-century recovery, the economic boom of the sixteenth century, and the seventeenth century downturn.[6] Such a long time period is necessary to include both events of the fourteenth century (widely regarded as pivotal for later agrarian change, especially in England) and the onset of the agricultural revolution in England. The focus on agrarian and agricultural change is justified because throughout this period the majority of people in Europe worked on the land, and all national economies were overwhelmingly rural economies. As Robisheaux notes (1994, 79), the main engine of European economic development remained rural and agricultural throughout the early modern period. The bulk of traded goods was also agricultural: wheat, rye, wool, malt, timber, wine; even textiles were based on agricultural products such as wool and linen. This was true even of highly urbanized regions such as the Low Countries, where nearly 60 percent of the entire population was engaged in agriculture in 1550 (see Wrigley 1987, table 7.8, 182). In England about 75 percent of the population was involved in farming in 1520 (Overton 1996, 22). Higher percentages of the population were still involved in farming in early modern Germany, France, and Sweden. As a result of this focus, I devote only a little attention to rural industry and manufacture. This mostly amounted to the textile industry, which met the most essential need, after food, in temperate climates (van Houtte 1977, 32). Yet even the textile industry was always a minor part of each country's economy. The whole English cloth industry, one of the major cloth industries of the day, reportedly employed only some fifteen thousand persons in 1400 (Pounds 1990, 198). For this reason I do not examine patterns of rural industrialization in any detail, although data suggest that agricultural development in a region made the appearance of rural industry more likely. There was also a correspondence between textile regions and regions of less-communal or enclosed field systems.

Five areas in western Europe are examined: those areas that correspond approximately to the modern-day nations of England, France, the Netherlands, Belgium, Sweden, and Germany. These areas were selected because they make up the core of "northwestern Europe," which shared many common characteristics (similar dry agriculture and agricultural technology, a similar history, religion, involvement in wars, similar culture) over the period. This similarity crudely serves to hold constant other factors not directly examined here that might be hypothesized to effect economic outcomes. In addition, the selection of areas ensures variation in both dependent and independent variables. For the dependent variable they provide two positive cases of rural development (in England and the Netherlands) with three largely negative cases (in France, Sweden, and Germany). The latter saw delayed "agricultural revolutions" in the nineteenth and twentieth centuries. The selected areas also provide variation in factors hypothesized to influence development outcomes: local institutions, ecology, population, market access, class relations, state institutions, and political oppression. Such variation helps us to discern the effects of local institutions net of these other factors. Last, there is no reason to believe that the addition of other European countries would change the conclusions of this study.

I divide each of the countries into regions according to type of local institution, using a threefold classification: communal open field, less-communal open field, and enclosed field systems. This classification follows precedent in the historical literature, particularly Bloch (1966a). For analytical purposes this classification is then collapsed into two categories: communal (i.e., the communal open field system) and less communal (including both the less-communal open field and enclosed field systems [see chap. 2]). The communal (open field) systems were found most typically in midland and central England (1), northern France (2), southern Germany (3), the border regions of the southeastern Netherlands (4), and eastern and southern Sweden (5). Other types of less-communal systems were found in eastern (6), southwestern (7), northern and western England (8), Normandy (9), the far north of France (10), western (11) and southern France (12), the northern (13) and southern Netherlands (14), eastern (15) and northwestern Germany (16), and most of western (17) and northern Sweden (18). This gives a total of eighteen, regions, or "cases." Although these cases are by no means fully independent (Clark 1995, 4), as distinctive regions they are meaningful units, and the use of such units is the best way to begin untangling causality at the regional level. I analyze these eighteen cases with respect to crucial variables described in chapter 3: local institutions and the field systems they gave rise to, local class relations, ecology, population, market access, state policies, and the legal delineation and protection of property rights. Initially, I compare regions within national frameworks. The decision to continue to use the national frameworks, even though they are often less than meaningful in the historical periods under consideration, is based on the following reasoning. First, in many cases there was a national state that, however diminutive (Mann 1988), did influence all regions within its sphere of influence in similar ways. Second, traditions of national scholarship mean that much of the groundwork of comparing regions within national frameworks has already been accomplished and can be utilized here to present the case for the effects of local institutions.

In comparing outcomes across countries (see chap. 9), I follow Mill's method of similarity and method of difference (Ragin 1987, 36–39). That is, I compare both similar regions with similar developmental outcomes (e.g., eastern England and the Netherlands) and similar regions with very different developmental outcomes (e.g., these regions with eastern Germany) and note how they compare on theoretically relevant factors. I also avoid a static, variables-oriented analysis, however, by providing a narrative discussion of the historical process of agrarian change in each country. This process itself plays an important causal role, because it is often the timing of events, and not merely the events themselves, that is crucial for determining final outcomes. For example, agricultural revolutions, which occurred in all regions after the English agricultural revolution, were greatly influenced by the English experience. Thus, attention to the historical process also helps deal with the problem of the lack of independence between cases.

I use a variety of types of evidence. Some evidence is qualitative and draws primarily from regional and national histories and monographs. This tells us the nature and process of agrarian change in different regions and how local institutions and other factors impinged on that change. Some evidence is quantitative and consists of statistics collected by economic historians and others. Relevant information includes population densities, urbanization figures, export statistics, farm sizes, and cereal yields. The dependent variable, "agrarian change," is defined as changes in agricultural productivity as well as changes in the relations of production and structure of landholding. Change in agricultural productivity refers to change in crop yields, in agricultural productivity per capita, in peasant prosperity, and in the use of intensive agricultural techniques and procedures. Change in relations of production refers to change toward "capitalist" contractual relations of production and terms of tenancy. Change in the structure of landholding refers to changes such as consolidation and enclosure of landholdings.

When I report evidence of cereal yields I typically use yields for wheat as the benchmark, except in Sweden, where little wheat was grown before the nineteenth century (Söderberg 1996, 28). This is somewhat controversial, as wheat was the grain of the rich and was only rarely consumed by the broad mass of population. It was typically, however, an important export crop. Furthermore, it is encountered frequently in the accounts of religious institutions and larger manors and thus often provides the best and sometimes the only figures for yields and prices (van Houtte 1977, 67). This brings us to the fact that almost all the quantitative evidence on yields and other measures of agricultural productivity come from manorial or estate records. In heavily manorialized regions this is not a problem. But in areas where manors and estates are few, or nonexistent or no longer exist, it poses a problem. It means that in regions where there is a great deal of peasant agriculture we typically have no direct measures of the productivity of peasant farms. Yet, since manor or estate practices and levels of productivity typically reflect local practices and local productivity, I use the available evidence from manors as reflecting conditions in the region. Given that there is evidence that smaller, freehold farms were more productive than estate farms in many regions (Allison 1957; Britnell 1991; Kirby 1990, 248), the use of manorial evidence may understate differences in productivity between regions. Of course, besides this problem, none of this evidence is as systematic or comprehensive as one could wish for in a study such as this one. Nor does it always lend itself readily to comparison, either between regions within countries or across countries.

These problems are unavoidable, given the research question, the time periods under consideration, and the nature of the available evidence. A survey of historical agrarian issues in several different countries, across such a wide time span, would have been impossible otherwise. Such an approach may contribute to errors of fact and/or judgment in my analysis, yet these are unavoidable in such a large-scale enterprise. My hope, how-ever, is that any such errors are minor in nature and that the value gained from such a comparative study more than outweighs any losses so incurred.

In chapter 2 I begin by discussing regional differences in rural eco-nomic organization and the role of ecology (and other factors) in creating those differences. In chapter 3 I set out the new institutional theoretical approach, apply it to regional differences in economic organization across Europe, and present the working hypotheses that follow from this theoret-ical approach. These hypotheses predict a regional pattern of agrarian change, correlating with regional differences in local institutions, although influenced by local class relations, ecology, demography, and political and market factors. In subsequent chapters I discuss evidence from the various countries and regions. In chapters 4 through 8 I first discuss the two coun-tries with positive outcomes, England and the Netherlands, then the three latecomers, France, Germany, and Sweden, respectively. Of the two posi-tive cases I put England first, primarily because England shows most vari-ation in the independent variable of most interest—local institutions—while there was little variation in this factor in the Low Countries. France is discussed next, as it is the closest comparison to England and the Netherlands, yet, unlike those countries, its rural economy stagnated, and it saw a delayed agricultural revolution. Chapter 9 summarizes the findings of the previous chapters, compares outcomes across countries, and draws final conclusions.

CHAPTER 2

# Explaining Regional Differences in Economic Organization across Europe

> Only a society of great compactness, composed of men
> who thought instinctively in terms of the community,
> could have created such a regime [the communal open
> field system].
> —Marc Bloch, *French Rural History*

The differences in economic organization that existed across rural Europe have long been known in English as differences in "field systems." This name is somewhat misleading, as it suggests the layout of the fields and no more. The layout of the fields, however, reflected the social organization of the farmers, and each field pattern was thus associated with distinctive social relations and agricultural practices. Thus, in practice the term *field system* denoted an entire social system, what Marc Bloch referred to as an "agrarian civilization." To remain consistent with the historical literature, however, I use the term *field system*. In this chapter I give an overview of the various types of field systems in preindustrial Europe and discuss reasons why they differed from place to place.

## Field Systems in Preindustrial Europe

Any given map of field systems in preindustrial Europe is likely to give a very detailed and confusing picture of differences in field systems across regions in Europe (cf. Huppertz 1939; Smith 1967, 218, 237, 276). First, the nature of local field systems is not always known with any certainty (Overton 1996, 26). Second, even within regions field systems could vary quite dramatically from one place to the next. Given these limitations, however, field systems across Europe may be classified parsimoniously, and regional patterns may be identified, as Bloch did for France (1966a). Since most of the various types of field systems across Europe can be fit within this simple categorization, I use Bloch's typology here.

Bloch identified three distinct types of field systems: systems of regular open fields (*open field system* in English, *Gewanndorf* in German, *champs ouverts* in French); systems of irregular open fields; and enclosures (*woodland* in English, *bocage* in French). The most important dimension underlying this classification is the "extent of communal control over agriculture," or simply "communalism." That is, field systems range from the most communal (the regular open field system) to the least communal (*bocage*). Thus, to avoid confusion, what Bloch calls the regular open field system I call the "communal open field system"; what Bloch calls the irregular open field system I call the "less-communal open field system"; systems of enclosures and privatized agriculture I call "enclosed field systems." In what follows I discuss typical characteristics of each type of field system. This general discussion necessarily cloaks much of the variability in field systems in various regions, some of which will be discussed in later chapters. Yet, although field systems varied somewhat according to circumstance, in all cases fitting them into the threefold classification, based on the extent of communalism, is fairly straightforward. In my later analysis I group together the less-communal open field and enclosed field systems into one less-communal category. But, first, it is necessary to describe the three different systems to show why less-communal open field systems and enclosed field systems may be meaningfully classified together.

The *communal open field system* was, from a modern point of view, the most unusual system. In this system the arable land of the village was typically split up into many long thin strips of land: each strip called a *lanière,* in French; *Streif,* in German; and *teg,* in Swedish. Strips could be very long indeed, sometimes up to a kilometer in length, although very narrow. They were divided by grassy balks (unplowed ridges), by boundary stones, and by the pattern of ridge and furrow left by the plow. Each cultivator had a share of strips of land in all parts of the village land. These strips were grouped into furlongs (*quartier* in French, *Felder* in German) and organized into one, two, or three large fields depending on the type of rotation system used by the village. Crop rotations ranged from more extensive to more intensive use of the land. The most extensive form of agriculture was to have no fallowing or rotation of fields and simply to abandon land when the soil was exhausted. This was the one-field system, in which all the village land was contained in one large unit, or field. When abandoning land was not feasible, a two-course rotation could be used, which let half of the land sit fallow each year. In this case all the village land was arranged into two great fields, and one field was cropped while the other lay fallow. The following year the fallow field became the cropped field, and vice versa. The most intensive form of agriculture left only a third of the land fallow each year. In this case there were typically three great fields, and two fields were cropped while one lay fallow. The next year the fields were rotated.

By and large, by the late medieval period a three-field system dominated in regions of communal open field agriculture, that is, in the midlands of England, eastern Denmark, northeastern France, and southwestern Germany. Exceptions are the communal open field regions of Sweden, where a one-field or two-field system was more common, and parts of the Rhineland in southwestern Germany, where a two-field system (with a two-course rotation) was common (Heckscher 1954, 28; Abel 1978a; Rösener 1992, 119).[1]

It is important at this point to distinguish between a three-field system and a three-course rotation. Although a three-field system always followed a three-course rotation and a two-field system always followed a two-course rotation, the reverse was not true. That is, it was possible to have a three-course rotation and yet not have three great fields; in fact, this was typical in less-communal regions. In the latter regions rotations were typically based on subdivisions of fields, not whole fields, so the number of fields and the number of rotations were unrelated. Thus, in these regions the type of rotation simply tells us the amount of land left fallow every year (a three-course rotation means that one-third of the land sits fallow each year, two rotations means one-half, etc.) and does not refer to the number of fields or to the field system per se.

The great fields of the village were referred to as *sols* in French, *Zelgen* or *Schläge* in German, and *vångar* in Swedish. Typically, strips were organized in a regular way in the fields, often going in a clockwise direction (the course of the sun in the northern hemisphere) in the same order as the houses along the village street. This way every farmer's strips in the fields were adjacent to those of his neighbors in the village. In Denmark this sun division (*solskifte*) of strips in the fields was referred to in the saying "The toft is the mother of the acre." That is, the position of the house garden, or *toft,* gave rise to the position of the strips in the open fields (Homans 1941, 97). Similarly, in Sweden the medieval Provincial Codes expressed this as "Lot is acre's mother" (Heckscher 1954, 26; Söderberg 1996, 27). Within the fields strips were grouped into blocks, called *furlongs* in England, *quartiers* in France, and *Gewänne* in Germany (Smith 1967, 197). This pattern of strips gave the fields a familiar checkerboard pattern as well as a pattern of ridge and furrow that can be seen still engraved on the landscape in many of these regions today (Beresford 1979; see photograph 1). Figure 2 shows a stylized depiction of that field pattern.

Strips of land were cropped individually yet were subject to communal rotations and (typically) communal regulation of cropping. Under a three-field system one field would be fallow, one field would have the spring crop (e.g., barley or oats), and one field would have the winter crop (e.g., wheat or rye). The next year the three fields would rotate. This meant that each

**Photograph 1. Ridge and Furrow at Wimpole Hall and Park, Cambridge-shire. (Copyright © British Crown Copyright/MOD. Reproduced with the permission of Her Britannic Majesty's Stationery Office.)**

farmer was required to follow the same time schedule for planting, harvest-ing, and fallowing his strips in the open fields (although the choice of crops was not always constrained). In addition to communal cropping, fallowing, and rotation, villagers had to allow the village herd to graze on their land at certain times: on the fallow field and on the arable fields after harvest. All of this was regulated by a central body or council of some sort, called the *byelaw* in England, *marken* in the eastern provinces of the Netherlands (Van Houtte 1977, 14), the *Dorfgenossenschaft* (or other name) in Germany

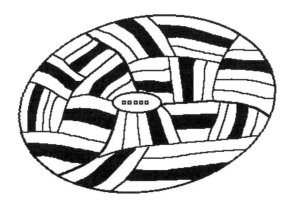

**Fig. 2. Communal open field system, depicted without common. Shaded area represents one landholding. (Adapted from Dodgshon 1980.)**

(Rösener 1992, 46), and *bystämman* in Sweden (Moberg 1973, 40). This council was responsible for coordinating cropping, harvesting, grazing, and field rotations as well as appointing village shepherds and fence keepers. It was also responsible for sanctioning those who violated the rules. If admonishment by the village council was not enough, seigneurial law and the seigneurial court further enforced agricultural rules. Such regulation and enforcement served to maintain the system, because unless all farmers followed the rules the entire field system would break down.[2]

The size of holdings in the common arable fields differed somewhat from region to region and from country to country. The basic unit in England was the hide, which was more or less equivalent to the German *Hufe,* the French *manse,* and the Swedish *mantal* (Rösener 1992, 126). These were measures of land large enough to support a family and its dependents. In all countries these units tended to fragment over time (until they eventually disappeared), and most cultivators had some fraction of this unit to farm. In late medieval England a typical farm size was a *yardland,* or virgate (quarter-hide, or about 30 acres [see Homans 1941, 75]). The Swedish equivalent of the English hide was the *mantal,* although as in England actual farms were usually some fraction of a *mantal,* perhaps about 9 or so hectares (about 22 acres) (Heckscher 1954, 164; Mead 1981, 37). Average farms in Germany may have been about the same size in the late Middle Ages (Rösener 1992, 126). In France the *manse* ranged in size between about 5 and 30 hectares in the Middle Ages (Bloch 1966a, 154), with an average holding size of perhaps 13 hectares (about 32 acres).

Animals were grazed not only on the common arable fields but also on the commons proper of the village. The commons proper was separate from the arable fields and could include rough grazing land, marshland, woodland, and wasteland. Sometimes there was also a high-quality hay meadow. Everyone in the village had at least some rights to the commons and to products of the common land such as wood and hay. Regulating the use of the commons and the resources of the commons was another important responsibility of the village council. It is important not to confuse the commons proper with the common arable fields of the field system. This distinction becomes particularly important in later years, when attempts to break down the communal system were made. Partitioning the commons was much easier than partitioning the common arable fields. While the former was completed by the end of the eighteenth century in France, for example, it took until the mid-twentieth century for the common arable fields to be entirely partitioned.

Characteristics of the communal open field system for England have been summarized by Thirsk (1964, 143), but they apply to communal open field systems across western Europe. They are:

1. the scattering of the strips of a landholding;
2. common grazing and common cropping on land organized into two or three great fields (although in Sweden there could be just one field);
3. common waste (unused land) for village grazing and common meadow; and
4. the presence of disciplinary assemblies to oversee the working of the system.

The communal open field system spread across the great plains of Europe, through the midlands of England, through eastern Sweden, parts of Denmark, northeastern France, and southwestern Germany (see map 1). These were all regions of great fields, divided into very long narrow strips. Because there were few enclosures and little use of fences and hedges to mark boundaries, the general aspect was of wide-open country, hence the name "open field."

*Less-communal open field systems* were often similar in outward appearance to communal open field systems, as they typically included few fences or other enclosures. The major difference between regions of less-communal open fields and regions of communal open fields was the differing extent of community coordination and cooperation in agricultural matters. While this was limited in the former, it was pronounced in the latter. Less-communal open field systems displayed greater variability in

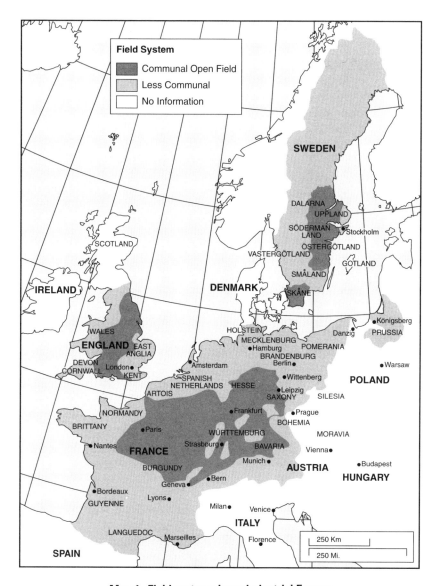

**Map 1. Field systems in preindustrial Europe**

form than the communal open field system. In what follows I discuss two of the more typical forms found in late medieval Europe.

In some less-communal open field regions farmers' strips of land were not neatly organized into discrete fields and furlongs and could be short and wide rather than long and narrow. In regions of dense population and partible inheritance these parcels of land could be tiny in size. Strips or parcels of a single farmer's holding often were concentrated in one part of the village land and not scattered evenly across it, as in the communal open field system. This feature facilitated practices of private cropping and grazing. In some such regions animals would be tethered on each farmer's land, rather than allowed to roam free across the common fields under the care of a common shepherd. Rotations could be collective, but the rotating unit was typically a "shift" (some designated area of land) or a furlong rather than an entire field. This method of rotation only required the cooperation of a small group of farmers and did not entail the cooperation of the entire village. Such less-communal open field systems were found in both East Anglia and the southwestern counties in England, in southern France, eastern and northwestern Germany, parts of the northern and southern Netherlands, and Sweden. These field systems may also be depicted schematically (see fig. 3).

Another common pattern for less-communal open field systems was the "fishbone" pattern, or row village type, with the houses aligned along the roadway with their fields stretching out behind and around them. These fields often were made up of wide, rectangular blocks of land rather than the ribbonlike strips common in communal open field regions. This was the typical pattern of the street village of eastern Europe (also known as *Strassendorf*) and was found in many other places in western Europe as well (such as Normandy in France) (see fig. 4). Communal rights and communal cooperation in farming typically were limited in these kinds of villages. Extreme variants of this row village type were the *Waldhufendorf, Hagenhufendorf,* and *Marschhufendorf,* in all of which the farmhouse was located in the middle of the farmland, which extended in a long strip on either side of the farmhouse (Huppertz 1939, 126; Aubin 1966, 465; Mayhew 1973, 73–77). The farm contained all its own land—meadows, pasture, and arable as a self-contained unit—and farming was privatized. *Waldhufendorf* commonly were found in parts of eastern and central Germany, while *Hagenhufendorf* and *Marschhufendorf* were common in both the Netherlands and the northern coasts of Germany (Mayhew 1973, 68).

The remaining general type of field system in preindustrial Europe is the *enclosed field system.* Areas of enclosures were characterized by almost completely privatized systems of agriculture. Most fields were entirely enclosed; there was often no communal participation in farming, and no

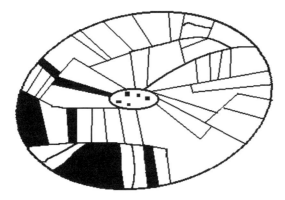

Fig. 3. **Less-communal open field system, depicted without common. Shaded area represents one landholding. (Adapted from Dodgshon 1980.)**

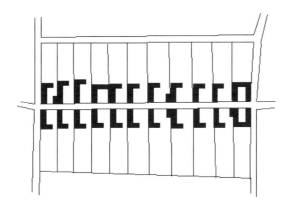

Fig. 4. *Strassendorf* **(street village), depicted without arable fields and common. (Adapted from Abel 1978a.)**

communal regulatory bodies at all. In such regions houses typically were scattered across the landscape. Villages tended to be smaller and less compact than in other regions, and there was often no central grouping of houses in a village or hamlet. As a result, the village church often stood alone and isolated in some prominent natural location. Fields were fenced (either with hedges, trees, or stones), and little land was left open. Since many fences were live hedges or included many trees, this gave the landscape a wooded appearance. This earned such regions the name of woodland regions in England, *bocage* in France. Fields also tended to be smaller in enclosed regions, giving the landscape the smaller and more delicate scale described in the quote by Thomas Hardy in chapter 1. It was quite dramatically different from the wide-open spaces characteristic of regions dominated by the communal open field system.

Areas of enclosures were found throughout the northern and southern Netherlands and in Brittany and Normandy, parts of eastern and southwestern England, parts of southern France, and some places in Germany and Sweden. In mountainous areas enclosures usually were associated with a pastoral economy. Pastoral regions in nonmountainous areas also typically were enclosed, and, as a result, it is, and has been, a common misconception that enclosed regions were *always* pastoral regions. Regions of enclosures, however, did not necessarily have a pastoral focus. Many were regions of mixed farming (as were the majority of all regions in preindustrial Europe) that included both arable and pastoral husbandry. Enclosed fields could be used just as easily for arable agriculture as for pasture farming, and cows and sheep would alternate with small fields of wheat, barley, oats, or rye in the same enclosure. Many such enclosed regions had highly productive arable agriculture and often produced a surplus of grain for the market, a point to which I will return later. Thus, it is an error to think of all enclosed regions as pastoral regions, although the reverse was typically true.

## Field Systems and Local Cultures

In regions of communal open fields communal regulation of agriculture and land use was accompanied by strong traditions of communitarianism. In these regions villages tended to be large and compact, and people lived side by side. The church, centrally located within the village, was often the center of the life of the community. In many villages the village associations met in the church, something that is understandable, given the fact that the church was typically the largest public building in the village. (Although other locations could be used—e.g., under the linden tree was common in southwestern Germany.) These were regions where people "thought instinctively in terms of the community," as Bloch puts it (1966a, 45). In England, Homans writes, open field villagers "felt that they were bound to help their neighbors and do what they could, each man in his office, to further the common good of their village" (1941, 308; see also Overton 1996, 45). Communal solidarity was reflected further in the custom, common in communal open field regions, of holding all members of a village responsible for the debts of one member (Homans 1941, 338;

Root 1987, 31, 40). In England wakes—large village festivals only found in communal open field regions—were occasions when a village celebrated its collective identity (Homans 1941, 374). Other celebrations and ceremonies that took place at various times in the agricultural year were more common in communal villages than in less-communal villages (Overton 1996, 37).

While regions of communal open fields were regions of well-developed communities, regions of less-communal field systems and enclosures were regions where a more individualistic or familistic ethic often reigned. Visitors often remarked on the individualism of regions of less-communal open fields and enclosures. For example, Kentishmen (from a region of enclosed and less-communal field systems) long had a reputation for clannishness and suspiciousness in their dealings with strangers (Fryde and Fryde 1991, 774). In the early modern period Swiss, Frisians, and peasants of Ditmarsch were well-known for their individualism (Downing 1992; de Vries 1974, 55). Similarly, less-communal and enclosed regions of the south of France were considered the most individualistic in France (cf. Poland 1957, 12; Bloch 1966a; Prince 1977, 151), as popularized by the character of Cyrano de Bergerac, the Gascon hero of the Rostand play of the same name. The Normans and Bretons also gained a reputation as individualists.

The individualism of more privatized regions did not, however, preclude a strong civic associational life.[3] As we shall see in later chapters, these regions often contained active peasant associations. The heresies of the late medieval period, and later Protestantism, often flourished in these regions, and these served to promote the extensive development of both civic and religious associations (Zaret 1985; Schilling 1991; Hopcroft 1997). In fact, under Protestantism it could be argued that more economically individualistic regions were characterized by more community control over individuals (at least when it came to moral issues) than the more economically communitarian regions. This community control could extend even to economic matters. Thus, in some cases the association of "individualistic" field systems with individualistic cultures requires much qualification.

## Economic Organization and Class Relations

Different field systems were associated not only with different cultural mores but also with different class relations. While regions of communal open fields tended to be heavily manorialized, the reverse tended to be true of regions of enclosures and less-communal open fields.

In communal open field regions the influence of the feudal lord pervaded all aspects of rural life, economic and social. Ties between lord and peasant were reflected in the structure of landholding. Strips of land of both lord (the demesne land) and peasant often were intermingled in the open fields. Most peasants were customary tenants, that is, those who farmed land considered to belong to the manor and/or those who were considered to be bound personally to their lord in some way, for example, as villeins or serfs. In these regions there were few freeholders who owned their lands outright and were largely free of manorial obligations (although there are conspicuous exceptions to this—e.g., in Sweden; see later discussion). Customary tenants were responsible for cultivation of the lord's land as well as their own land. There was also often a separate demesne attached to the manor house, and this too was farmed by customary tenants. In addition, customary tenants were tied to their lords by a variety of other rules and obligations. In addition to labor dues, all customary tenants were held responsible for a variety of other feudal dues in kind, fees, and services. These often included money rents for using the land, mandatory fees for the usage of manorial facilities—the mill, ponds, ovens, etc.—as well as dues when land or goods were transferred through sale or inheritance, and a miscellany of other taxes and dues (see Bloch 1966a, 80; Moeller 1977, 30; Overton 1996, 31). By the late medieval period the use of labor services had dwindled in most of the Continent, although they continued to be commonly used in England. Other dues and obligations remained, however.

Customary tenants were also subject to the authority of the manorial court, that is, the court run by the feudal lord. In midland England there was typically only one lord per village, although on the Continent it was quite common for several lords to share jurisdiction over a village and its lands. This became more common in times of rising population, first in the thirteenth century and again in the later fifteenth and sixteenth centuries. The manor court judged any conflicts and disputes that arose in the village. The lord sometimes attended his court and served as judge, although often such duties were delegated to manorial servants chosen from among the peasant community. Similarly, other lordly duties—supervision of cultivation of the demesne, for example—were often delegated to well-off members of the village community. Village governance typically worked in conjunction with manorial officials, and vice versa. Thus, the *byelaw* in medieval England depended on the manorial court for enforcement of its rulings and punishing noncompliance (Homans 1941). The same was true in northern France and southern Germany (Bloch 1966a; Rösener 1992). By the sixteenth century, however, the legal functions of the manor courts had largely been taken over by regional *parlements* in France and by provincial court systems in southwestern Germany. By this time in France the royal government depended on local village governing bodies to keep order in the provinces (see Root 1987), as did the princes in southwestern Germany (Robisheaux 1989, 33).

Conversely, in regions of less-communal open field systems and enclosures manorial control over rural affairs typically was weak. Once again, the separation of lord and peasant is reflected in the structure of landholding. Demesne lands often were physically removed from peasant holdings. Furthermore, usually few or no labor services were required of tenants. In regions of less-communal open fields and enclosures in England and parts of the northern Netherlands, much of the peasantry was free of any kind of feudal obligations, as there was a large proportion of freeholding peasants. Similarly, manorial control was relatively weak in much of the southern Netherlands, Sweden, southern France, and Normandy. In these regions manorial dues and services were traditionally light or nonexistent.

There are, however, exceptions to these generalizations. The association of the communal open field system with strong manorial control was not found everywhere. All of Sweden remained lightly manorialized throughout the late medieval and early modern periods, despite extensive communal open field systems in much of southern Sweden. Nor were less-communal field systems always associated with weak manorial control. Brittany, a region of enclosures and less-communal open fields, was also a region where seigneurial control was strong and serfs (*mainmortables*) existed nearly to the end of the ancien régime. Many of these serfs were subject to especially heavy feudal dues and labor services (Goubert 1973). Yet even in Brittany there were places where there was a large free peasantry (see chap. 6). Another exception is eastern Germany, a region of less-communal open field systems. There, before the sixteenth century, manorial control was very light and the peasants relatively free. Events of the sixteenth century, however, changed this. The obligations of the peasantry were increased and their freedoms curtailed, in a process often referred to as the second serfdom (see chap. 7).

Despite these exceptions, the general association between class relations and field systems has led many scholars to suggest that there may have been some causal connection between them. For example, many attribute the formation of the communal open field system to actions of the lord of the manor, which would explain why communal open field regions also tended to be highly manorialized regions. Others have argued, however, the reverse pattern of causality—that is, that the field system determined class relations (Homans 1988c, 155). According to this argument, it was easier for lords to take power in regions where there were centralized villages in which most people lived and where there were strong village organizations that could be controlled. It was much harder to dominate people who lived scattered in hamlets and individual farms, and this explains why such regions were typically weakly manorialized. This brings us to the knotty problem of why regional differences in field systems and settlement patterns existed at all.

### Local Economic Organization and Ecology

Ecology appears, at first glance, the most likely factor to explain variation in field systems across Europe. As discussed previously, this has become one of the most widely accepted explanations for regional differences in preindustrial Europe (see Thirsk 1967; Clay 1984; de Planhol and Claval 1994, 140). Thus, it is necessary to address it directly. I begin with Bloch's (1966a) argument for France, in which he argued that different field systems were a product of both ecology and plow technology (although he noted that the argument was not entirely adequate [see 45]).

Bloch suggested that the shape of the fields, and consequently the organization of agriculture, was influenced by the type of plow used in the region. This in turn was determined by the regional ecology. In hilly, sparsely populated areas of poor soil the *araire,* or stick plow, was used; this gave rise to areas of square fields and less-communal field systems or enclosures. These fields were most conveniently farmed in an individualistic fashion; hence, a noncollective system of agriculture emerged. The wheeled plow was used in areas of better and heavier soils, because the ridge and furrow pattern the plow produced served to drain the soil.[4] As the heavy wheeled plow was difficult to turn, fields were arranged in long strips, with each strip being the equivalent of a day's plowing. Scattering of the strips of a holding was implemented so that each cultivator had a share of each different kind of land and therefore all cultivators shared the same risks and opportunities. The resulting long, narrow, scattered strips of arable were farmed most conveniently in a collective fashion. Therefore, areas where the heavy wheeled plow was used were areas of communal agriculture and the communal open field system.

Bloch's ecological and technological argument works best for his native France, but to some extent it also fits evidence from other regions. Throughout Europe there was a correspondence between the use of the heavy wheeled plow, long strip fields, ridge and furrow cultivation, and the communal open field system (cf. Kerridge 1992). Since use of the wheeled plow represented a substantial investment in capital and effort that could rarely be undertaken by one farmer alone, it is very plausible that communal agricultural practices would most likely have arisen in areas where the wheeled plow was used. This is what we find. Much of northern France, midland England, and southern Germany was characterized by use of the wheeled plow, long strips of land, and communal open field systems (Smith 1967, 240). In central Sweden, southern France, and other Mediterranean regions, where soils tended to be poorer, the *araire* was used. In these areas square fields were the rule, and there was little communal involvement in agriculture.

The argument, however, is not valid for all regions in France or elsewhere. By and large the use of the wheeled plow was dominant north of a line running through Bordeaux in southern France through the Alps to Italy (Smith 1967, 203). Yet within this wheeled plow region many areas of good soil were *not* characterized by the communal open field system—for example, much of Normandy (Delisle 1903, 34) and parts of England, Sweden, the Netherlands, and Germany. Thus, use of the wheeled plow did not lead necessarily to the development of communal systems of agriculture. Furthermore, the existence of long strips of land in the fields was not necessarily a sign of either the use of the wheeled plow or communal agriculture. In parts of central France and Sweden land was divided into many long narrow strips, even though it was not worked by a heavy plow (Smith 1967, 200). In most of communal open field Sweden with the *solskifte* system of land division the moldboard (wheeled) plow was absent (Göransson 1961, 82). In such regions sometimes land would be worked collectively in some way, sometimes not. Thus, there was not always a direct correspondence between plow type, existence of strip fields, and degree of communal control of agriculture (Dion 1934, 96–110; Smith 1967). Bloch himself conceded that use of the wheeled plow and fields of long strips alone could not account entirely for the strength of communal regulation present in communal open field regions and suggested that communal regulation was the product of "an attitude of mind" that was absent in areas of less-communal fields and enclosures (1966a, 59).

Ecological arguments not referring to plow technology also have been made. For instance, Thirsk (1967) relates regional differences in field systems to local ecology, the agricultural specialization best suited to this ecology, and the local population density (see also Clay 1984; Goldstone 1988; de Planhol and Claval 1994, 140). She suggests that areas of fertile soil were most suitable for grain growing and therefore also densely populated. It was in such areas that the communal open field system evolved. High population density created a situation in which grazing land was in short supply; hence, the communal system was implemented by the village community to ensure adequate grazing land for all. Areas of poor soil and unfavorable ecology, however, tended to have low population densities and a more pastoral focus. In such regions there was a plentiful supply of grazing land and thus never any need for communal grazing and communal organization of agriculture. As a result, these regions were characterized by less-communal field systems and/or systems of enclosures.

This argument seems to have much to recommend it. The fertile plains of northern France, southern Germany, and central England were all devoted primarily to the growing of cereals and were all characterized by dense populations and communal systems of agriculture. In addition, the argument that enclosed and less-communal regions were pastoral regions fits the areas where the ecology was highly inhospitable—such as the high-altitude, wet, and cold areas of Scotland and Wales, parts of Brittany, and the Massif Central and Pyrénées regions of southern France. These regions were suitable only for pasture farming. This ecological explanation also appears to fit the more marginal lands of southwestern England, parts of East Anglia, some of the northern and eastern Netherlands, parts of the north German plain, and parts of western and northern Sweden fairly well. These were lands of poor soils, moor, marsh, or heath with low population density, an emphasis on animal husbandry, and less-communal systems of agriculture (Bailey 1989).

Yet not all fertile, densely populated, cereal-growing regions were regions of communal agriculture. This ecological explanation breaks down when applied to parts of eastern England, the coasts of southwestern England, part of the southern Netherlands, northwestern Germany, or Normandy in France. These were fertile grain-growing regions in the late medieval period, with a temperate climate (see chaps. 4–7). They had some of the highest population densities in Europe, yet none were ever farmed according to a communal open field system of agriculture (Douglas 1927; Titow 1965; Smith 1967, 263; Hallam 1981).[5] Conversely, communal agricultural systems were found in some ecologically marginal areas of Europe. For example, the western, southern, and eastern edges of the Parisian basin are marginal and infertile regions yet were characterized by the communal open field system (de Planhol and Claval 1994, 142). Similar exceptions may be found all over Europe. In some cases different systems of agriculture could be found in regions that were adjacent to each other and very similar ecologically. There was no *necessary* association between agricultural specialization, population density, and communal participation in agriculture (Blum 1961; Chayanov 1986; Bois 1984; Overton 1996, 61; see also Hopcroft 1995).

In sum, ecology is a good first attempt at explaining regional differences in economic organization across Europe. Ecology was associated with regional differences in field systems, as the most naturally fertile land of Europe typically was characterized by communal systems of agriculture. Yet there are important exceptions that call into question the proposed relationship between ecology and field systems.

## Alternative Explanations of Communal Open Field Systems

To date most scholars who have offered nonecological explanations of field systems have been interested in explaining the origins of the communal open field system. This is the most distinctive of the European field systems, and hence its evolution is seen as being most problematic. Given the paucity of evidence, all such explanations are somewhat speculative. In what follows I review and critique these explanations of the communal open field system and offer an explanation of my own.

### Ethnic Settlement

Early studies attributed differences in agrarian structures across Europe to the different groups that settled in the different areas (see Meitzen 1895; Gray 1915; Homans 1987). The most famous of these early studies was the early work of Meitzen entitled *The Settlement and Agrarian Structure of the Western and Eastern Germanic Tribes, Celts, Romans, Finns and Slavs* (English translation of German title). In this work Meitzen argued that communal open field villages had their origin in early Germanic society and the institution of the German "mark community." Over the years this explanation has been roundly criticized. For example, Bloch criticized Meitzen's work for oversimplifying and covering up the complexity involved in the evolution of field systems. He wrote: "Quite apart from his various misconceptions, he made the mistake of confining his attention to the historic peoples, the Celts, Romans, Germans and Slavs. But one would need to go much further back in time than this, to the anonymous prehistoric groups of men who first created our fields. 'Race and 'people' are words best left unmentioned in this context; in any case, there is nothing more elusive than the concept of ethnic unity. It is more fruitful to speak of types of civilization" (1966a, 62). Given that Bloch wrote those words in about 1930, a time when nationalism was on the rise throughout Europe, it is understandable that Bloch was uneasy about the concepts of "race" and "people."

Bloch's criticisms of the ethnic explanations of field systems have found echoes in more recent works (Thirsk 1964; Smith 1967, 262; Rösener 1992, 48; de Planhol and Claval 1994, 135). These works criticize ethnic explanations for suggesting that agrarian structures were transported fully fledged from one region to a new region of settlement, when there was abundant evidence of evolution and change over the years. For example, Rösener criticizes Meitzen's theory as follows: "Recent research in the history of rural settlement has shattered this theory by showing in great detail that nuclear villages with their open field system developed only during the high Middle Ages and that they were preceded by smaller settlement types in the early Middle Ages" (1992, 48). Thus, since the communal open field system in its "classic form" was a phenomenon of the high Middle Ages, it cannot be traced back directly to the time of the Germanic invasions of the early Middle Ages.

These and other criticisms have meant that ethnic explanations have fallen largely from favor. They have been replaced with more materialist explanations that attributed the development of communal open field systems either to functional requirements of farming scattered strips of land or problems caused by population growth.

### Scattering

Many scholars have suggested that the communal open field system was a product of the scattering of each farmer's strips of land throughout the land of the village. Scattering itself has been theorized as product of joint plowing (Vinogradoff 1892; Gray 1915), as a means of equalizing shares of land among villagers (Seebohm 1890), as a product of the colonization of new land (Bishop 1935), and as a result of land fragmentation caused by partible inheritance (Thirsk 1984). A risk-aversion argument for scattering was put forward by Marc Bloch (1966a) and later supported mathematically by Donald McCloskey (1976).[6] More recently, Fenoaltea (1988) suggested scattering was an efficient system of landholding because it prevented shirking on plowing duties by agriculturalists.

Such explanations typically assume that, given scattered plots of land, an organized and communal rotation of crops and fallow soon would be devised as an optimal solution to agricultural problems created by scattering. This would lead inevitably to the evolution of a communal open field system of agriculture. Yet this assumption cannot be made so easily, as empirical evidence shows that scattering of plots of land per se does not lead necessarily to the development of a fully fledged communal open field system. A comparison with other field systems in preindustrial Europe shows that scattering by itself was not unique to the highly communal system of agriculture but was also found in less regular and less-communal field systems. Farms in regions of less-communal open field systems, as described earlier, typically were made up of scattered plots of land. Nor was scattering unusual in areas of enclosures (Juillard, Meynier, de Plan-hol, and Sautter 1957; Dovring 1965; Dodgshon 1980). Similarly, a wider comparison with evidence concerning preindustrial agricultural systems worldwide shows that scattering of land plots is very common. Scattering of farm plots is characteristic of much of the agriculture of contemporary Africa, Latin America, and Asia (Meynier 1959; McCloskey 1975). In most of these cases scattering is accompanied by minimal communal regulation of agriculture. Thus, since scattering of plots of land is prevalent among preindustrial agriculturalists and does not lead necessarily to communal regulation of agriculture, then scattering of landholdings cannot explain the emergence of highly communal open field systems.

## Population Growth

Population growth often has been suggested as the primary catalyst for the development of the communal open field system in Europe. The argument associates this with the replacement of more extensive systems of agriculture by more intensive systems, especially through the introduction of a three-course crop rotation in place of a two-course crop rotation (Abel 1955; de Planhol 1957; Blum 1961; Slicher van Bath 1963b; Braudel 1990; Rösener 1992, 51). A three-course rotation allows the possibility of two cereal crops a year, rather than one, and hence increases agricultural productivity. This happened early with the population growth of the eleventh to the thirteenth centuries in western Europe and perhaps as late as the sixteenth century in northern Russia (Robinson 1932; Blum 1961). Population growth also stimulated nucleation of villages at this time. Archaeological evidence from England, Sweden, and Germany shows that nucleated villages characteristic of open field regions were preceded by systems of scattered habitations more characteristic of less-communal and enclosed field areas (Dodgshon 1980; Abel 1955; Braudel 1990; de Planhol and Claval 1994, 135).[7] Thus, both the three-course rotation and the nucleated village characteristic of communal open field systems are attributed to population growth.

Thirsk (1984) puts forward a variation on this argument that complements her ecological argument. She describes the development of communal open field systems under pressure of population growth, in combination with inheritance customs. She suggests that population growth caused a shortage of pasture land for grazing animals, while partible inheritance customs (dividing land among all the heirs) led to fragmentation of landholdings into many narrow, scattered strips. In response to difficulties of grazing animals on so many scattered fragments of land, farming communities developed the communal open field system. The village land was rearranged so as to group all the arable land of the village into two or three large fields. This would ensure that every year there would be one large block of land (the fallow field) for the village herds to graze, although it also necessitated communal cropping. Thirsk suggests that this occurred gradually, through neighborly agreements, and as evidence of this process she cites cases of agreements between neighbors in late medieval England. In short Thirsk suggests that the communal open field system was implemented by the village community because it offered advantages in the form of communal grazing to all cultivators (Thirsk 1984; see also Dion 1934; Beckett 1989; de Planhol and Claval 1994, 135).

Communal grazing had several advantages. First, it saved each villager the time, effort, and cost of fencing his or her fallow field individually. By grouping the entire village herd into one large field, only one fence needed to be constructed to keep the herd from the growing crops. Second, it saved on supervision costs: only one shepherd was necessary to watch the entire village herd, rather than each villager having to watch to make sure his or her animals did not stray into fields under cultivation (Clark 1988; de Planhol 1957). Communal grazing, however, also had disadvantages. Costs of common grazing included uncontrolled livestock breeding and endemic disease (McCloskey 1975; Godoy 1991). Overgrazing was also a possibility, although village rules usually prevented this. Other indirect costs of common grazing were that each farmer was subject to communal control of his or her planting and harvesting.

Insofar as the communal open field system represented a more intensive agricultural system, capable of supporting more people than formerly, this population growth explanation is certainly true. The introduction of a three-course rotation was clearly a response to population growth. Yet it should be remembered that it was possible to have a three-course rotation and not have a communal open field system, just as it was possible to have a communal open field system without a three-course rotation (e.g., in Sweden, where a communal open field system coexisted with no rotations at all). Population growth in medieval Europe may have promoted the transition to a three-course crop rotation, but it did not lead necessarily to the implementation of the communal open field system. For example, it has been documented that in eastern England land was divided into smaller and smaller parcels in response to population growth (as Thirsk's theory would predict), yet these small strips of land never were arranged in a regular two- or three-field system through neighborly agreements. Instead, a chaotic arrangement of small strips of land was the final result (Williamson 1988; Titow 1965, 86–192; Campbell 1980, 174–92). Similar processes occurred in other areas of Europe that were characterized by growing populations and less-communal field systems, for instance, areas in southern France, northern Italy, and the Low Countries. In these regions land division, or dispersed new settlements in regions of less dense population, were the typical products of population growth—not communal farming systems (de Planhol and Claval 1994, 141). Nor were nucleated villages a necessary product of population growth, as population growth frequently led to the dispersal of populations, not their concentration. Thus, population growth may have been one of the conditions under which the communal open field system emerged, but it is not sufficient to explain the particular form the system took.

### The Problem of Process

In addition to challenging the plow technology, scattering, and population growth explanations with empirical exceptions, we also can challenge assumptions they make about the behavior of preindustrial cultivators. These arguments all suggest that cultivators created the communal open field system from less-communal and more individualistic systems of scattered strips because the open field system offered them several advantages in terms of common plowing, common grazing, and other labor-saving conveniences. Yet, even if we accept those advantages, it cannot be assumed that changing to the new system was relatively unproblematic. On the contrary, there are reasons to doubt that the implementation of an open field system would have followed easily from the recognition of its advantages for the collective.

The communal open field system could have been adopted by two possible processes. First, it could have evolved gradually. This would have occurred presumably in response to a change in another factor—population size being most likely. Yet, as we have seen, evidence from eastern England contradicts this hypothesis. In addition, it seems doubtful that a system as regular as the open field system would have evolved naturally. The system embodies conscious planning and design (Bloch 1966c, 276). The planned nature of the open field system is perhaps best illustrated by the common use of the *solskifte,* or "sun division," to designate each villager's holding in the open field, as noted. In the fields cultivators' strips occupied a set order, so that each cultivator always had the same persons owning the adjoining strips. Similarly, the glebe lands—lands belonging to the church—usually occupied the same relative position in each furlong (Homans 1941; Rowley 1986, 101). A person given land "toward the sun" had strips in the east or south of each furlong, while a person with land "toward the shade" had strips in the west or north of each furlong. This practice of sun division apparently had religious (or superstitious) significance (Homans 1941; Göransson 1961, 80–101; Dodgshon 1980).

The regularity suggests the second process by which the communal open field system may have been implemented—through a major rearrangement of land at a single point in time. The process, however, cannot simply be assumed. Suppose that prior to such reorganization each individual farmer's strips of land were not held in any regularly distributed fashion throughout the land of the village. In order to create the communal open field system farmers would have had to have given up some familiar plots of land in exchange for unfamiliar strips of land. In addition, cultivators would have had to agree to communal regulation of when and what they planted and when it was to be harvested and to submit to rules and regulations governing agricultural practice laid down by village bylaws. The process would have inevitably involved other short-term costs for cultivators, such as disruption of the year's agricultural schedule and the time involved in sorting out the logistics of equitable land exchanges.

Moreover, there would have been little assurance that the newly rearranged system would prove superior to the older, more disorganized system. In addition, many farmers undoubtedly would have feared that such a major land exchange would provide an opportunity for richer and more powerful villagers to profit at others' expense. Such risks probably would have been unacceptable in a population practicing subsistence agriculture, in which one failed harvest could spell disaster. Implementation of a communal open field system would have required the cooperation of most people in the community, yet it is unlikely that almost everyone would have agreed to pay the costs and accept the risks of implementing such a major change (Scott 1976; Campbell 1981). In the absence of coercion it seems that risks and costs of implementing the open field system would have outweighed the potential benefits for many farmers—at least for enough farmers to prevent such a system from being implemented very often, if at all.

Empirical support for this analysis is found in the fact that, despite the labor-saving benefits of the communal open field system, it was not universal in northern Europe, as indicated by the widespread existence of more individualistic field systems composed of enclosures or less-communal fields. Also, we have no direct evidence of any major reorganization of a village field system from a noncommunal to a communal two- or three-field system in preindustrial Europe. The rarity of the communal open field system can be illustrated further by contemporary agrarian societies, in which, despite scattering of land holdings, communal grazing is rare, and cultivators usually settle for more individualistic and less efficient means of grazing their animals on their own plots of land (Despois 1957; Pignede 1966, 133; Toffin 1984, 88).

## The Role of the Feudal Lord

In recognition of these problems, social factors have been invoked to explain the emergence of communal open field systems. It has been suggested that individual farmers may have been forced into reorganizing their lands, by a feudal lord or other powerful body. According to Campbell and Godoy (1986), this probably occurred sometime during the ninth and tenth centuries and was implemented as a response to labor shortages caused by declining population (see also Dodgshon 1980; Campbell 1981). There is also evidence that labor control was the motivation for the creation of common-field agriculture in the Andes in the early modern period. Kerridge also suggests that labor shortage was responsible for the manumitting and "hutting" of former slaves in Anglo Saxon times and suggests this was an important precursor to the growth of communal field systems in midland England (Kerridge 1992).

Some circumstantial evidence for the role of manorial authorities in the creation of communal open field systems is provided by the fact that areas of communal open field agriculture tended to be heavily manorialized areas, as noted earlier (Campbell 1980; Williamson 1988). There are many reasons to suppose that a communal system of agriculture was in the lord of the manor's interest: it made assessment of taxes easier and promoted stability in landholding, both of which were desirable from the lord's point of view. Much evidence from the late medieval period suggests that it was monitoring by the manorial court that preserved the regularity of the agricultural system from century to century (Homans 1941).

Such an explanation, however, also has problems. Although evidence is plentiful (from the late Middle Ages) that the feudal lord maintained and regulated the system, there is little evidence that he was responsible for its original organization. We can question the ability of the lord to effect any major changes in established agricultural systems. Many studies of late medieval villages show that force of custom restrained the lord from abusing his position, from exploiting villagers without limit and having his way in general in the village (Raftis 1964, 209; Dewindt 1972, 10). By extension it would have been very difficult for feudal lords to effect major changes in agricultural organization, especially if cultivators were loathe to part with their parcels of land for the reasons discussed previously. A major reorganization would have been possible in the case of conquest; and perhaps it is in such cases that this explanation is most correct.

There are other problems with the argument that the communal open field system emerged as a response of the feudal lord to declining population. In a period of declining population there would have been no necessity for village animals to graze on the fallow field. Animals could have been herded communally on uncultivated lands. This would have avoided some of the problems of grazing on the fallow, mentioned previously, and yet still offered the labor saving advantages of communal grazing. Without the necessity of a compact area of land for fallow grazing, there would have been little reason to organize a communal open field system. In support of this point, there is evidence that the three-field system was abandoned in northern Russia for more extensive agricultural systems in the time of declining population of the late sixteenth century (Blum 1961, 166). Moreover, the initial change to a less-communal common-field system would have involved less upheaval, and thus less resistance by cultivators, than a change to a more communal system.[8]

Thus, with manorial lords we have a problem similar to that for individual cultivators. How could they have—and why would they have—managed to introduce a communal system of agriculture in some regions? Moreover, why was such a system never developed in other, ecologically similar regions?

## A "Path-Dependent" Explanation

Here I offer a path-dependent explanation that sees the creation of a communal two- or three-field agricultural system as a response to shortages of pasture land created by population growth but only in regions where initial conditions meant it was not costly. This may or may not have involved the feudal lord at some point. The following discussion outlines a plausible scenario in which it would involve minimal costs and risks for individual farmers to implement a communal open field system.

The scenario can begin in different ways. For example, imagine a situation in which new land for cultivation was cleared by a village as a collective and then divided up among individual farmers in a systematic fashion or one in which a group took over another group's lands then shared the conquered land out among themselves in the same systematic fashion. Alternatively, imagine a situation in which a feudal lord divided up his lands in a regular fashion among his former slaves (as proposed by Kerridge 1992). We should presume that the landholdings of a single family or individual would be scattered throughout the area in question, to ensure that each family had its share of the risks and/or benefits associated with different pieces of land.

Add to this initial land division a continuation of customs of communal clearing and land division and furthermore add inheritance rules, which ensured that each plot of land was divided equally among heirs or, alternatively, was inherited by only one person. If such customs were followed, eventually each holding of land would be scattered regularly over the land belonging to the community. Add to this the use of a wheeled plow, which, because it was difficult to turn, meant that fields tended to be much longer than they were wide. The division of land under population pressure, in this scenario, would result naturally in long strips of land, rather than shorter, square fields. The strips of land would not constitute a communal two- or three-field open field system, however, as there would be no common rotation and perhaps no communal grazing.

With the passage of time and the growth of population the number of strips of land would multiply, until at some point the difficulties of grazing animals on the fallow of so many different narrow strips of land would become acute. In other words, the incentive for reorganization into a system with only one large fallow field would increase, perhaps exacerbated by the diminishing area of natural pasture or unused land for grazing animals.

In this scenario, however, reorganization would involve little upheaval. Since each cultivator already would have a plot of land in all sections of the village land, creating large coterminous sectors or fields of uniform cropping and fallowing would involve no land exchange. It would involve simply an alignment of cropping schedules of individual farmers. In addition, if farmers who shared land collectively already had some village administrative apparatus, the process of reorganization would become even simpler. If the village administration then undertook the task of maintaining the communal system of agriculture and enforcing inheritance rules, then the long-term survival of the system would be assured. In this scenario not only might the benefits from the communal open field system have outweighed the costs to each individual farmer of contributing to its formation, but its implementation would have involved little or no risk or uncertainty. Note that it also would have been relatively easy for manorial authorities to bring about the new system, if they had desired to do so (cf. de Planhol and Claval 1994, 136).

In short, it is probable that the communal open field system emerged among people who adhered to a tradition of communal clearing or the systematic sharing of new land or newly conquered land. Such customs certainly were found in communal open field regions in the late medieval period (Dion 1934, 45; Beresford 1979). But did they predate the system itself? There is some evidence that they did. Ine's law of the eighth century (in England) equates common land with "deal land," or land divided out in equal shares. That these shares were regularly distributed is documented by other evidence from the ninth, tenth, and eleventh centuries. For instance, charters from the tenth and later centuries specifically granted or leased every second, third, eighth, or ninth acre in the fields (Kerridge 1992, 22). Thus, there is clear evidence that regions of communal open fields were regions where there had long been customs of dealing out land in a regular and equitable fashion—at least going back to the eighth century.

We may trace these customs back even earlier to various Germanic groups that settled different parts of Europe. Customs of egalitarian land division may have been brought to England and other places in Europe by Germanic groups that invaded western Europe in the fifth and later centuries. This is supported by much circumstantial evidence. For instance in France, place name evidence suggests that the region later characterized by the communal open field system was a region heavily settled by Germanic peoples during invasions of the fifth and sixth centuries (Bonnaud 1977; de Planhol and Claval 1994, 63, 67). Similarly, archaeological evidence shows that the incidence of Anglo-Saxon burial places is most frequent in the midland and central regions of England. This suggests that battles were bloodier and thus Anglo-Saxon settlement was thicker in those regions that were later home to communal open field systems (Kerridge 1992; Williamson 1988). It appears that, wherever certain Germanic groups settled in large numbers, communal open field systems later emerged. This suggests they imported into those regions the cultural precursors of the communal system. It is important to note, however, that the argument presented here does not depend on regular systems of land division being a particularly Germanic trait. It appears to have been shared by many tribal groups of early Europe. For instance, the organization of the Russian family commune seems to have resembled the organization of Germanic tribes (Blum 1961, 25).

This brings us back to the ethnic explanations of Meitzen (1895), Gray (1915), and Homans (1987a), but with a twist. That is, this explanation does not suggest that agricultural systems were brought in full-fledged by the different groups that settled different regions. Nor does it deny that they evolved and changed given the demands of new situations and rising population. Thus, considerations of defense, access to water, the nature of the new terrain, preexisting settlement patterns, and pressures of population growth doubtless helped determine the form and evolution of each settlement. The explanation does suggest, however, that groups that settled in the various regions brought agricultural customs with them that later made it more likely that certain systems of agriculture (and not others) would emerge in those regions.

How do we explain the customs themselves? Customs of communal clearing, land division, and prescribed inheritance rules are not uncommon among preindustrial cultivators. It is quite possible that they may have taken a particularly regular form in parts of northern Europe. We may surmise that both familial and community organization were strong in the face of the severities of winter in the inland areas of northwestern Europe. In turn, strong village communities may have worked to maintain the regular nature of land division and inheritance rules, assuming that they operated on democratic or both democratic and hierarchical principles. We then can imagine that groups maintained these customs when they migrated to other regions and that these customs later facilitated the emergence of communal open field systems across the plains of Europe. At this later time feudal lords also had their own reasons to oppose changes in the structure of landholding and methods of inheritance. We know, for example, that feudal lords typically enforced inheritance rules of primogeniture.

In sum, I have suggested that the communal open field system in preindustrial Europe would have been most likely implemented in those areas where agriculturalists maintained collective habits of a regular system of land sharing. Other considerations, in particular population growth, no doubt played a major role in the final implementation of a communal open field system. Yet an initial regular division of land (by a feudal lord or by the village community itself) and the continuation of customs of regular land division and inheritance laid the basis for its later emergence. Such customs and their enforcement by the village community or the feudal lord also maintained the communal open field system once it was created. If this argument is correct, we can see the communal open field system was in part a *social* creation, as Marc Bloch had anticipated.

### Origins of Less-Communal Open Field Systems and Enclosed Systems

Compared to the attention lavished on the origins of communal open field systems, less scholarly attention has been focused on explaining less-communal field systems and enclosed field systems, perhaps because they are less unusual to modern eyes and their origins therefore are seen as less problematic. These field systems, however, also had distinctive characteristics that differed from area to area: for example, the size and shape of the fields, the extent of rights in common, agricultural customs, names given to fields and pieces of land, customary land measures, and so on. How do we explain these variations? As we have seen, ecology often can help explain the form of field systems, but ecology does not always account adequately for the nature and distribution of field systems across preindustrial Europe. In the preceding discussion I suggested that sociocultural factors must also be invoked to explain communal open field systems. Are such factors also involved in the origin of less-communal open field systems or systems of enclosures?

Like the explanation of communal open field systems, early explanations of less-communal field systems and enclosures traced them back to different groups that settled in various regions (e.g., Meitzen 1895; Gray 1915). As noted earlier, however, these early explanations may have oversimplified the issue. It was not a simple matter of a certain group bringing a certain system to an area, because waves of different invasions over the centuries brought different groups to the same regions of Europe. Moreover, it was never a matter of groups bringing full-fledged agricultural systems with them but, rather, a question of them introducing new ways of doing things, which evolved in the new context, often in interaction with preexisting systems.

This being said, we can see that customs of specific groups could play a role in shaping the form of field systems. For these reasons let us review some of the linkages that have been made between agrarian regimes in particular regions and specific groups known to have settled in that area. These explanations tend to be controversial, mostly because of difficulties with the evidence on which they are based. This evidence includes archaeological evidence, institutional evidence, linguistic evidence, evidence of place names, and evidence from popular history (e.g., the English monk Bede's *History of the English Church and People*) and mythology. It is sketchy at best, and in all cases there is much that we can never know for sure. The invasions and great migrations of Europe took place at a time about which little is known, in large part because all the upheaval meant few people were bothering to record events as they took place.

Homans (1987b) used archaeological, place name, linguistic, and institutional evidence to link agrarian forms in East Anglia and Kent to Frisia and southern Denmark. To account for these similarities he suggested that Germanic invaders who came to England in the seventh and eighth centuries were not uniformly "Angles and Saxons" and may have arrived in several waves. Specifically, he suggested that Frisians, Franks, and Jutes came in earlier waves and settled the eastern seaboard in East Anglia and Kent (which were the regions of England closest to them). They brought with them the cultural complex that produced the less-communal field systems characteristic of eastern England. These people were mistakenly known in England as "East Angles" (hence East Anglia) and "East Saxons" (hence Essex). Angles and Saxons (from further toward the heart of Germany) came in subsequent waves and circled around the first new settlements in Kent and East Anglia to settle behind them on the midland plain. They brought with them the cultural precursors of the communal open field system. These people were known as the "Middle Angles," "Western Saxons," and "Southern Saxons" (hence, Wessex and Sussex). In later years parts of East Anglia and northern England also were settled by large numbers of Danes (in an area that became known as the Danelaw). Homans argued, however, that, although Danish influence served to modify the established field systems of East Anglia and northern England, it did not substantially change them.

Homans further argued that characteristics of rural social organization in East Anglia were remarkably similar to those found in Frisia—the region of the Continent closest to East Anglia. He summarizes his findings on the East Anglia-Frisia similarities thus:

> In the absence of the open-field system, in the concentration of the holding in one part of the village fields, in the customs of inheritance of land, and in the structure of the joint-family—the two are, it is not too strong a word, identical. Less precise, but none the less strong, are the similarities in structure and function of the larger social units above the holding, especially the small hundred or leet as a folk court and as a group of plowlands and vills. There are even traces in East Anglia of a double duodenary arrangement of territorial units from the plowland up. Still less clear, but still present, are hints of survival of the Frisian social classes. . . . Finally, East Anglia and Friesland share a more general characteristic, which may have been a resultant of the others: a high proportion of free tenures, a resistance to manorialization in the form of the *maneriolum.* East Anglia, indeed, is culturally more closely related to Friesland than it is to its nearest English relative, Kent. (1988a, 180–81)

Another piece of evidence for the connection between eastern England and Frisia is linguistic, as the language most similar to English is Frisian. According to Homans, these similarities are best explained by extensive Frisian (aka East Anglian) settlement in East Anglia. He concluded that, "if Frisians did not cross the North Sea, they certainly ought to have done so" (1988a, 159).

Not all regional patterns have been traced to invading groups. The distinctive field systems of southwestern England (Devon and Cornwall), Scotland, and Wales have been traced to the persistence of large numbers of Celtic peoples in those regions after the invasions (Gray 1915). While Angles and Saxons (and perhaps Franks, Frisians, and Jutes) settled in eastern England and the midland areas, they never settled in large numbers in lands further west or north (see the *Times Concise Atlas of World History,* 34). Partly thanks to the natural barrier posed by hills and mountains, the Celtic peoples in the west and far north were largely left unbothered. They therefore maintained their language, culture, and agricultural customs. For this reason, field systems of the west and north consisting of small square fields, many enclosures, and agricultural practices involving few common rights are often called "Celtic" systems. Similar field patterns are found in Ireland, western France, and Man (northern and central Sweden), and these may also be traced to the continued existence of Celtic peoples in those regions (e.g., Flatrès 1957; de Planhol and Claval 1994, 86 [Celtic-type field systems are described in more detail for France and Sweden in chapters 4 and 6]).

The distinctive field systems of Normandy in France have been attributed to the large numbers of Scandinavians who settled there in the ninth century (Bloch 1966a, 38; see also *Times Concise Atlas of World History,* 37)—hence, also the name: Normandy, land of the north men. Scandinavians cleared many new lands in Normandy and settled in places previously unsettled (such as the Cotentin Peninsula). In these and other areas Scandinavian influence is apparent in place names. This is especially so in the Pays de Caux, around Rouen, on the north coast of Normandy, and in the Cotentin Peninsula (Smith 1967, 160; de Planhol and Claval 1994, 87). Unlike much of northern France, in these places, *bocage* (enclosures) with small or large fields predominates (Brunet 1955).

The south of France, like Normandy, avoided extensive Frankish settlement and influence. In Provence and Languedoc continuity from Roman times was most complete (Smith 1967, 139; *Times Concise Atlas of World History,* 34; de Planhol and Claval 1994, 48). This may account for the distinctive settlement forms of enclosures and less-communal open fields in southern and western France. In addition, the difference between the northern linguistic region of *langued'oui* and the southern region of *langued'oc* in France also may be traced in part to heavier Germanic influence in the north and lack of such influence in the south (de Planhol and Claval 1994, 125; see chap. 6 for more on French field systems).

In the Netherlands natural barriers of river and marsh helped protect native groups from the influx of invaders over the centuries. This also helped preserve high levels of peasant freedom, particularly in the northern Netherlands. This can help explain the endurance of the native customs and traditions of the Frisians in the northern Netherlands. Only in parts of the southern Netherlands was feudalism ever established, no doubt by Germanic overlords as in northeastern France (Smith 1967, 145). The distinctive field systems of the Netherlands are described in more detail in chapter 5.

Better documented than these early Germanic, Celtic, and Scandinavian settlements is the later Germanic settlement of eastern Germany from the twelfth through the fourteenth centuries (Holborn 1959, 8). Migrants from densely populated regions of the Netherlands and Frisia led the colonization movement and may be responsible for the distinctive nature of the east German field systems (van Houtte 1977, 8; Rösener 1992.)[9] Local lords brought in these migrants in an effort to increase their yields by clearances and by the introduction of techniques that were unknown to the natives. When forests and moorland were cleared in Brandenburg, Pomerania, and other parts of the German lands, the work was probably done by colonists from Brabant and the Meuse or Walloon regions of the Low Countries.To this day there is a region to the southwest of Berlin called Fläming, after the Flemings who settled there. The Dutch and Flemish were particularly important wherever marshes were drained, as in Holstein, or where river courses were diverted, as with the Elbe and many of its tributaries (van Houtte 1977, 8). New immigrants set up planned, open field systems of a character quite different from the highly communal open field systems of the west (see Carsten 1954; Rösener 1992). The new field systems embodied more private property rights and much less-communal regulation of agriculture and best fit the description of "less-communal open field systems." (The settlement process and the resulting field systems are described in more detail in chap. 7.)

My point in discussing these ethnic influences in various regions has been simply to note that they may have influenced agrarian structures in the various regions and not to present ethnic settlement as a complete explanation of field systems. We will never know for certain the extent to which ethnic factors influenced the form of field systems in various regions. Yet, as with the communal open field system, it is reasonable to suppose that, while ongoing considerations of ecology, population, politics, and defense shaped the evolution of field systems, they did so in conjunction with the social customs and traditional practices of the societies of people who settled in the various regions.

Field systems across preindustrial Europe differed dramatically in field shape and form but most notably in the extent of communal property rights and communal control over agriculture. Ecology, plow technology, type of agriculture, scattering, or population density cannot entirely explain these regional differences. We may never know exactly what caused regional differences in field systems. In the second part of this chapter, however, I argued that the different field systems of preindustrial Europe had, at least in part, a basis in the customs and culture of the different groups that settled in the various regions. Yet, although we may never be sure of their origins, that regional differences in field systems were (and still sometimes are) quite real is not in dispute.

CHAPTER 3

# The New Institutional Economics, Field Systems, and Economic Change

That men act in a social frame of reference yielded by the groups of which they are a part is a notion undoubtedly ancient and probably sound.
—Robert Merton and Alice Rossi,
*Social Theory and Social Structure*

When we describe rights of ownership, or of use, or of tenancy, we are talking about relationships between people. Rights imply duties and liabilities, and these must attach to people. A hectare cannot be sued at law, nor is a boundary dispute a quarrel with a boundary.
—John Davis, *Land and Family in Pisticci*

In the previous chapter I reviewed regional differences in field systems and discussed their possible origins. We saw that field systems in much of pre-industrial Europe may be categorized on a continuum that ranges from highly communal to noncommunal, with regular open field systems at one end and systems of enclosures at the other. Field systems shaped the lives of farmers in various regions of Europe, and we can imagine that they would have influenced development outcomes in different regions. This is what the new institutional economics suggests. That is, this theory suggests that the set of property rights embodied in any field system would shape the opportunity set of farmers. I turn now to an overview of the new institutional approach to development, from which I draw six general hypotheses. Later chapters examine whether the predictions derived from the new institutional economics are supported by regional outcomes in the different countries.

## The New Institutional Economics and Economic Change

The new institutional economics (NIE) builds on the neoclassical economic model of behavior. Thus, the standard version of NIE accepts the neoclassical premise that individuals in all societies, on average, prefer more wealth to less, all else being equal (Williamson 1975, 1985; North 1981, 1990a; Eggertsson 1990, 6; 1996; Clague 1997, 14–17). It should be noted that suggesting that people tend to prefer wealth does not imply that all people in all societies prefer wealth all the time. Nor does it imply that including wealth as an individual preference excludes the possibility that individuals also have other preferences, such as social status and acceptance, reproductive success, etc., that may at some times conflict with a preference for wealth. It does mean that enough people prefer wealth, enough of the time, to shape development outcomes in somewhat predictable ways (see also Olson 1997, 62). According to the neoclassical model, the total output of a society (which we may use as a proxy for level of development) may thus be conceived as maximization of some wealth-preferring function, subject to constraints imposed by current levels of technology, population, and resources (Cameron 1982; Ransom, Sutch, and Walton 1982).

The major contribution of the new institutional economics is to incorporate institutions into this model. It does this in the following way. In the neoclassical model constraints imposed by current levels of technology and resources may be considered "costs." For example, if resources are scarce, their costs are consequently high. This raises the total costs of production and thus inhibits development. NIE suggests that other costs also affect development including *transaction costs.* Transaction costs are *socially created* costs involved in production and exchange. They include *costs of defining and enforcing property rights* ("the right to use, to derive income from the use of, to exclude others, to exchange"); *of measuring the valuable attributes of what is being exchanged, and of monitoring the exchange process itself* (Coase 1960; Williamson 1975; North 1981; North 1990a, 27, 1990b, 184).[1] Transaction costs exist because information is costly and because uncertainty is inherent in the definition and enforcement of rights and in exchange.

This is how institutions are introduced into the neoclassical model, as institutions shape transaction costs. *Institution* is a word that in social science can have a wide variety of meanings; therefore, a narrow definition of institution is in order here. Institution is defined as a system of social rules that are accompanied by some sort of enforcement mechanism. Rules may be formal: for example, constitutions, laws, the specification of property rights, and so on (Coase 1960, Barzel 1989; North 1982, 23); or informal: norms, customs, mores (North 1990b, 192; Knight 1992), although the two categories often overlap. According to NIE, institutions, by defining property rights and rules of exchange and enforcing them, help determine levels of uncertainty and hence determine social costs involved in transactions—that is, transaction costs (Coase 1960). Institutions that maintain high levels of uncertainty increase transaction costs and thus inhibit development. Institutions that reduce levels of uncertainty decrease transaction costs and hence encourage development.

Institutions themselves exist (in part) because of the existence of positive transaction costs (North 1990a). That is, because transacting is costly, social groups develop rules to try to lower those costs and enforce those rules. The rules include property rights (who owns what) and rules of exchange (what is fair and what is not). No transacting may occur in a state of total anarchy, that is, in which there are no rules or conventions, informal or otherwise. Yet rule systems, and hence institutional forms, differ, and some institutions do a better job of lowering transaction costs than others. Thus, according to NIE, development outcomes are a product of not just individual maximization given existing levels of resources and technology but also the nature of existing institutional arrangements. Furthermore, institutions become fixed as various interests become aligned with particular institutional forms. This means that institutional change is often slow, difficult, and almost always follows a path-dependent course. That is, new institutions typically are determined in part by preexisting institutions (North 1994; Greif 1995).

### Field Systems, Transaction Costs, and Development

Using the terminology of this theoretical approach, we may consider field systems in preindustrial Europe as a *product of local institutions.* That is, we can conceptualize field systems as the product of systems of both formal and informal social rules and their enforcement by the village community: norms of house and building location, rules specifying the extent of individual versus communal rights over land, norms of fencing, rules specifying agriculture practice, and norms of individual economic behavior. Implementation of these social rules (in conjunction with other factors) produced the set of property rights and associated field and settlement patterns we call field systems.

Clearly, these rules and enforcement systems were very obvious in regions of communal open field systems. Everyone was forced to conform to village norms of cropping, harvesting, and building by the village organization and, presumably, informal pressures. Anyone who did not conform was punished accordingly. In regions of less-communal field systems and enclosures, in contrast, there was a different set of formal and informal rules regarding the disposition of property. Compared to communal regions, property was considered to be more private in the modern sense, as cultivators had more individual rights over the land. Common rights were fewer, or absent altogether, and communal regulation of agricultural activities was typically minimal. There was often no body formally over-seeing cultivation as in communal areas; thus, rule enforcement in less-communal regions could be more informal and provided by the members of the community, a local court, or a higher authority such as the state.

Applying this theory to different field systems, we can see that com-munal open field systems embodied higher transaction costs than other types of field systems. This is primarily because costs of defining and pro-tecting rights over property were higher. This increased uncertainty and discouraged development. Why was this so? First, in communal systems of agriculture the individual right to use the land was carefully defined by vil-lage bylaws. In practice, however, rights were attenuated and subject to great uncertainty due to problems of monitoring and enforcement in the communal system. For example, in a system in which each farmer always had neighbors on each side of every strip of his land and in which there were rules forbidding fences, neighbors could "free-ride" on his agricul-tural efforts. Piers Plowman was referring to this when he said, circa 1378:

> If I go to the plough I pinch so narrow
> That a foot of land or furrow fetch I would
> Of my next neighbour, take of his earth;
> And if I reap, overreach, or give him advice that reap
> To seize to me with their sickle what I never sowed.
>
> (William Langland,
> *The Vision of Piers Plowman*)

There was always a temptation for farmers, sight unseen, to take a lit-tle of a neighbor's crop. Piers Plowman also mentions the temptation for "devourers of furrows" (see also Bloch 1966a, 37). These were people who, by driving their plow a little over the boundaries of their own furrows into their neighbors' furrows, could eventually appropriate additional land for themselves. Bloch notes that there is at least one instance of a parcel of land that was enlarged to more than a third of its original size in the course of sixty years (1966a, 38).[2] Common grazing deterred the private growing of forage crops, which not only provided animal food but also provided benefits for the soil. Free-riding by putting more than one's share of ani-mals into the common herd was another potential problem that could wreak havoc on common grazing areas. These problems created disincen-tives for long-term investment in land.

Second, neighboring farms created externalities (difficult to prevent even when there were rules against the practices) that could spoil efforts of individual farmers to improve agricultural output or the quality of their stock animals (cf. Thornton 1991). For example, communal grazing meant that it was impossible for individual farmers to control either stock breeding or the spread of disease. This made it difficult for farmers to improve the quality of their livestock. The close proximity of farmers' strips of land meant that a neighbor's negligence in weeding or maintaining his land could bring all of a farmer's efforts to rid his own land of weeds and unwanted bugs to nought. This also made it difficult for any farmer to improve the quality and productivity of his land (Clay 1984, 115) and deterred long-term investment.

We know about all of these difficulties of enforcing rights from the village laws and rules banning such practices and from court records that elaborate disputes over just these issues. The manorial court and the village organizations were organizational attempts to enforce and protect rights in the communal system and thus decrease transaction costs. Yet both the manorial court system and the communal regulatory bodies themselves served to increase opportunity and other costs for some farmers. For example, village regulations prevented individual cultivators from responding to market demands for particular crops, as the village community regulated the types of crops that could be planted in the common arable fields (cf. Biddick 1985). Village regulations also prevented experimentation with new techniques or tools that would disrupt the operation of the communal system. Village regulations also prevented the free exchange of land, as there were always strong rules and customs prohibiting the sale of family land. Likewise, withdrawal of land from the communal system was forbidden. This was because, if one person enclosed his or her land, then the whole system of agriculture would experience difficulties. In these ways the community organization and the manorial court, by actively opposing any changes in the existing agricultural system and preventing a free market in land, raised costs faced by those who might wish to change and improve agricultural practices. Further, manorial and other court systems, designed to decrease transactions costs by protecting and enforcing property rights in the communal system, could actually have the reverse effect. This was because of the complexity of rights in communal systems. Courts could become forums for endless negotiations over complicated property rights and thus could increase, not decrease, uncertainty over rights.

The communitarian ethic associated with the communal agricultural system may have helped decrease costs of enforcing communal rights. Yet, by discouraging the growth of economic inequality and the concentration of wealth in a few hands, it may also have discouraged efforts to increase production. Economic activities in communal open field communities were dominated by "what can only have been a desire to maintain the equality of the members of the community in economic opportunity" (Homans 1941, 337) and a desire for "ensuring that everyone got a share in the relatively scarce resources upon which they all depended for their living "(Clay 1984, 65) . One can surmise that such sentiments were often antithetical to the individual search for profit and the accumulation of private wealth. This may have deterred production for the market, and thus efforts to increase agricultural productivity. The common custom of holding the richest in the village accountable for the debts of all also may have discouraged accumulation of wealth.

Given these liabilities of the communal agricultural system, it may seem astonishing that such a seemingly inefficient system of agriculture ever evolved in the first place. It must be remembered, however, that the system ensured adequate pasture, and at least some harvest, every year for all in the village. It was a system that minimized subsistence risk (Bloch 1966a; Clay 1984, 65; Robisheaux 1994, 82). Furthermore, a communal system, and a strong communitarian spirit, meant that the poor were always provided for so that none were completely without means of survival. For example, even the landless typically had gleaning rights and rights to straw left in the common fields after harvest or could send a few animals into the common flock. Last, common ownership and intermixed land tenure was not merely an obstacle to individual initiative but also was a guarantee against conspicuous mismanagement (Østerud 1978, 147; Overton 1996, 167).[3] In early stages of the development of the system these benefits may have more than outweighed any loss of productivity. At later stages, particularly with a large increase in population density, the reverse may have become true. At this point, however, too many people had an interest in preserving the existing system for it to be dismantled without difficulty.

In less-communal and enclosed field systems the grouping of landholdings in one part of the village land, fewer common rights, and sometimes fences lowered the costs of protecting and enforcing property rights and hence transaction costs. Cultivators did not have to be concerned that communal agricultural practices would ruin the results of their hard work. Free-riding of neighbors could still be a problem, especially in regions where farms were made up of scattered strips of land. If a neighbor's practices were infringing on a farmer's land, however, he or she could put up a fence or even sell the land.

Opportunity costs were lower in less-communal and enclosed field systems. There were fewer restrictions on the exchange or sale of land. This made the consolidation of strips of land easier and thus facilitated the expansion of farms. It also meant that land could find its way to those who would use it most productively. There was little or no regulation of crop-ping or agricultural practices, so there was little to hinder innovators or those who wished to adopt more productive methods. Moreover, unlike in communal open field regions, there was no strong spirit of communitari-anism to inhibit pursuit of individual profit and wealth.

In sum, transaction and other costs were higher in regions of commu-nal field systems than in regions of less-communal and enclosed field sys-tems. This meant that there were more incentives in less-communal and enclosed areas than communal areas to increase and diversify production and invest in one's land and equipment. Private enforcement costs were lower. That is, individuals could spend more of their time on productive activities and less time protecting their rights, whether in court or else-where. Last, the costs of land exchange were lower in less-communal and enclosed areas, which meant that land could be used optimally. These con-siderations lead us to *expect more agricultural development and agrarian change in less-communal and enclosed regions than in regions of communal open field systems, all else being equal.* This is hypothesis 1.

I should note that here, for analytical reasons, I group the enclosed field systems with less-communal open field systems into one "less-com-munal" category. This differs from the classification of many past ana-lysts, who have pointed to the inefficiencies of the communal open field system and the efficiencies of enclosed systems. Here I point out that what was important for economic development was not enclosure per se but the nature of property rights. Less-communal rights were more efficient than communal rights; thus, what was important was not whether fields were open or enclosed but whether the property rights were communal or not. This goes beyond a simple division between open and enclosed systems and draws attention to the really important factor influencing economic change, which was not fences but the socially constructed rights governing economic behavior. This is a major point of departure of this analysis that needs to be stressed.

### The Role of Local Class Relations

In chapter 2 I noted that communal regions of preindustrial Europe tended to be regions where feudal control was strong. Associated with manorial control were courts provided and run by the feudal lord, and these courts often decreased transaction costs of defining and enforcing communal rights. Yet these same bodies often served to increase transac-tion costs, as courts became forums for the negotiation of less than clear property rights to land and rules of exchange.

There were other more straightforward costs associated with over-lordship. Feudal dues and taxes tended to be heavy in communal open field regions, and this meant that cultivators had little reason to produce a surplus on their own land, where it could be taxed away (although this was less true when dues were fixed in kind or in cash). Nor did they have any reason to produce a surplus on the lord's land for the lord himself. Feudal regulations also limited labor mobility, as they tied customary tenants to their holding and to the feudal lord.

In less-communal regions, on the other had, manorial exactions were proportionately lower. In fact, taxation in general (rent seeking and otherwise) was harder in such regions. Scattered habitations and smaller villages in regions of enclosures and less-communal open fields meant enforcing taxation was often more difficult than in regions of communal open fields. It is much easier to tax farmers in nucleated villages than it is to tax farmers scattered across the countryside, if only for the simple reason that it is easier for the latter to evade the tax collectors physically. Farmers in nucleated villages are easily accessible and have few places to hide either themselves or their goods. Farmers in scattered habitations and small villages are less accessible and have more places to hide themselves and their goods. Tax collectors often have to cover long distances to reach those who neglect to pay their taxes, often for little or no gain. For this reason residents of these regions were able to avoid taxation more than residents of communal open field regions. In the case of taxation to fund common goods—the building of roads, bridges, and other infrastructure—this would inhibit development. Yet in the case of rent-seeking taxation, of which much preindustrial taxation consisted, the difficulties of collecting taxes would have done a great deal to promote development.

In addition to a lack of taxes there were few other feudal restrictions on cultivators' activities in less-communal regions. Thus, not only were farmers relatively free of feudal dues and taxes, but they were free to move around, to buy and sell land, and to bequeath it to whomever they wished. This leads us to hypothesis 2: *agrarian change and development will be more likely in areas where overlordship is minimal.*

It could be argued that this factor alone reduced the productivity of communal regions. That is, the effect of communal institutions is spurious; rather, low agricultural productivity was a result of heavy overlordship typical of communal regions. Thus, it is instructive to look at the case of Sweden, which combined communal field systems with minimal or no overlordship in many regions. As we will see in chapter 8, even without extensive overlordship there is evidence that communal systems hindered agricultural development.

## Ecology, Market Access, and Demography

The new institutional economics draws attention particularly to the effects of social institutions on costs and as a result on economic development. Yet this does not preclude a role for more traditional factors such as resources, market access, technology, and demography. These shape regional development outcomes in the same way local institutional conditions do, by shaping costs and benefits for farmers. In preindustrial Europe basic agricultural technology did not differ greatly from region to region, but resources, as determined by ecological conditions (soil, terrain, and climate and other geographical factors), and demographic factors did. Proximity to markets for agricultural goods also differed, and this also influenced costs faced by producers. These factors have loomed large in previous analyses of economic change in preindustrial Europe. As noted earlier, many regional differences in agrarian change have been ascribed to such factors. The point here is not to disregard such factors but to separate their effects from the effects of local, socially created conditions.

With regard to ecological and geographical factors, we may expect that an inhospitable ecology (soil and climate) and a remote geographical location will inhibit development. Thus, we expect little rural development in mountainous or highly infertile regions, for example, mountains of the Massif Central in central France, northern England, the moors of southwestern England, northern Sweden, and so on. At the same time, ecological and geographical factors often influence development in unexpected ways, as some ecological difficulties can be turned into opportunities and resources. For example, no region has a more precarious ecological existence than the Netherlands, yet its ecological marginality has been in many ways an important positive factor in that region's economic success, as it enabled inhabitants to resist conquest and full incorporation into an external state. Furthermore, even the harshest physical environment may have some comparative advantage that can be turned into economic gain, as Bailey showed with regard to marginal lands of the Norfolk breckland (Bailey 1989). For this reason it seems unwise to make hard and fast predictions on the basis of the local ecology. We may note, however, that *development will be most likely in countries and regions with ecologies (soil, climate, and location) favorable for agriculture* (hypothesis 3).

Ecological and geographical factors are perhaps most important where they affect costs of market access. A remote location and an inhospitable ecology will increase the costs of access to markets, while access to navigable waterways will lower such costs. These considerations lead us to expect little development in remote and inhospitable regions that do not have easy access to markets for agricultural commodities. The availability of markets for agricultural goods will be influenced also by local population density and urbanization. In general we would expect increased population density and urbanization to increase demand for agricultural products and hence to spur higher agricultural productivity per unit of land (Boserup 1965). Hypothesis 4 states that *development will be most likely in countries and regions that have access to markets (urban and otherwise) where there is a high demand for agricultural commodities.*

### Factors Specific to the Protonational Setting

In addition to regional factors such as ecology, market access, and population density, there are also the factors specific to protonational settings that influence development in predictable ways. Like local factors, they influence costs and benefits associated with various economic behaviors. In past applications of the new institutional economics to economic development, the role of protonational legal and financial institutions has been particularly stressed (Barzel 1989; de Soto 1989; Campbell and Lindberg 1990; Bates 1990; North 1990a). According to NIE, where these state-made institutions increase transaction costs, development is less likely. Conversely, where these state-made institutions reduce transaction costs, development is more likely.[4] Of particular importance is state protection of property rights by means of appropriate legal institutions and court systems. When a reasonable set of property rights are enforced, contracts are made secure, and the outcome of both production and exchange becomes more certain. North and Thomas note that protection given to property rights was a notable aspect of states in preindustrial England and the Netherlands (1973, 64). In both countries such legal protection dates back at least to the thirteenth century and was an important cause of subsequent development in both countries.

North (1981) has shown further that in history there is a tension between the state's desire to increase wealth, which means creating institutions that serve to define and protect rights and thus lower transaction costs, and the state's desire to maximize its power and control, which involves creating institutions that lack consistency in the definition and protection of rights and thus increase transaction costs. States often choose the latter over the former, at the expense of economic growth (Eggertsson 1996, 12). For example, for short-term reasons autocratic (and other) governments may cease protecting property rights and even confiscate property. This increases uncertainty and hence transaction costs for many years to come. Similarly, high levels of corruption in state institutions increase uncertainty and thus transaction costs. Thus, hypothesis 5 suggests that *development will be most likely in countries and regions where state institutions (particularly legal institutions) and policies decrease transaction costs involved in production and exchange.*

Besides its role in shaping institutions that influence transaction costs, the state also can influence development through taxation (and other) policies. High levels of taxation and other exactions by the state (in addition to those imposed by local elites) can limit incentives for increased production (Jones 1988). This is the case when taxation is used not for purposes that might promote commercial activity—the building of roads, bridges, and other infrastructure; provision of welfare, policing, and defense functions, etc.—but purely for the private purposes of the rulers (conspicuous consumption, patronage, etc.). This is the typical pattern in history, and here I call it "rent-seeking taxation." Rent-seeking taxation could take the form of direct taxes on production, indirect taxes on sales, or disguised taxes such as manipulation of the currency and government monopolies (which also have the effect of increasing uncertainty and hence transaction costs). Another common occurrence is for autocrats and others to regulate and control prices, particularly of basic foodstuffs, in order to maintain stability and hence their own position. This is tantamount to a tax on producers, as it limits the prices they can demand. Hypothesis 6 suggests that *development will be most likely in countries and regions where state institutions and policies limit state taxation.*

### The State and War

Nowhere is the tension between the state's desire to maximize its power and control and the state's desire to increase its wealth in the long term more evident than in warfare. Warfare severely damages the wealth creation ability and potential of the regions in which it takes place, yet throughout the preindustrial period in Europe states repeatedly engaged in it. While there are long-term economic losses for the region or regions affected, there are short-term power, status, and other gains for individual autocrats, as warfare gave autocrats opportunities both to expand their domains and to consolidate their personal power (Tilly 1989, 1992; Downing 1992).

Wars damaged regions through destruction of crops, farm animals, and other capital goods and through disruption of the agricultural year. Wars also directly increased transaction costs, by way of increasing the frequency of trade embargos, controls on trade, piracy, brigandage, plus more frequent debasements of the currency and control of bullion flows (Munro 1994, 154).

The ability of regions to avoid warfare itself is affected by a variety of different factors, particularly geopolitical considerations. An island like England always has had greater protection from invasion than an inland region such as Germany. Similarly, the rivers and marshes of the northern Netherlands and the relative isolation of Sweden have protected those lands from invasion and warfare. Thus, all else being equal, we can expect more economic development in a place like England, which has not suffered an invasion since 1066, than in one like Germany, which long has been the battlefield of Europe. Similarly, we would expect more economic development in the northern Netherlands, with its natural protection, than in vulnerable northern France, which historically has seen nearly as much warfare as Germany. Thus, as a corollary to hypothesis 6, we can state that *development will be less likely in countries and regions where warfare is common.*

Given this reasoning, on the one hand, we generally would expect the most rural development in regions with less-communal field systems, little feudal control, very favorable ecologies, dense populations, access to markets, and, at the national level, relatively impartial legal institutions, low levels of rent seeking, and little warfare. On the other hand, we would expect the least development in regions with highly communal field systems, strong feudal control, unfavorable ecologies, sparse populations, little access to markets, and, at the national level, a lack of impartial legal institutions, high levels of rent seeking, and periodic warfare. In practice no region had exactly these combinations of factors. The analysis is often confounded by the fact that the factors that favored rural development frequently co-existed with factors that were highly detrimental to rural development. For example, as mentioned previously, the most desirable land of the European and English plains—with dense populations and the most access to markets—was characterized by strong feudal control and highly communal field systems. Sovereignty over these areas was often contested, and thus they experienced periodic warfare. Conversely, much of the least desirable land of Europe—with thin populations and little access to markets—was characterized by weak feudal control and less-communal field systems. These areas were able to escape warfare better than other areas. In both cases, however, the effects of the positive factors were typically outweighed by the effects of the negative factors, so the outcome was little rural development. There were some regions where the conjunction of factors was more serendipitous; in parts of eastern England, the Netherlands, Normandy, parts of the south of France, and northwestern Germany, there were regions where less-communal field systems combined with little feudal control, ecologies that did not pose insurmountable difficulties for agriculture, dense populations, and access to markets. In such cases, where circumstances at the national level permitted, sustained rural development was possible. In subsequent chapters I discuss these cases—from England, the Netherlands, France, Germany, and Sweden—in much greater detail.

## CHAPTER 4

# Rural Institutions and Agrarian Change in England

More profit is quieter found
(where pastures in severall be)
from one silly acre of ground
than champion makes of three.
Againe what a joye is it knowne
When men may be bold of their owne

The champion liveth ful bare
When woodland full merry doth fare.
—Thomas Tusser, *Fiue hundreth points of good husbandry Vnited to As many of good huswiferie*

Agricultural development in early modern England has earned the name the "agricultural revolution," not because agricultural achievements in England were greater than in places like the Netherlands but because they were sustained for long enough to facilitate the first industrial revolution. Further, all later Continental agricultural revolutions, including that in the Netherlands itself, were largely inspired by what had already taken place in England. It may be argued that, without the English example, these other periods of agrarian change would never have occurred at all. For these reasons the case of England is particularly important.

In this chapter I show how regional differences in field systems played an important role in shaping the course of agrarian change in late medieval and early modern England, just as Tusser (1965 [1573]) says they did. The more prosperous regions of England tended to be regions of less-communal open fields and enclosures (woodland), while communal open field regions (champion) lagged behind. Moreover, the less-communal regions led the way in agrarian change in England and thus were in part responsible for the agricultural revolution itself.

In what follows I first examine regional differences in ecology, population, and market access. Next, I note the regional difference in rural structures and class relations and then examine the effects of these regional differences on agrarian change for both the late medieval and the early modern period. Last, I examine the role played by factors particular to the national setting—state institutions and policies as well as warfare—in shaping rural development outcomes and, ultimately, the agricultural revolution.

## Ecology, Population, and Markets

Much of the best agricultural land in England is found in southern England in the midlands and central zone (incorporating much of the counties of Yorkshire, Derby, Nottingham, Lincolnshire, Rutland, Leicestershire, Staffordshire, Warwickshire, Northamptonshire, Cambridgeshire, Huntingdonshire, Bedfordshire, Buckinghamshire, Berkshire, Oxfordshire, Gloucestershire, Worcestershire, Hampshire, Sussex), while agricultural conditions are often inferior in parts of the east (Norfolk, Suffolk, Essex, Middlesex, Surrey, Kent), southwest (Cornwall, Devon, some of Somerset, Dorset), north (Cumberland, Westmoreland, Northumberland, Durham), and west (Lancashire, Cheshire, Shropshire, Herfordshire [see map 2]). Most of southern England is a flat and temperate zone. The best soil is found in the midlands or central area (clays and loams) (Grigg 1989). This region is also well watered and rarely suffers drought (Grigg 1989, 32). The eastern and southwestern parts of southern England are less well-endowed by nature. East Anglia in eastern England (i.e., Norfolk and Suffolk) may have the poorest ecology, with poor soil and climate. The soil of Norfolk, for example, is sandy and was frequently disparaged by medieval writers, as the following twelfth-century verse indicates:

> Every land and every sea
> Have I crossed, but much the worst
> Is the land of Norfolk cursed.
> That the land is poor and bad
> I the clearest proof have had
> If you plant the choicest wheat
> Tares and darnel you will meet.
>
> Satan on the road to Hell.
> Ruined Norfolk as he fell.
>                                    (Qtd. in Riches 1967, 35)

In the seventeenth century Charles I and Charles II are supposed to have remarked that Norfolk's soil was such that it should be divided among other counties to make the high roads (36). Norfolk is also subject to

**Map 2. The counties of England**

drought in the summer (Riches 1967; Grigg 1989) and is swept by cold winds coming off the North Sea in the winter. Other parts of the east are better endowed than East Anglia. For example, Kent, in the southeast, has better soils than Norfolk, although they are sandy in some places and alkaline toward the coast. Compared to the midland regions, the ecology is poor also throughout much of the southwest. Limestone rocks promote an alkaline soil in Devon and Dorset. Devon and Cornwall contain the moors. High, foggy, and windswept, the moors make particularly poor agricultural areas. The north and far west of England (often referred to as the "highland zone") has the least favorable ecology. Here the terrain is hilly and mountainous, the climate both cooler and wetter than elsewhere, and the soils relatively poor, so that only limited areas of land are suitable for arable agriculture (Clay 1984, 53).

In the late medieval period England was comparatively sparsely populated. Average densities were rarely more than about 40 people per square mile, as compared to northern France, where they reached 75 to the square mile, and the plain of Flanders, where they were often well over 130 to the square mile (Pounds 1990, 149). English population densities, however, were higher than in Sweden and much of the German lands (with the exception of parts of the west) at the same time. Within England population densities were highest in the eastern and midland counties (Russell 1948; Campbell 1984; Britnell 1991, 611). The poll tax of 1377 shows a population density of over 40 people per square mile in two eastern areas, Norfolk and part of southern Lincolnshire, and two midland counties, Northamptonshire and Bedfordshire. The southwest had a much lower population density—about 20 to 29 people per square mile in Cornwall and 30 to 39 people per square mile in Devon and Dorset (Darby 1969, 232). Population densities in the north and far west were lowest of all. This distribution of population did not change greatly until the industrial revolution (see Braudel 1984, 576), when concentration shifted to industrial regions of the north.

By the late medieval period the densely populated regions of the south and east also had the greatest access to markets. For the year 1500 (which typically marks the end of the medieval period) de Vries (1984, 160) found the area with the greatest urban potential or involvement in an urban system in England to be the southeastern region around London. Areas around London had easy access to the huge London market, as did the southern midlands (by river) and East Anglia (by sea). The south coast and southwest also had access to the London market by sea, although it was a longer voyage.

### Field Systems in Late Medieval England (c. 1200–1500)

Communal Open Field Systems

In late medieval England communal open field (champion) field systems were found in the fertile and densely populated midland and central regions (see map 3).[1] The communal system of central England approximated the "ideal type" of a communal open field system described in chapter 2, perhaps more so than communal systems anywhere else in late medieval Europe. In this region the great arable fields of the farming community, in addition to the commons proper, spread out around a large, compact village. Agriculture and grazing on the arable fields and the commons were communal and were regulated by a central body called the "byelaw" (Clay 1984, 65; Overton 1996, 26). This body coordinated cropping, harvesting, and grazing on the arable fields and on the commons and appointed village shepherds, fence keepers, and other village officials. The byelaw, in conjunction with the manorial court, typically enforced customs of primogeniture (inheritance of all land by eldest son) or the "borough English" custom (inheritance by youngest son). Such customs were widespread in communal regions. They kept individual landholdings (and hence the entire field system) intact across generations (Homans 1941, 110; King 1973, 170). This helps account for the "ideal-typical" form of the system in central England at this time. Also sustaining the system was a strong communitarian ethic, as was typical of regions of communal agriculture.

### Regions of Less-Communal Open Fields and Enclosures

To the east and west of the communal region of southern England were regions of less-communal open fields and enclosures. Here soil and climate were often poorer than in the midlands. In regions of less-communal open fields, crop rotations were typically not by field but usually by "shift" or a smaller section of land. Similarly, common grazing on the arable fields was often organized by shift. For example, the celebrated East Anglian *foldcourse* system was one such system. Each grazing shift would be fenced temporarily with wattles to keep animals from straying. In some places common grazing and common cropping on the arable fields were absent altogether. Even in the absence of common grazing and cropping on the arable fields, however, most villages had at least a small commons where animals were herded together. Some villages also possessed other common areas, such as a hay meadow or wood. As in communal open field areas, the community governed use of such commons. Compared to communal areas, however, community control of agriculture was minimal in these regions. This promoted greater diversity in farming arrangements and a greater variety in crops.

Because of the poor soils as well as the presence of the moors (in the southwest) and marshes (in the east), it often has been suggested that all these areas were primarily pastoral areas. This in turn has been used to account for the distinctive social organization found in these regions (e.g., Thirsk 1967; Clay 1984; Goldstone 1988, 296–97; Somers 1993). Yet, while pasture farming was certainly the predominant agricultural specialty of the moors in the southwest and some parts of the east, such as the Forest of the Weald and the East Anglian Breckland (Campbell and Power 1989;

Field System

▨ Communal Open Field

☐ Less-Communal Open Field

**Map 3. Field systems in England. (Adapted from Gray 1915.)**

Bailey 1989; Mate 1991, 134), the description pastoral does not fit most of eastern England and many places in the southwest.[2] Eastern England was a major producer of cereals at an early date. By the thirteenth century eastern Norfolk in particular was an important cereal exporter, producing barley and malt for an international market (Campbell 1983, 1991; Britnell 1991, 59–65). The ports of Boston (in Lincolnshire) and Lynn (in Norfolk) were primary outlets for grain from Norfolk and other parts of eastern England (van Houtte 1977, 39). Despite its poor soils and coastal marshes, Norfolk was not primarily a pastoral region by any reckoning, nor did it have a high ratio of livestock units to cereal acres (Campbell and Power 1989; Campbell 1991, 153, 163). The emphasis on cereal production continued in eastern Norfolk even after the demographic decline of the fourteenth century, which prompted change to pasture farming in many other regions of England (Campbell 1991; Britnell 1991). Nor do other parts of eastern England fit the pastoral description. Essex and southern and eastern Suffolk were all important wheat producers in the late medieval period (Britnell 1991, 61). Kent (with parts of Sussex) was another important grain-producing region in eastern England in the late medieval period and beyond (Mate 1991, 125).[3] In the southwest the predominant use of the moors was for pasture (Fox 1991, 157). In lower-lying areas and along the coast, however, pasture farming gave way to productive arable agriculture. Already in the late medieval period parts of coastal Cornwall and Somerset were important grain producers (Fox 1991, 160). Thus, particularly in the east, it is erroneous to associate less-communal field systems and enclosed field systems with a regional focus on pasture farming, although this was true to a large extent of parts of the southwest.

Areas of enclosures were areas where fields were fenced (either with hedges, trees, or stones) and little land was left open. They were concentrated in mountainous areas in the west and north, although they also could be found in parts of East Anglia, Essex, and Kent as well as (to a lesser extent) in other parts of England. In mountainous areas they usually were associated with a pastoral economy, although in the east and later in the southwest enclosed fields could be used just as easily for arable agriculture. In regions of enclosures most fields were entirely enclosed and private. Since many of the fences were live hedges or included many trees, this gave the landscape a wooded appearance and earned such areas the name of "woodland" regions.

In both regions of enclosures and those of less-communal open fields, inheritance customs tended to be partible and customs of primogeniture, or "borough English," uncommon (Homans 1941, 1988c, 148; Dodwell 1967). This can help explain the irregular and diverse nature of landholding in these regions, as farms were often split up into many pieces upon the death of the owner. It also can account for the small size of fields in such regions. Particularly in the east, in places like Kent, partible inheritance customs led to the proliferation of tiny fields and microscopic farms.

In regions of less-communal open fields villages tended to be smaller and less compact (hamlets rather than villages) than in communal open field regions. Regions of enclosures often contained no villages at all but, rather, farmsteads scattered across the landscape. One other distinctive feature of less-communal settlements was that, unlike in most communal communities, the village church often stood alone and isolated in some prominent natural location, rather than as the focus of the village center. A modern-day traveler can observe this phenomenon in many regions to this day. For example, a traveler going from Cambridge (a communal region) to Norwich (a less-communal region) still can observe the change from a region of compact villages and centrally located churches to a region of more scattered habitation and isolated churches. Local cultures were more individualistic in regions of less-communal field systems and enclosures. This was expressed in religious choices. In the east in particular, and in the southwest around Bristol, individualistic religious beliefs gained popularity at an early date—first Lollardy, later Protestantism and Puritanism (Zaret 1985; Dickens 1987).

## Regional Pattern of Class Relations

As was typical in other countries, communal regions in England tended to be heavily manorialized regions. Each village usually had only one lord, who dominated its economy and society (Overton 1996, 46). His demesne land was intermixed with tenants' land in the open fields. Most tenants held their land by custom of the manor, meaning they were not freeholders. He or his agents were the chief justices in the manorial court, which decided justice in the village and enforced manorial rules. These rules prescribed wages, labor services, and various other feudal payments and dues; they limited tenant mobility and otherwise constrained tenant behavior. Most people in the village were subject to these manorial rules, since freemen who owned their lands outright and were free of manorial restrictions were few in these regions (although not unknown).

In both regions of less-communal open fields and those of enclosures the tyranny of the manor was less than in communal regions. The lord's land (his home farm or demesne) was often separate from tenant holdings. Sometimes more than one lord was represented in a village (particularly in the populous east [see Overton 1996, 46]). The presence of several lords attenuated manorial power as they contested territorial and other rights of lordship, a situation peasants could turn to their own advantage. Each lord ran a manorial court; thus, tenants frequently could take legal cases to their choice of several manorial courts (Campbell 1981). Perhaps for these reasons customary tenants owed few labor services to the lord, and even these were commuted to money payments at an early date. Wage labor rather than customary labor was used on all great estates in the east by the thirteenth century, while in other areas use of customary labor services persisted (Homans 1941, 414; Campbell 1983). In the less populous north and west a single lordship could encompass many villages (Overton 1996, 46). This also served to attenuate the power of the manor in these regions, if for opposite reasons. Likewise, this may have promoted the change to contractual labor arrangements in some parts of the west. Use of wage labor was also in evidence in the southwest by the fifteenth century (Fox 1991). Feudal dues and taxes also tended to be lighter.

In these regions there was often a large proportion of freeholding peasants (Overton 1996, 34). That is, much of the peasantry was entirely free of feudal obligations and manorial restrictions. This was particularly true in the east, where there was a very large free peasantry. In East Anglia the free population (including the poorer freemen, or *sokemen*) reached 80 percent in some areas. Kent also was characterized by a majority of freeholders (Gray 1915; Douglas 1927; Dodwell 1939; Britnell 1991, 618). In England not only were freeholders free of many feudal restrictions; they also had substantial legal rights. Most important was the right of appeal to the king's courts, in place since the twelfth century (Hyams 1980; see later discussion). The king's courts frequently had no reason to take up the interests of the feudal lord and often did not. This made property rights of freeholders stronger than those of customary tenants, as customary tenants could take cases only to the manorial court(s) and therefore lacked the protection of the common law.

### The Regional Pattern of Agrarian Change in Late Medieval and Early Modern England

Given the regional pattern of field systems and the hypotheses developed in chapter 3, we would expect to find the greatest agricultural development and agrarian change in the less-communal regions of the east and west, while we would expect the least development and change in the communal regions of the midlands and the remote and inhospitable regions of the north and west. There is evidence of such a regional pattern throughout the late medieval and early modern periods.

A word about evidence is necessary before preceding. In general, there is much more evidence of agricultural matters available for England than for Continental Europe. This is in part because the persistence of direct farming of demesnes in England through the late medieval period meant that English lords were much more likely than their Continental counterparts to keep detailed records of their estates. It is also because the records that were kept on the Continent (in the late medieval period and after) were more likely to have been destroyed during war and other periods of turmoil than they were in England (van Houtte 1977, 72).

In England the preservation of manorial records means that we actually know more about farming in the late medieval period than the early modern period. Manorial accounts provide ample documentation of farming and agricultural productivity on manorial demesnes up until about 1400, after which time they taper off, coinciding with the rapid decline in demesne farming at this time. There is nothing equivalent to the manorial records for the early modern period, thus after about 1500 documentation of rural affairs of all sorts is much sparser. Some private estates kept detailed accounts, but they are fewer and less detailed than those kept by medieval manors. Most data on farming and productivity for this period come from probate inventories of private farmers (Overton 1990; 1996, 78). These were inventories of a farmer's goods and possessions made at the time of his death. For obvious reasons the data such records supply are not entirely adequate, and the proper use of such records for estimating agricultural productivity is debated. There is much about agricultural productivity and farm management in the early modern period that may never be known. Consequently details of regional differences are also less clear. It was not until the nineteenth century that national surveys of agriculture and agrarian issues were undertaken (Overton 1996, 70), by which time the marketization of England and the demise of many early agrarian structures had begun to obliterate regional differences.

### Agrarian Change in the Late Medieval Period

As noted, evidence of agriculture in late medieval England comes from the records of manors and estates. There is little or no documentation of agriculture on the freehold farms in this period, which were very numerous in the east in particular. Assuming that agriculture on manorial estates reflects local practices and that freehold farms were likely to be both more productive and innovative than manor farms (assumptions for which there is evidence [see Allison 1957; Mate 1986; Britnell 1991]), we can conclude that manorial evidence provides a reasonable, if conservative, picture of regional differences in agricultural productivity.

Given their favorable ecology, dense population, and easy market access we would expect to see greatest development in the southern midlands and the region in the immediate vicinity of London. There was early development in the London region (i.e., Middlesex and Kent). Yet in the late medieval period there was comparatively little development in the communal midland regions. Instead, greater development took place in the more distant and less well-endowed, but less-communal, regions of the east and southwest.

One measure of agricultural productivity per unit of land is cereal yields per acre. In the late thirteenth century studies of manors in the less-communal regions of eastern England show yields per acre that were higher than in most other areas of the country, attaining 20 bushels per acre for wheat. Seed/yield ratios (a measure of the ratio of yield to seed) were also exceptionally high by medieval standards and reached 7 to 1 (and higher) for wheat (Campbell 1983, 1988, 1991; Stacey 1986; Mate 1986, 1991, 277; Britnell 1991, 206).[4] In contrast, wheat yields in the communal regions of England typically averaged less than 5 to 1 (Slicher van Bath 1963a, 30–33). In the southwest, the other less-communal region, yields per acre in the late medieval period were less outstanding than in the east, reflecting both a lower population density and more of a pastoral focus in this area. Seed/yield ratios in the southwest were as good, however, as in the communal parts of the country (4 and 5 to 1 in the early fourteenth century [see Slicher van Bath 1963a, 37]).

Agricultural methods in the east at this time were also quite sophisticated. High levels of agricultural productivity were accomplished by many of the same methods that in later centuries helped produce the agricultural revolution. Methods included extensive use of leguminous plants (mostly peas in the early period), multiple plowings, use of the horse rather than the ox, intensive soil fertilization and liming, and complex crop rotations that left a smaller proportion of land fallow each year. All were in evidence as early as the thirteenth century on manors in parts of East Anglia and Kent (Stone 1956, 347; Langdon 1986; Hallam 1981; Mate 1986, 1991; Stacey 1986; Britnell 1991).

It should be noted, however, that all these developments in agricultural methods in the east were not really innovations. Most of these techniques—the growing of legumes, complex rotations, and so forth—were not new. Their use has been documented in many places in late medieval Europe. Many had been known since Roman times (Parain 1941). In addition, they were improvements in crops and cropping practices rather than labor-saving innovations. All the new practices required labor inputs over and above those required by more traditional agricultural practices. For example, growing legumes or grasses on the fallow field requires more effort than leaving the fallow with no crop at all. Thus, increased agricultural production at this time was due primarily to the increased land productivity, rather than to increased labor productivity. This remained true until the eighteenth century (Overton 1996, 131).

It has been argued that poor soil drainage and a lack of adequate drainage technology prevented similar early agricultural development in the midland region of England at this time (Chambers and Mingay 1966, 65; Grigg 1989). Given the feats of drainage performed contemporaneously in the Netherlands and in the fenlands of eastern England, where large acreages were reclaimed from the sea for agricultural use, this seems a poor explanation (Te Brake 1985, 186). It seems that it was not technology for drainage that was lacking but some other factor.

There is little evidence of agricultural improvement in the north and west at this time. These sparsely populated and inhospitable regions remained primarily pastoral (with a specialization in oxen [Miller 1991, 184]). Arable land was scarce, but was characterized by extensive agricultural systems (infield-outfield systems) in the late medieval period. Infield farming was characterized by intensive and continuous cultivation of a small infield, made possible by the abundant use of manure, with periodic temporary cultivation of the outfield, which included pasture, waste, and common (Smith 1967, 213). Little is known of cereal yields, but they were presumably not particularly high.

In sum, in the late medieval period conditions were most propitious for agricultural change in southern England. Yet within this region it was the less-communal regions of the east that had the most productive and innovative agricultures, and the communal areas of the midlands lagged behind in comparison.

## Late-Fourteenth-Century Changes

The Black Death of 1350 (and epidemics periodically thereafter) caused severe population decline in all regions of England. Low population levels created a labor shortage, which improved the bargaining power of workers. As a result, wages tended to increase and working conditions tended to improve all over England. Low population levels also made more land available, which led to an increase in farm sizes everywhere. Yet all these changes—rising rural prosperity, changes toward more favorable terms of tenure and large farms—were more dramatic in the east and southwest than in the communal regions of southern England. The far north and west remained largely a pastoral zone and did not participate in the rising prosperity of the southern areas during this period (Miller 1991, 52).

In the east there had been an active land market involving both small and large plots of land since before the Black Death, as in these regions farmers could buy and sell land as they wished and manorial restrictions on the land market were few. Partible inheritance customs also stimulated the land market, as people who had inherited only a small piece of land often either tried to buy land to enlarge their property or sell their own smallholding and enter a nonfarming occupation. After the Black Death this land market boomed. Peasants rapidly accumulated land and often began the process of consolidating it into a single compact unit. Since landholdings in these regions tended to be concentrated in one area of the village land anyway, consolidation of farms into a single unit was relatively uncomplicated. The same process occurred in the southwest, if to a lesser extent.

Historical evidence (again culled from manorial records) shows the regional difference in farm expansion after the population decline of 1350. For example, in less-communal Devon and Cornwall in the southwest, tenant farms increased in size during the fifteenth century until more than half of all tenant holdings were over 36 acres (15 or 30 acres were common farm sizes in thirteenth-century England). Tenant farms of 150 to 200 acres have been documented in the area by the mid-fifteenth century.[5] In addition, figures from various manors in Devon and Cornwall consistently show a decline in the number of holdings of less than 15 acres to as few as 10 percent of all holdings, with very few holdings of less than 5 acres (Fox 1991, 724, 725). Likewise, tenant farms increased in size on manors in less-communal Norfolk (Campbell 1984, 125) and Kent. They could reach several hundred acres in size, although large numbers of very small farms of less than 5 acres remained in these areas. Once again, little is known about the size of freehold farms, but we can assume that they increased in size at the same time and for similar reasons.

Communal regions also saw an increase in the size of tenant farms, although the change was not as dramatic. For example, tenant farms in the midlands and in central England often increased in size to 30 or 60 acres but rarely exceeded 100 acres (Tawney 1912, 64–65; Kerridge 1968, 289; Miller 1991, 703, 706, 712). Within the confines of the communal open field system it was difficult for them to become much larger. In addition, in these areas consolidation of farms into compact units was uncommon. Highly scattered strips of land made it difficult for farmers to consolidate their farms or to benefit from any economies of scale if they did so.[6]

### Enclosure

Enclosure for both arable and pastoral purposes also occurred early (before the sixteenth century) and with little complaint in the less-communal regions of the east and southwest (Leonard 1962, 251; Thirsk 1967; Britnell 1991, 613; Fox 1991, 152). In these regions there were typically no restrictions on enclosures. Fencing also was made cheaper by the consolidation of landholdings, a process that was already under way in the east and southwest.

In contrast to the experience in the east and southwest, enclosure in the midland and central regions was a long, drawn-out, and difficult process. Enclosure did not begin here until the fifteenth century (Wordie 1983). The economic depression of the fifteenth century struck the midland and central regions with particular severity. Cereal prices in these regions fell and stayed low (Coleman 1977; Campbell 1991; Dyer 1991, 80–87). Conversely, wool prices were relatively high (Clay 1984, 67). Many farmers and landlords switched to producing the more profitable commodities of wool, meat, and milk. These activities also had the advantage of using less labor, which was in short supply in these regions at this time (Dyer 1991, 80; King 1991, 72). For these reasons the midland and central regions saw a severe contraction of the acreage under crops at this time. This change to pasture farming prompted farmers and landlords to attempt to enclose their fields in these regions. Enclosers were often tenants who wanted to enclose their own lands in the common fields to raise sheep or graze cattle. This began in the fifteenth century and continued on into the next and was particularly prevalent in the midland counties (Wordie 1983, 493), most notably the counties of Northamptonshire, Leicestershire, Warwickshire, Buckinghamshire, Bedfordshire, and Lincolnshire (see also Clay 1984, 75).

Unlike in the east and southwest, enclosure caused great social distress in the midland and central regions. Many smallholders in these regions depended on common grazing rights for their livelihood, and enclosure meant the end of communal grazing on the common fields and/or the commons proper. Enclosure thus met a great deal of resistance in these regions. Some of this resistance was legal; that is, peasants who owned common rights took enclosers to court. This was possible when there had been breaches of manorial custom, in which case peasants combined to bring civil suits against their lord or his demesne lessee. They had some success with this strategy (Clay 1984, 77; Overton 1996, 205). If not, enclosure was resisted in more rudimentary ways. Enclosure riots had become common by the end of the fifteenth century (Robisheaux 1994, 102). Resistance to enclosure was not always successful. As most of the tenantry in these regions were customary tenants, it was often possible for a lord to evict his tenants legally (and illegally) (Kerridge 1969, 96). The commission of 1517 revealed many cases of forced evictions of tenants in previous years in the midland or central regions (Dyer 1991, 88). Sir Thomas More complained in his *Utopia* (1516) that the large landowners "leave no grounde for tillage, thei enclose al into pastures, thei throw doune houses, thei pluck downe townes, and leave nothing standynge but only the churche to be made a shepe-howse" (qtd. in Slicher van Bath 1963b, 165; see also Coleman 1977, 34–36).

Nevertheless, enclosure in communal regions proceeded more slowly than enclosure in less-communal regions. By the sixteenth century the regional difference in enclosure was clear. It was noticed by a writer in Tudor times who noted the predominance of enclosure in the east and southwest (and also remarked on the relative prosperity of the enclosed areas): "We se that countries where most Inclosures be, are most wealthie, as essex, kent, devenshire and such" (Lamond 1549).

### Rise of Contractual Labor Relations and Industry in Less-Communal Regions

Local institutions in the east and southwest also promoted the emergence and spread of (more efficient) contractual labor relations after the Black Death. Copyhold tenure also was established early in both regions. Copyhold tenure meant that tenants possessed a copy of the terms (as entered in the manorial court role) on which their land was held from the lord of the manor (Overton 1996, 31). In earlier centuries these terms usually included labor services as well as the usual customary dues and payments, although use of labor services had vanished in most places in the east and southwest by the thirteenth century. Copyhold tenure afforded tenants some legal support for their property rights; thus, copyholders were more secure than most customary tenants. For customary tenants in the east copyhold tenure was widespread by 1450 (Britnell 1991, 621). Moreover, copyhold of inheritance was common in eastern England, a tenure that approximated that of freehold (fee-simple) land. Copyhold tenure was also common in the southwest by 1500. For example, in Dorset almost 90 percent of tenants were copyholders, and in some cases these copyhold tenures were equivalent to freehold tenures (Overton 1996, 35). The customary tenants in the midland and central regions also became copyholders in the early sixteenth century, but then it was often a relatively disadvantageous tenure of a copyhold for life (Hoyle 1990, 6, 10; Overton 1996, 154).

The regional pattern of the rise of contractual labor relations is paralleled by the regional pattern of the development of rural industry and nonagricultural occupations. The east and southwest were characterized by very prosperous textile industries by the fifteenth century (Pounds 1990, 196). These industries produced luxury woolens, mostly for the colder climes of northern Europe, especially the Baltic area (Munro 1994, 156). By the early fifteenth century English broadcloths also began to be sold in Levantine markets as medium-quality but generally lower-priced woolens than those available contemporaneously from Flemish manufactories (Munro 1994, 159).

Along with flourishing textile industries there were a variety of other industries: for example, brewing, salt making, fishing, shipping, tanning, baking, carpentry, and tiling (Campbell 1984; Mate 1991). In the southwestern counties of Devon and Cornwall these included tin mining (Fox 1991). Commercialization of agriculture, agricultural change and improvement, and development of rural industry in the east and southwest promoted high levels of rural prosperity (Clay 1984, 57). These regions saw the highest rates of growth of lay wealth over the period from the fourteenth to the early sixteenth century, as map 4 shows.

In communal regions, on the other hand, local institutions discouraged production for the market and agrarian change as well as the emergence of more contractual labor relations in these areas. Subsistence farming dominated in the region (Clay 1984, 59). Rural prosperity lagged behind that of less-communal regions. It is also significant that most evidence of deserted villages in the post-plague era comes from this area (Beresford 1979). Very few villages were deserted in either the east or southwest at this time, a reflection of a greater prosperity in those areas.

## Multivariate Analysis of Regional Differences in Economic Growth in Late Medieval England

So far I have suggested that the effects of the social organization of agriculture on agrarian change in late medieval England were independent of factors such as ecology, population density, and market access. We can test this conclusion in a multivariate analysis, using variables for the period 1334 to 1515, a period for which comparable statistics on economic growth from tax figures are available. After this date tax figures are no longer comparable (Schofield 1965). The analysis is further limited because it does not use direct measures of agricultural development or agrarian change. This is because comprehensive, comparable data on the productivity of all the factors of production—land, labor, and capital— for all the English counties are not available for the late medieval period (cf. Overton and Campbell 1991). In lieu of this I use economic growth, assuming that any wealth stemming from industrial production is itself indirect evidence of agricultural development (see earlier discussion). Certainly, evidence of economic growth will capture any gains in the productivity of land, labor, and capital.

In this analysis I control some of the other important factors to assess

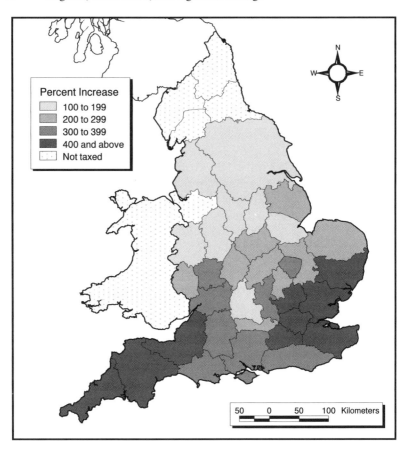

**Map 4. Rates of growth of lay wealth in England, 1334–1515. (Adapted from Schofield 1965.)**

the effect of the local social organization of production on economic growth for the period. I evaluate the effects of market access, industrial development, population density, agricultural organization, and technological change on economic growth over this period.

## Data and Variables

In this analysis the unit of interest is the (premodern) English county ($N = 44$). The dependent variable is the rate of growth in wealth of the county (GROWTHRATE), excluding clerical wealth. This is measured between

1334 and 1515, as these are the dates of the two closest comparable tax assessments (Schofield 1965). Wealth refers to "assessed wealth"—a measure used to determine the tax rate. Unfortunately, as with all measures based on tax returns, it is no doubt subject to considerable measurement error.

Most of the independent variables are measured for the late fourteenth century, the rationale for this being that these are the factors that help determine the course of economic change over the period 1334–1515. Market access is measured by indicators of the number of sea ports (#PORTS) and the number of places with assessed wealth of over 225 pounds in 1334 (TCENTERS). The latter are almost all market centers (Darby 1973). The presence of industry is measured by the number of cloths produced per year by the late fourteenth century (CLOTHIND [from Darby 1973]) and the number of centers of the wool industry (WOOLCENTER [from Gilbert 1968]). Population per square mile (POPSQM) is used to measure the influence of population density and comes from the poll tax returns of 1377 (Russell 1948).

The local social organization of agriculture is measured by a dummy variable that indicates whether the county is a communal open field county or not (OPENFIELD [from Gray 1915]). This variable also serves as a proxy for local class relations and types of tenure, as communal open field villages were more heavily manorialized and had proportionately fewer freemen than areas of enclosures or less-communal open fields.

As a measure of agricultural innovation, the percentage of horses used on manorial demesnes is used (%HORSES). The horse is a more efficient, if more expensive, work animal than the ox, and the use of horses is a sign of agricultural innovation (Langdon 1986).[7] Such innovation was most common outside of the communal open field regions. Controlling for this variable will help determine if the primary influence of the social organization of agriculture came about through technological change.

### Results and Discussion

Results of this analysis suggest that the most important determinants of regional differences in economic development before 1600 were the degree of industrial development, the population density, and the local social organization of agriculture. In what follows I describe these findings in more detail.

Preliminary analysis of the data showed that both the variables TCENTERs and WOOLCENTER had little direct influence on economic growth, and thus these variables were omitted in the final analysis presented in table 1. Any effects of these variables are captured by other variables in the analysis. The results imply that access to market centers alone was not the crucial determinant of economic growth. Table 1 gives results of the final regression analysis. Population density is a strong predictor of later economic development, as expected, thus supporting the hypothesis that population density is an important factor fueling economic development. Industrial development is also important in explaining later economic development, as demonstrated by the positive effects of CLOTHIND (the number of cloths produced per year) on GROWTHRATE.

The variable OPENFIELD, which indicates the communal open field system, is strongly negatively associated with later economic development. This supports the hypothesis that the social organization of agriculture was an important factor in economic growth. It is also evidence of the role of class relations in shaping economic change. Communal open field regions were all heavily manorialized regions. These regions saw little economic growth over the late medieval period.

The variables #PORTS and %HORSES were associated significantly with economic growth but in the direction opposite from that predicted. A look at maps of the distribution of both use of the horse and ports explains this apparent anomaly. First, horses were concentrated outside of communal open field regions but mostly in the southeastern corner of England. The use of the horse was less common in the southwest, yet this area was characterized by high rates of economic growth over the next two centuries—thus, the apparent anomaly of a negative relationship between %HORSES and GROWTHRATE once OPENFIELD was controlled. A similar argument can be made for the anomalous results for the variable #PORTS. Ports were most common outside of communal open field

**TABLE 1. Regression Analysis of the Rate of Growth of Lay Wealth in Late Medieval England, 1334–1515**

| Variable | B (S.E.) | Beta |
|----------|----------|------|
| POPSQM | 2.45[b] | .46[b] |
|  | (6.23) |  |
| OPENFIELD | −3.31[b] | −.84[b] |
|  | (4.94) |  |
| %HORSES | −4.17[a] | −.35[a] |
|  | (1.56) |  |
| #PORTS | −1.11[b] | −.32[b] |
|  | (3.93) |  |
| CLOTHIND | 7.46[a] | .29[a] |
|  | (2.77) |  |

*Note:* Explained Variance = .70; $N$ of cases = 35
[a]Significant at .05 level
[b]Significant at .01 level

regions yet mostly in the eastern and northeastern parts of England. Thus, the fast rates of growth in southwestern England, which were not associated with either the use of the horse or the availability of ports, explains these two anomalous findings. These findings imply that, first, the effects of social organization of agriculture on economic growth were not just mediated by one important technological innovation: the use of the horse. Second, ports and the access to international markets they provided were not essential to economic growth, probably because most traded commodities were not transported by sea or intended for overseas markets. Trade by river or road was always more important in England than trade by sea. Overton notes that port books indicate that the volume of corn shipped to London via the coast circa 1700 was only about 20 percent of the total carried to the capital (Overton 1996, 141–42).

## Sixteenth Century and After

Because of their reliance on human labor, many innovative agricultural methods that had been in use in the late medieval period went out of service in the east and southwest during the depression of the later fourteenth and the fifteenth centuries. As a result, cereal yields fell. In later centuries most of these techniques were revived in these regions, causing cereal yields to rise again. In the early modern period the less-communal regions of the east and southwest led the way in agricultural improvement in England.

Convertible husbandry (also called "up and down husbandry") was in evidence in the southwest by the early fifteenth century (Finberg 1951; Fox 1991, 313). Convertible husbandry is a flexible use of fields that involves "converting" fields from arable to pasture, and vice versa. Legumes are typically grown on the field before it is converted to pasture, so both the nitrogen-fixing properties of legumes and the dung of animals serve to fertilize the ground (see Kerridge 1968). Similar techniques involving legumes in rotations continued in the eastern counties at the same time. Turnips were first introduced into England in the eastern counties in the sixteenth century (Chambers and Mingay 1966; Overton 1991). Clover appeared there in the seventeenth century (Overton 1991, 320). The advantages of root crops such as turnips were that they provided food for animals, which in turn provided more manure, and that the hoeing and weeding necessary in their cultivation served to cleanse the field of weeds. The advantages of the leguminous grass crops (such as clover) were that they helped replenish nitrogen in the soil as well as served as a source of hay for animal fodder. The introduction of these new crops in rotations obviated the need to leave land fallow for periods of time and thus made for a much more intensive cultivation of the soil, with larger and better-quality outputs being the result. Besides these new fodder crops, a variety of new specialized crops began to be grown in these regions by the sixteenth century. These included fruit and vegetables, hops, tobacco, industrial crops such as coleseed, flax and hemp, woad and weld, teasels, licorice, and saffron (Clay 1984, 135). These innovations all led to improvements in land productivity.

Other improvements in agricultural technology occurred first in eastern England. The replacement of oxen by horses in this region continued apace. By the fifteenth century horses rather than oxen were widely used in eastern England; for example, in Norfolk, over 70 percent of draft power was provided by horses (Overton 1996, 126). There were also improvements in plow technology. By 1600 the lighter, two-horse Dutch plow was to be found in parts of eastern England and reduced plowing times. Labor productivity was improved by these changes. Labor productivity was also improved by the custom, common in East Anglia in eastern England as early as the sixteenth century, for laborers and plowmen to work two "journees" (half-days) per day rather than one, as was customary elsewhere (Riches 1967).

By the seventeenth century the new agricultural methods were being introduced in the midland and central regions (Allen 1992). Diffusion of new agricultural techniques is difficult to document fully, as few records have been kept on the process. It is well-known, however, that turnips, originally adopted in East Anglia in the sixteenth century, began to spread all over England in the seventeenth and eighteenth centuries. Techniques of convertible husbandry, first developed in the east and southwest in earlier centuries, likewise were diffusing through communal regions by the seventeenth century (Kerridge 1968, 194; Clay 1984, 129; Overton 1996, 117). Likewise, the use of the horse began to spread. Horses had largely replaced oxen all over the country by the mid-eighteenth century (Overton 1996, 126).

In communal regions the need for communal agreement for any proposed change retarded the pace of agricultural change (Clay 1984, 134). As a way around the problem of communal regulation, enclosure of the midlands began in earnest. Innovators and landlords who wanted to implement the new methods often first had to enclose their lands to withdraw them from the communal farming system. By the seventeenth century low cereal prices and high wool prices encouraged farmers to enclose their land and turn to pasture farming (Clay 1984, 68; Dyer 1991; Campbell 1991). In many respects the seventeenth century saw a repeat of what had occurred in the fifteenth century, although to an even greater extent, as the seventeenth century is regarded as having the fastest rate of enclosure (Overton 1996, 148). Again, there was much resistance among the smallholders to enclosure. Again, landlords sometimes overcame this resistance with force, simply evicting tenants who protested enclosure and incorporating their land into large farms. These evictions helped precipitate a series of enclosure riots and a serious rebellion in the midland revolt of 1607 (Johnson 1909; Wordie 1983; Dyer 1991, 637; Martin 1983). This has been called the last peasant revolt in England (Martin 1983).[8] Writers from Tudor times on have described this process, which became an important element in many accounts of the rise of agrarian capitalism in England (e.g., Marx 1906, 794).

Eventually enclosure was forced by Acts of Parliament (mostly in the eighteenth century). These had the greatest impact on communal farming regions, which generally had over 40 percent of their land area enclosed by Act of Parliament, more than any other region (Wordie 1983, 500). Most parliamentary enclosures occurred in the south and east Midlands and central areas, with more than half of Oxfordshire, Northamptonshire, Huntingdonshire, Bedfordshire, Leicestershire, and Cambridgeshire being enclosed by legislation (Clay 1984, 85; Beckett 1990, 36).[9] Once again, complaints against enclosure were loudest in the midlands.

Complaints against enclosure were not unfounded, as enclosure did contribute to the decline of the smallholder in regions such as the midlands. From the seventeenth century on enclosure had the effect of reducing the number of smallholders in the midlands and central regions, while the number of middle-sized and large estates grew (Johnson 1909, 132; Grigg 1989, 121; Beckett 1990, 40; see map 5). Smallholders who could not support themselves without access to the commons sold out, and their holdings were added to existing farms (Grigg 1989, 126). They began to swell the ranks of the industrial proletariat. Cottage industry began to develop in the midland counties only after the enclosure movement of the seventeenth and eighteenth centuries (Jones 1968, 62; Braudel 1984, 560; Clay 1984, 99) as the newly landless or land-poor became available as cheap sources of labor. The decline of the smallholder was accompanied by the decline of arable farming in many of these regions. Some counties that had been wholly arable in the sixteenth century (such as Leicestershire and much of Northamptonshire, Bedfordshire, and Buckinghamshire) had become largely pastoral counties by the eighteenth century (Clay 1984, 116).

There were few parliamentary enclosures in the eastern and southwestern counties (as well as the far north and west) (Leonard 1962; Beckett 1982; Wordie 1983).[10] Enclosure that did occur in these regions tended to have the effect of actually increasing the number of smallholders (Johnson 1909, 59). Although the number of very large estates increased, many small farms persisted (Fourquin 1990; Britnell 1991, 617; Mate 1991, 702).

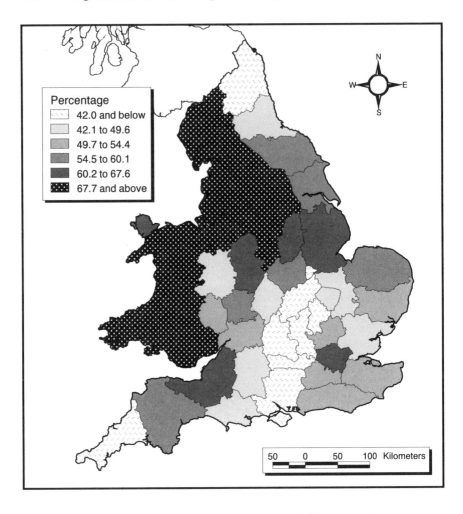

**Map 5. Farms of 5 to 100 acres, as a percentage of all farms over 5 acres, 1851. (Adapted from Grigg 1989.)**

Both the east and the southwest still had proportionately more small farmers (in the 5- to 100-acre range) as late as the mid-nineteenth century (see map 5).

The persistence of small farms is testimony to the strength of peasant property rights in these regions. Furthermore, these small farms may have played a crucial role in the continuation of agricultural development in the east and southwest. There is evidence that larger farms in those regions borrowed innovations that had proven their effectiveness on the many smaller farms. For example, innovative crops such as turnips and legumes, which were later to be much heralded by English agronomists, were crops with long histories among smallholders of eastern England (Allison 1957; Campbell 1983; Britnell 1991, 210). In addition, more prosperous small farmers also constituted a pool of capable tenant farmers for the large farms of great estates, which tended to grow in size over subsequent centuries (Du Boulay 1965). Finding capable tenant farmers was always a problem for owners of the large cereal-growing estates in northeastern France (Forster 1970), for instance, where the tendency during the same period was to divide the great estates further among many farmers. Prospective tenants had to have some of their own resources as well as the ability and motivation to undertake the running of a large farm and to turn a profit. Better-off small farmers of eastern and southwestern England frequently had these qualities. Historical research can follow certain families from origins as small-time tenant farmers to later status as major landowners themselves and prominent local figures. Examples include families such as the Townshends in Norfolk and the Knatchbulls in Kent. These families first appear in historical records as tenant farmers in the fourteenth and fifteenth centuries, respectively. Several hundred years later the same families formed the local nobility (Du Boulay 1965; Moreton 1992). Thus, it may have been the existence of such an enterprising class of small farmer that was an essential precondition for the further growth of large farms.[11]

At the same time, the east and southwest became home to a large population of landless or land-poor people who served as workers either on larger farms or in local industrial occupations. This was particularly true in the east. Customs of partible inheritance of land, which were very common in the east, contributed to the numbers of land-poor people. The successive division of land among children over several generations left many with plots too small to sustain them (Campbell 1980, 187). Bad harvests, epidemics, market fluctuations, and such also could bankrupt smallholders. Yet, as long as the economies of the east and southwest prospered, the majority of such people could find nonagricultural work and were not indigent. Many found work in the textile industries, which continued to flourish in the east and southwest. By the 1640s the "New Draperies" of East Anglia had come to dominate European markets (Munro 1994, 180). The development of market gardening and the growing of specialty industrial crops also provided smallholders with occupations in these regions. For example, fruit and hop growing sustained many smallholders in Kent during the sixteenth and seventeenth centuries (Clay 1984, 117).

**The Agricultural Revolution**

By the seventeenth century agricultural productivity was rising all over England, although the precise timing of the agricultural revolution throughout all of England is a matter of contention within the scholarly literature (Overton 1996, 6). Some suggest that increased agricultural production throughout England was associated most closely with the industrial revolution of the eighteenth century (Chambers and Mingay 1966; Crafts 1985, Harley 1992; Overton 1996, 8, 69); others posit a slow rise beginning in the sixteenth century (Jones 1965; Allen 1992); while still others argue that by 1700 the rise in agricultural productivity had already peaked in England (Kerridge 1968; Clark 1991). English yields of wheat per acre (a measure of the productivity of land) showed a rapid rate of increase before 1800, although there is much debate over whether this occurred before or after 1700 (see Allen 1988a, 143; 1988b, 125; Clark 1991). Wrigley has estimated that the productivity of workers in agriculture (i.e., labor productivity) probably roughly doubled between 1600 and 1800 in England (Wrigley 1987, 191). Qualitative historical evidence (e.g., contemporary accounts, last subsistence crisis,[12] last peasant revolt) points to the earlier dates (i.e., late sixteenth century) for the beginning of the agricultural revolution in England, with an acceleration of production throughout the seventeenth and eighteenth centuries. By the late seventeenth century England was exporting grain on a larger scale than ever before (Clay 1984, 102–4). By 1800 little more than a third of the English labor force was involved in agriculture. This was much less than in other European countries, where the closest rival was the Netherlands, with 55–60 percent of the population engaged in agriculture (Wrigley 1987, 189).

Long at the forefront of agrarian change in England, the eastern regions played an important part in the English agricultural revolution (Mate 1991, 135; Campbell 1991; Fox 1991).[13] East Anglia, in particular, became notable for agricultural innovation and improvement. Norfolk was responsible for the development of the Norfolk fourcourse, a rotation of wheat, turnips, barley, and clover, in the eighteenth century (Overton 1991, 318). This technique was to be copied widely around England and abroad (Overton 1996, 119; Turner 1982; Braudel 1982, 281). The use of this technique caused grain yields to double. Other innovations were first introduced in eastern England. The Rotherham plow made plowing quicker and easier (Overton 1996, 122). This plow was in use in Norfolk in the 1760s. Another eighteenth-century development was the seed drill and the horse hoe, as popularized by Jethro Tull. His method was to sow seed in rows with a drill and hoe between them with a small plow (the horse hoe). This method reduced the amount of seed used by 70 percent. The seed drill was common in Norfok and Suffolk (and Northumberland and Durham) at the turn of the nineteenth century, before it began to spread to other regions (Overton 1996, 122).

As a result of these changes, Norfolk, with its poor soil, "fit only to make the high roads," became the major supplier of both bread and meat for England. In the eighteenth century the French encyclopedia written by Diderot described Norfolk as the "model agricultural economy." In Norfolk and Suffolk agricultural output rose considerably more than in English agriculture as a whole at the same time (Overton 1991, 322). By 1794 Norfolk was exporting more grain than all the rest of England combined— in fact, nine-tenths of the total amount exported by the whole country. The profitability of farming in Norfolk is reflected in the rise of the price of leases. Young estimated that the general rise of rents in Norfolk during the last twenty years of the eighteenth century was about 27 percent. Rents on some estates rose by extraordinary amounts. For instance, the Holkham estate rental increased from 10,000 pounds a year to 20,000 pounds a year between about 1776 and 1796 (Riches 1967, 3, 75). As late as the nineteenth century, yields of wheat in the east (Norfolk and the London area) were the highest in the country, while yields in the former communal regions were generally lower (Turner 1982; see map 6). At this point the southwest lagged behind as a productive agricultural region, (Wilmot 1996, 105–35), although map 6 shows that in 1800 wheat yields were very good in Devon and Cornwall (around 24 bushels per acre for wheat).

## Factors Specific to the Protonational Context

The agricultural revolution in England was at least in part a product of national factors in the late medieval and early modern periods that influenced agrarian matters everywhere. These include state institutions (both legal and financial) that lowered transaction costs, comparatively low levels of taxation, lack of warfare on English soil, and the enduring power of Parliament. Many authors have credited them with the ultimate success of English development. Although such factors cannot explain the regional differences, they provided necessary conditions for the changes I have described and were crucial for ultimate development outcomes. I briefly review them here.

### Legal and Financial Institutions

As noted, of particular importance was the development and protection of exclusive rights to land by freeholders and copyholders (Hoyle 1990;

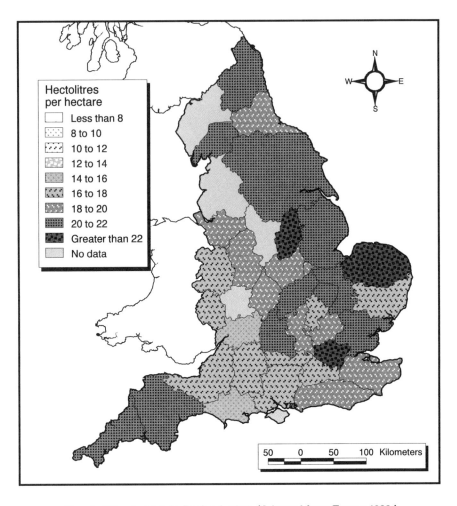

**Map 6. Wheat yields in England, 1800. (Adapted from Turner 1982.)**

Fryde 1991; Sayer 1992, 1399). Legal protection for freehold dates back to the twelfth century, at which time freeholders were granted substantial legal rights under English common law, including the right of appeal to the king's courts (Kerridge 1969; Hyams 1980). Over the course of the thirteenth century freehold land also became freely alienable (North and Thomas 1973, 63). As North and Thomas note, with the exception of the Netherlands, these developments in England were unique in the feudal world. The king's courts were the common law courts, and cases were heard by traveling justices sent out from Westminster. Although they could be corrupt and biased in elites' favor, more typically they gave a fair third-party opinion of the cases that they heard. They offered freeholders substantial protection for their property and other rights, something most customary tenants did not have. These rights contrast with those of customary tenants, who could take their cases only to the manorial court. This court was run by the manorial lord and could be expected to pass decisions in his favor. By the end of the fifteenth century similar protection was awarded to copyholders, that is, those customary tenants who owned a copy of the terms on which their land was held according to the manor court roll (Kerridge 1969; Fryde and Fryde 1991, 819; Overton 1996, 31). Copyholders had fewer rights than freeholders, as they were not considered to "own" their land. They could, however, sue a landlord in common-law courts for personal trespass if the landlord infringed on their land rights (Kerridge 1969, 71; Hoyle 1990).

By the seventeenth century almost all former customary tenants in England had become "copyholders" and received some protection for their property rights (Fryde and Fryde 1991; Overton 1996, 32). Evidence from eastern Germany (see chap. 7) shows what could happen in the absence of such legal protection for both free and customary tenants. Local justices of the peace also supplied local justice in England (in cases of all misdemeanors and felonies). Yet, unlike the jurisdictional lords in the eastern German lands, they were appointed by the monarch and operated within the framework provided by national statutes, and their activities were closely watched by the King's Council and traveling justices. Furthermore, individuals could appeal legal decisions to these royal courts (Sayer 1992, 1406, 1399). Thus, although justices of the peace were representatives of the propertied class, they never were able to abuse their judicial powers to the same extent as local landlords in parts of Germany during the sixteenth and seventeenth centuries.

State-supplied legal support for property rights decreased uncertainty and transaction costs for agriculturalists all over England. At the same time, it helped slow the shift to more efficient property rights in the midlands and central regions. As noted earlier, peasants (particularly freeholders in the open fields) often used the legal system to resist efforts of landlords and others to enclose the common fields. For example, freeholders in the open fields of the manor of Cotesbach, in Leicestershire, petitioned James I in 1602 to prevent the landlord's proposed enclosure of the open fields. Although the state found for the landlord and enclosure did occur, it was at considerable cost to the landlord, who had to buy out the freeholders (Overton 1996, 157).

Not only did the central government provide basic legal support for rights of freeholders and copyholders, but in later years it provided a variety of institutional arrangements that diminished transaction costs and created a more favorable environment for agriculture, trade, and economic development in England. These included a stable currency, legal guarantees for credit instruments and, after the seventeenth century, a variety of novel financial institutions that facilitated trade.

Of primary importance for economic development was a stable currency. The English currency had been fairly stable since the fourteenth century. Parliament, which met regularly by this time, strongly protested any debasement of the coinage and insisted that the king only debase the coinage with its approval. Thus, when Edward III debased the coinage in 1335, it was the first time it had been done in sixty years, and he did it with parliamentary approval (Spufford 1965, 123). In 1344, and again in 1351, Edward III reduced the value of the coinage without parliamentary consent. This created a great outcry. In response, in 1352 the Statute of Purveyors stated that the current coinage "shall never be worsened, neither in weight nor in fineness." Not for another half-century was the English coinage altered and then only as a strictly defensive measure by Parliament (Munro 1972, 35).[14] Thereafter debasement was a rare event in England. It occurred most notably in the sixteenth century, during the reign of Henry VIII. Finally, parliamentary aversion to this debasement culminated in Elizabeth I's fixing the value of the pound sterling at four ounces of sterling silver, a value that remained essentially unchanged until the twentieth century. No other European country did likewise (Braudel 1984, 356).

England was also one of the first countries to institute legal changes that permitted credit instruments to become negotiable, that is, transferrable to others. This made possible a dramatic increase in both public and private credit. In 1437 a London court ruled that the bearer representing a bill for collection on its maturity had as much right to payment as the original payee in the bill (Munro 1994, 173). A variety of other reforms and changes created institutions and policies in England that promoted economic development. It is significant that the campaign to reform English institutions was often led by people from more progressive (less-communal) regions of England, for example, Edward Coke from Norfolk. Coke's seventeenth-century campaign against the granting of royal trading monopolies culminated in the Statute of Monopolies in 1624 (North and Thomas 1973, 148).[15] This statute effectively prohibited the hitherto common practice of granting royal trading monopolies. Other institutional innovations introduced at later points in time included the elimination of surviving feudal laws, the first patent law, development of the joint stock company, development of the coffeehouse (a forerunner of organized insurance), development of the bank note, and creation of a central bank, in 1694 (Braudel 1982; North and Thomas 1973, 155; van Houtte 1977, 216; van der Wee 1993, 26). All these institutions reduced transaction costs and facilitated rural production and trade throughout England.

These early innovations promoted a fall in interest rates. The seventeenth century saw a long-term decline in the rate of interest obtainable from moneylending, which made it easier for agriculturalists (and others) to borrow money to finance improvements. Changes in mortgage policy after 1620 also facilitated access to credit by landowners. The principle of the equity of redemption was developed, which made it possible for mortgages to remain outstanding indefinitely. Lenders who wanted their principal back could assign their security to another, who would assume the role of creditor in their stead. Thus, borrowers did not need to fear sudden foreclosure from creditors who decided they wanted their principal back (Clay 1984, 124).

In addition to a regime of institutions and policies that lowered transaction costs, general levels of taxation remained low in England throughout most of the period under study here. The tax assessment of the early 1300s remained in effect, essentially unchanged, in England until the early seventeenth century (Fryde 1991). This meant that levels of direct taxation actually declined over the period and were never an onerous burden on the small peasantry. Taxes did not begin to rise in England again until the later seventeenth century (Clay 1984, 78).[16] In addition to direct taxes, indirect taxes were regularly levied on sales and exported commodities. Producers could evade them more easily, however, than direct taxes (cf. Bates and Lien 1985). Further, indirect taxes fell primarily on merchants, traders, and landlords who had some political power because of representation in Parliament and who could therefore force the Crown to trade favors for revenue (North and Thomas 1973, 83). Such low levels of taxes on producers preserved incentives for continued agricultural production and kept capital and investment flowing into the agricultural sector throughout the early modern period.[17]

### Lack of Warfare and the Maintenance of Democracy

As important as state institutions and policies was the lack of warfare on English soil throughout the late medieval and early modern periods (see Downing 1992; Tilly 1989). Luck in geography and geopolitical considerations kept England free of invasion after the eleventh century. Even civil wars and other disturbances were relatively few (the Civil War of the seventeenth century being a notable exception). Such minimal warfare created a comparatively stable and peaceful environment in which agriculture, trade, and industry could develop. This is best illustrated by comparison to the southern Netherlands, France, and Germany, which periodically were devastated by armies over the same period. Lack of warfare and unrest also helped preserve constitutional institutions such as Parliament (Downing 1992).

The role of Parliament in creating financial institutions and shaping taxation demonstrates the importance of Parliament's continued existence and its continued ability to shape national policy on fiscal and other matters. Parliament formed the mouthpiece by which commercial landlords, farmers, and the landed gentry eventually were able to influence law and taxation as well as to introduce the institutional innovations described earlier. Although not all parliamentary laws promoted economic growth, for example, laws that controlled the trade in agricultural commodities, such as the Corn Laws regulating grain prices, were not uncommon and may have done some harm. By and large, however, the control of Parliament facilitated economic development in England. That such a (nominally) representative government survived into the early modern period is itself extraordinary (Downing 1988; Tullock 1987). It meant that no autocratic government was able to arrest the growing prosperity of England through warmongering, confiscating property, debasing the currency, or imposing punishing levels of taxation (Olson 1997).

## Conclusion

In conclusion, England may be considered to have been doubly blessed: both local and protonational conditions were propitious for economic development. Local institutions in some regions of England created flexible systems of land tenure and individualistic property rights. In eastern England these regions were also characterized by a large free peasantry and a spirit of "individualism." Combined with a benign ecology and access to the huge London market, state protection for property rights, a stable currency and other financial institutions that facilitated trade and commerce, comparatively low levels of taxation, and a relative lack of warfare, these areas of southern England saw early agricultural development and agrarian change. Highly productive methods were in evidence at an early date, along with technological changes such as the use of the horse rather than the ox as a draft animal and the use of new grasses and fodder crops in more complex rotation systems. Labor relations became contractual, and the use of customary labor disappeared at an early date. All of this was particularly notable in the east, but the southwest also participated in early agrarian development. Enclosure and farm consolidation occurred early in both the east and southwest. In both the east and southwest agricultural development accompanied the development of nonagricultural industries, particularly cloth making.

In eastern England rising agricultural productivity served to spearhead the agricultural revolution of the seventeenth and eighteenth centuries. Agriculture in Norfolk in particular became the standard by which agriculture everywhere else was judged. The Norfolk rotation (consisting of wheat, turnips, barley, and clover) was widely adopted and contributed to rising agricultural productivity. At this point the southwest lagged behind the more dynamic eastern regions. Agricultural productivity was now rising all over England, however, and it facilitated subsequent industrialization.

CHAPTER 5

# Rural Institutions and Agrarian Change in the Netherlands

Que dirai-je d'une terre qui n'était il y a peu de temps
guère propre à la culture, mais que ton esprit inventif et
ton activité ont rendue fertile, au point de surpasser à cet
égard des terres naturellement plus aptes à la production.

[What shall I say of a land that only a short time ago was
scarcely fit for cultivation, yet which your inventive spirit
and your activity have rendered fertile, to the point of
surpassing in this regard lands more naturally suited to
production.]
　　　—Letter from Archbishop Gervais to the count of
　　　　　　　Flanders, middle of the eleventh century

If the islands of paradise lie anywhere on earth, they
must be here, because in the whole land we found nothing that smacked of poverty or filth.
—Frenchman Charles Ogier describing Holland, while
　　　on a journey from Amsterdam to Leiden (1636?)

The Low Countries, or Netherlands (see de Schepper 1994, 502), saw precocious agricultural development, often exceeding the high levels we have
seen in parts of southern England and was home to the first Continental
agricultural revolution. Although the Netherlands shared many of the
same conditions as the progressive parts of southern England, there were
differences that make it a useful comparison case. In particular, it allows
us to examine the effects of extensive warfare and political upheaval on
agrarian change, as the region was involved in warfare in much of the
period examined here. In this chapter I examine why and how agrarian
change occurred in the Netherlands, the role of local field systems, and
what happened to its early, promising development.

Physically, the Low Countries resemble Norfolk and other parts of
East Anglia across the channel. Most of the land is low lying, marshy, and
flat, with comparatively poor soil. Like Norfolk, the region was long set-

tled and densely populated by the late medieval period. Highly communal agricultural systems were practically unknown. The only exceptions were the border regions of the east and far south, where there were small sections characterized by the highly communal systems of northern France and southern Germany. Also like Norfolk, the Low Countries had a history of weak manorialization. Furthermore, some parts of the Low Countries had escaped entirely incorporation into territorial empires. The Low Countries also had the advantage of a coastal position at the mouths of several major river systems that gave easy access to the major European markets.

Given these conditions, according to the theory outlined in chapter 3, we would expect early agricultural development in the Low Countries. This is what we see. Agricultural development began in the south (what is modern day Belgium), the most promising agricultural region in the late medieval period, but it was not long until the north (what is the modern day Netherlands) caught up, and eventually surpassed, the southern advances. Furthermore, as we might expect, the only exceptions to this precocious development were in the communal border regions of the east and south, where agricultural progress lagged.

### Ecology, Population, and Markets

Ecologically, the Low Countries would appear to be unpromising as an agricultural region. In the south the land was divided by numerous streams and rivers and prone to flooding. In the north a large part of the land was ill drained, remote, and uninhabitable (de Vries 1974, 32). Soil in most of both the northern and southern Netherlands is comparatively poor, the only exception being in part of the south, which shares some of the loess deposits of northern France (de Vries and van der Woude 1997, 11–13). Despite this unfavorable ecology, the territory was one of the most densely settled in Europe by the late medieval period. At this time population was concentrated in the regions of more favorable ecology in the south. Population records for the Low Countries do not begin until after 1350 but then continue into the sixteenth century (Pounds 1990, 149). They show a region of dense population extending in the southern Netherlands from near Saint-Omer (Flanders) in the west to Liège in the east. Over large parts of this region in Flanders, Brabant, and Hainaut, densities of well over 130 people per square mile could be found. Densities were also high in the coastal areas of Holland. They were lower—below 50 per square mile—in the province of Luxembourg and in northern Brabant. In the northern Netherlands the population was also comparatively sparse, although the Frisian coastlands had a high density of population living on the *terpen,* man-made mounds reclaimed from the sea (van Houtte 1977, 3). The density of population in the Netherlands is one reason why, in the Middle Ages, the provinces of Friesland, Holland, and Flanders were notable areas of emigration (Slicher van Bath 1963b, 130; see map 7).

The high population density of the southern Netherlands reflects the early urbanization of the area. By the eleventh century a cluster of cities, reaching from Tournai and Valenciennes in the south to Bruges and Ghent in the north, had developed. By the thirteenth century the southern Netherlands was second only to Italy in its level of urbanization (Pounds 1990, 130). In contrast, towns were later coming to the northern Netherlands. The towns of Holland-Dordrecht, Leiden, Haarlem, Alkmaar, and Delft were not established until the thirteenth century. Early urbanization in the Netherlands was made possible by the prior development of agriculture there, which was in turn facilitated by the general absence of communal agricultural systems throughout most of the region.

## Field Systems in the Netherlands

### Communal Open Field Systems

The classic communal open field system of western Europe was largely absent in the Netherlands. Only in the southern and eastern borders (part of southern Artois, Hainaut, southern Brabant, Namur, southern Liège, Limburg and Luxembourg—see Huppertz 1939, Karte X; Sivery 1977–79) could extensions of the classic communal open field systems of northern France and southern Germany be found (see map 8).[1] In these border areas, the communal system faithfully conformed to the model described in previous chapters and more or less duplicated the situation in northeastern France and southern Germany. That is, there were two or three large fields, all subject to communal rotations and common grazing. Large, compact villages were typical. Here the seigneurial system was maintained, and the use of *corvée* labor persisted into the early modern period.

### Regions of Less-Communal Open Fields and Enclosures

Most of the Netherlands was characterized by less-communal and noncommunal systems of agriculture. In the southern Netherlands (modern-day Belgium) this was the case in Flanders, the north of Artois, and much of Brabant. Throughout the region, cereals, particularly rye and spelt (common wheat), were the predominant crops (van Houtte 1977, 66).

**Map 7. The Netherlands**

Field System

Communal Open Field

Less-Communal Open Field

Map 8. Field systems in the Netherlands. (Adapted from Huppertz 1939.)

These regions of the south were also lightly manorialized. The manorial system had been a recent introduction, probably dating to the ninth century (van Houtte 1977, 9). This system had some of the aspects of the classical manorial system: subject tenants owed agricultural services and various fees to the lord and were forced to use the lords' mills, ovens, ponds, breweries, and so forth. Services from villeins were fixed, as a rule, on the basis of the *manse,* which was usually a combination of arable and garden land with, occasionally, some pastures and woods. Each manor possessed between 10 and 40 *mansi,* but exceptional cases had as few as 4 or as many as 118 (van Houtte 1977, 10). Despite these outward forms, manorialization in the southern Low Countries (as in eastern England) was fairly weak. Serfs were few, and villeins were mostly "free" villeins or tenants (van Houtte 1977, 11). Furthermore, the system, introduced late, began to break down as early as the middle of the twelfth century. Many *mansi* dissolved, and demesnes followed suit (van Houtte 1977, 12); labor services disappeared (Ganshof and Verhulst 1966, 315). Since the demesne could no longer be cultivated by *corvée,* lords sometimes found it profitable to lease it. This occurred in Flanders by the twelfth century and extended all over most of the Low Countries in the following century (van Houtte 1977, 12–13). Leases customarily were fixed for a number of years, typically some multiple of three, particularly twelve or fifteen years. The extensive clearing of new lands and draining of the sea at this time of great population growth also hastened the demise of manorial control. In many cases, people who worked on clearing new lands were freed *en masse.* Serfs who participated in clearing also sometimes were able to buy their personal liberty.

By the late thirteenth century villeinage virtually had disappeared in the greater part of the southern Netherlands (in Flanders and Brabant) (Ganshof and Verhulst 1966, 337; van Houtte 1977, 15) . Apart from collecting his rents, the new type of lord at most could levy tithes and gather the income from a communal mill or brewery that peasants were forced to use. Typically, lords also maintained some kind of legal jurisdiction (van Houtte 1977, 15–16). In the country, a class of peasant proprietors arose and gained a large part of the land, both where villeinage survived and where there was a free peasantry. In 1335 the *échevins* of Ypres (in Flanders) could write: "Oncques n'avons oy de gens de serve condicion, ne de morte main, ne de quel condicion qu' il soient." (The old French may be roughly translated as "there have never been people of servile status, or in serfdom or any similar condition" [qtd. in Pirenne 1937, 83].)

In the eastern Netherlands (the provinces of Overijssel, Drenthe, Guelders, and part of Brabant) the soil was sandy and there were less-communal open field systems. Villages were often nucleated, and farmers had their arable holdings in open fields under some communal regulation.

There were also communal controls over village wastelands, which were extensive in these regions. Manorial control was likewise stronger (de Vries and van der Woude 1997, 196). In some parts of the eastern Netherlands there were systems of enclosures (Slicher van Bath 1963b, 56) associated with a more pastoral economy. Here cultivation was sometimes on *Esch* fields similar to those found in northwestern Germany (Smith 1967, 226; Bieleman 1990; see also chap. 7). The *Esch* was a small area of intensively farmed land made up of long strips of arable land which were owned individually. The entire *Esch* often was enclosed to keep animals from wandering onto the crops. The strips of land were fertilized regularly with sod cut from the heath in the village commons, which was enriched in turn with manure from animals that grazed there. The sod then raised the level of the strips of land so the *Esch* became elevated. Villages tended to be small (hamlets or *Drubbel*) with not more than three to ten farms. Agriculture was intensive. There were no fallow periods or common pasture on the *Esch* and no communal crop rotations.

To the north and west in the provinces of Holland, Zeeland, Utrecht, Friesland, and Groningen, and generally along coastal regions from Flanders to Friesland, isolated farms and non-communal agricultural systems predominated (Slicher van Bath 1963b, 55; de Vries and van der Woude 1997, 16). Coastal areas often had row villages similar to the German *Marschhufendorf* (Huppertz 1939; Sivery 1977–79 (see chap. 7 and map 8). In these villages, there was typically little communal control over agriculture, although there was communal cooperation in drainage matters. In this region the seigneurial system was either weak or absent altogether. Many settlements in these areas date only to the twelfth and thirteenth centuries when a large area of land in the Holland-Utrecht peat bog plain was made available for agriculture. This land had to be drained, and descendants of Frisian settlers specialized in this work of drainage and reclamage (TeBrake 1985, 117–18, 186). Their system consisted of digging drainage ditches that lowered the water table and left the ground dry enough for cattle grazing and even arable farming. Reclamation work was typically organized by a *locator,* who was responsible to a count and often served as local judge, just as he was to do somewhat later in eastern Germany (see chap. 7). As in eastern Europe, new settlers in these regions were given many special privileges and rights (van Houtte 1977, 15).

By the late thirteenth century serfdom and villeinage had virtually disappeared in the greater part of Holland and Zeeland. Further north, the manorial system was completely absent (van Houtte 1977, 9). The manorial system had never penetrated regions such as Frisia, Groningen, and Drenthe (de Schepper 1994, 513). In Frisia and neighboring Groningen, farmers were not only free but often enfranchised. By the late medieval period most of the population in this region had voting rights (de Vries 1974, 26). de Vries (26) describes this as follows:

> After about 1100, a system of administration developed in which *grietmannen* (in Friesland) or *redgers* (in Groningen) held judicial power over small districts through election by citizens. In contrast to the feudal system, the governmental system of the Frisians, such as it was, based itself on the voting rights of farmers. Frisians held voting rights through the ownership of a certain amount of land or the ownership of a farm invested by tradition with voting rights. Under this custom the bulk of the medieval population was enfranchised.

In Frisia and in other coastal provinces, community involvement in agriculture was limited to the work of draining marshy lands and protecting farmland from flooding. For this there was a group of officials known as *heemraden,* or dike reeves, who were responsible for the construction and maintenance of dikes and dams (de Vries 1974, 28; van Houtte 1977, 7; TeBrake 1985, 229). These officials were organized into higher water authorities (*hoogheemraden*) that were responsible for interregional cooperation concerning the waterworks. These organizations were also empowered to administer justice within their regions. Under the Burgundian-Habsburg rulers these were incorporated into the national judicial system as lower courts.

In the northern Netherlands and the coastal areas a lack of community control over agriculture, individual property rights, and a large free peasantry helped provide a general spirit of individualism in this region by the early sixteenth century. Descriptions of peasant society tend to stress individualism rather than communal spirit (de Vries 1974, 55). Protection of peasant rights from encroachment was at the heart of the many peasant rebellions in the Frisian region; for example, the Great Wars in West Friesland, Friesland, East Friesland, and Drenthe (in 1225, 1240 and 1324–28) (Slicher van Bath 1963b, 191).

## The Regional Pattern of Agrarian Change in the Late Medieval and Early Modern Netherlands

Flexible field systems coupled with light manorial control in both the north and south of the Low Countries encouraged agricultural development. Exceptionally high yields and innovative techniques were recorded in Flanders and other parts of the southern Low Countries from the Middle Ages. There was little evidence of such attainment in the communal regions of the south and east.

The polyptych of Saint-Pierre at Ghent in Flanders shows the existence of irregular cropping systems as early as the ninth century (Pounds 1990, 134.) Often land lay fallow not every third year but every fourth, fifth, or sixth year. Convertible husbandry also was used, the first known example being in 1323, in land just south of Ghent (Slicher van Bath 1963b, 179). Grass was sown after the fallow period, and after a few years (normally three to six) the artificial meadow was converted back to arable land and another meadow was sown elsewhere. There is also early evidence for the cultivation of pulses, vetches, and other "artificial" grasses and crops to be used as cattle feed on the fallow from the mid-fourteenth century (Slicher van Bath 1963b, 179; Pounds 1990, 194). Turnips were used northeast of Louvain (or Leuven, in Brabant) in 1404. In some cases the fallow period was dropped altogether and replaced by alternate harvests of feed crops (van Houtte 1977, 69). The earliest record of such intensive culture is 1328, in Bourbourg, northwest of Cassel (Flanders): 10.5 hectares were sown with wheat, oats, beans, and fodder crops. No mention was made of fallow (Slicher van Bath 1963b, 179).

There were also signs of innovation in agricultural implements. The light, one-stilt plow was introduced, which was drawn by a smaller team than the old plow and needed only one man, rather than two, to drive it. This plow was more easily turned at the end of the furrow than the former heavy wheeled plough (see also van Houtte 1977, 71). In addition, the Hainaut scythe slowly replaced the sickle for reaping (Slicher van Bath 1963b, 186; van Houtte 1977, 71; Pounds 1990, 195). This was a short scythe with a hook with which the straw was grappled. The peasants thus had more straw for bedding, which was all the more valuable since deforestation had limited the availability of leaves and similar material. In Artois and the polders (pastures reclaimed from the sea) north of Bruges the short scythe was known by 1326 at the latest (van Houtte 1977, 71). These practices and techniques spread, and the rotation systems of Flanders became the ideal for later agronomists.

Little is known of yields at this time, although available evidence suggests they were very high by standards of the day. The mean yield of wheat was 8.7 times the weight sown near Saint-Omer in the 1320s, 12.8 near Béthune in the Pas-de-Calais in the 1330s, and 8 around Douai between 1329 and 1380 (both in Artois). In the polders near Bruges, in the years 1359–68, the harvest was 4.3 times the sown weight of wheat. Around 1400 the yield was 8 to 1 for wheat around Brussels (in Brabant). These yields were much in advance of other countries, particularly England, about which there is much more information, due to the preservation of manorial records (van Houtte 1977, 72). They equal or exceed the best yields in eastern England at the same time (see chap. 4).

## Trade and Industry

Agricultural development made urban development in the southern Netherlands possible, and it also promoted the development of trade and industry. By the late medieval period this area had become the chief manufacturing and commercial region for cloth working outside Italy. Cloth in turn stimulated the export trade.[2] Merchants of the Meuse (or Maas, with an outlet at Dordrecht) and Scheldt (or Schelde, running through Antwerp) Valleys exchanged this cloth for products of northwestern Europe and the Mediterranean area. Their marketplaces were the fairs of northern France, towns along the Rhine, and London, to which they had easy access by water. In the thirteenth century the chief outlet for Flemish cloth was Champagne (van Houtte 1977).

At the same time, trade also was developing in the northern Netherlands. Utrecht had inherited much of the former trade of the Frisians, who had dominated trade in the Carolingian period and after. In the course of the thirteenth century, however, the trade route through Utrecht was abandoned gradually in favor of others between Dordrecht and the Zuiderzee. Merchants of Dordrecht, which was conveniently situated at the mouth of the Meuse and the chief branches of the Rhine, sailed up the rivers with salt from the Zeeland salines (salt-making areas) and cloth from Flanders and Brabant and returned with Rhine wines and metal goods.

Eventually, the traders from the north began to take over the Flemish trade. The overseas Flemish trade had declined, as now more and more foreign merchants undertook the journey to Flanders, instead of waiting for Flemish merchants to arrive. Merchants were primarily attracted to Flanders for its cloth, which was of a quality unrivaled in Europe and was in demand everywhere. The fair at Bruges became their meeting place. Around 1300 the large Italian banking and trading houses set up branches in Bruges and began to send their fleets to Flanders. Finally, English kings also sent their wool exports to Bruges and set up the wool Staple (primary market for English wool) there in 1325–26, 1340–48, and 1349–52. The presence at Bruges of Italians, Germans, and English made this city the most important business center in Europe north of the Alps in the fourteenth and early fifteenth centuries (van Houtte 1977, 99, 44–47).

## Fourteenth-Century Crisis

Unlike in other European countries, economic growth in the Low Countries did not stop in the late thirteenth and fourteenth centuries. Unlike most other European countries, the information available from tithes and agricultural rents in kind for the Low Countries in some regions shows increasing rather than stable returns between 1259 and 1350. The rate of growth slowed down, however, throughout the period (Slicher van Bath 1963b; Van der Wee 1993, 49). Furthermore, the deep wave of depression that engulfed the rest of Europe during the fourteenth and fifteenth centuries did not have the same paralyzing effect on the Low Countries as it did elsewhere (Thoen 1990, 31; Van der Wee 1993, 10). For a while, at least, the Low Countries truly may be dubbed the "Teflon" region, immune to crises afflicting everywhere else in Europe.

Much of the Netherlands appear to have escaped entirely the plagues of the mid-fourteenth century. Vast regions were unscathed. The Florentine Matteo Villani stated, with astonishment, that the plague spared Brabant. There was little evidence of a demographic collapse in the Low Countries and, consequently, few deserted villages. Nor did the Low Countries experience the seigneurial reaction common to many parts of Europe after the Black Death. This may have been due to the weakness of the epidemic or perhaps to the exceptional development of towns, which gave good refuge to peasants if their burdens were increased. Unlike elsewhere in England, France, and southern Germany, the emancipation of serfs proceeded apace (van Houtte 1977, 73, 75).

Even if areas were less affected by plague than elsewhere in Europe, the terrible ravages suffered by most regions of Europe did great harm to the export trade after 1350, as demand for grain tapered off. Low prices for grain did affect the farming sector. Yet what the Low Countries lost in long-distance trade appears to have been more than compensated for by domestic demand, which was still growing. Instead of generally decreasing as in other countries, in the southern Low Countries yields tended to stabilize in the years after the Black Death, from 1350 to 1437 (Van der Wee 1993, 49). Yields remained high, with seed/yield ratios in the neighborhood of Brussels between 1 to 7 and 1 to 9 (c. 1400, for wheat [see Slicher van Bath 1963a, 41]). Improvements in agricultural techniques continued with improved crop rotations and the use of fertilizer (Van der Wee 1993, 11).

There was increasing agricultural specialization in the Low Countries, reflecting in part changes in demand from other countries. Flanders began concentrating on production of butter and cheese in the fourteenth and fifteenth centuries; Holland and Frisia followed suit in the fifteenth to sixteenth centuries. The traditional focus on cereal crops declined. Around 1350 there was extensive cultivation of oleaginous plants for both food and lighting as well as manufacturing in Holland and around Utrecht. Rape and mustard were being harvested in southeastern Flanders by the fifteenth century. Hop growing appeared by 1360 or 1370 in Holland and northern Brabant and early in the next century west of Brussels as well.

The brewing industry expanded, particularly in the cities of Delft, Gouda, and Haarlem (in Holland). A great variety of vegetables, perhaps of Arabic origin, became common in markets of larger towns. Apples, pears, plums, cherries, chestnuts, and strawberries became more usual (van Houtte 1977, 68–69). Horse breeding developed, especially in Frisia.

A substantial domestic and European market remained for textiles; thus, there was little depression in the cloth industry. The linen industry underwent rapid development in the Low Countries at this time, and flax growing is mentioned more frequently in records. Growth of the linen industry in turn stimulated the growing of dye plants such as madder (for red) and woad (for blue). There is evidence of large-scale cultivation of madder in the Zeeland Islands and neighboring parts of northern Brabant in the fourteenth century.

Agricultural specialization in both Flanders and Holland was aided by the increase in imports of grain from abroad. An increasing proportion of grain now came from elsewhere, first from Artois and Picardy in northern France, later from the Baltic. Ghent, the town to which the Scheldt and the Lys carried most imports from northern France, set up a grain staple for downriver traffic in the mid-fourteenth century to ensure its own supply of grain. By the later-fourteenth century Baltic grain was imported regularly, particularly Baltic rye (van Houtte 1977, 66, 67).

At this time the seafaring towns of Holland and Zeeland began to embark upon a commercial expansion that by the sixteenth century would gain them economic ascendancy over their southern neighbors and the German Hanse. The inland waterways of these towns provided easy access by ship, which stimulated both maritime trade and coastal fisheries. Many ships of Holland and Zeeland came to be employed by the Hanse as supplemental carriers of Baltic cargoes between Hamburg and Bruges. Also at this time Holland-Zeeland towns gained an important lead in the herring trade. This was in part because they developed a type of large fishing craft that could spend a week or more in the abundant herring grounds far out in the North Sea. The Hollanders and Zeelanders also could acquire salt (a necessary ingredient in the preservation of herring) from the Bay of Bourgneuf more cheaply than Baltic Germans could (Munro 1994, 161–62). They were also involved in the export of beer made in Holland, which was exported to the southern Netherlands and to the Baltic regions as well.

### Late-Fifteenth-Century Downturn

Thus, productivity in the Low Countries did not collapse catastrophically from the high level reached at the beginning of the fourteenth century but, generally speaking, remained at a fairly high level during the entire European depression of the fourteenth and fifteenth centuries. Things changed in the later fifteenth century. In the last third of the fifteenth century the general trend of land productivity took a downward turn (Van der Wee 1993, 52; van Houtte 1977).

The death of Charles the Bold in 1477 and, even more so, that of Mary of Burgundy in 1482 opened an epoch of disorder and revolt against the rule of the duchess's widower, Maximilian of Habsburg. Flanders, Brabant, and Holland were ravaged by armed bands of both sides. Endemic insecurity made rural people seek refuge behind town walls. This unrest culminated in the Flemish War (1483–92), which disturbed many regions of the southern Netherlands (Yun 1994, 119; Van der Wee 1993, 53). In this period the plague appears to have struck the Low Countries with greater severity than it did in the mid-fourteenth century. Together with the general turmoil it contributed to a decline in population in the southern Low Countries. Most cloth towns of the south saw a fall in population—for example, Ypres. Many artisans emigrated, especially to London and to York. Of the major towns only Antwerp (1437–96) grew, as its commerce expanded. In secondary towns the total population also seems to have declined with the ruin of their export trades (van Houtte 1977, 61–63). The entire population of Brabant declined by some 20 percent in the sixty years from 1437 to 1496 (Van der Wee 1993, 54). Estimates based on *dénombrements* from Flanders, Brabant, and Hainaut suggest a decline in the total population of the southern Netherlands from 1.4 million in 1375 to 1.24 million in 1500, about 11 percent (de Vries 1974, 11–12). Economic recovery began, encouraging expansion of the population, only with the return of peace in the 1490s (van Houtte 1977, 123). Rental values of land revived rapidly. Nominal agricultural money rents rose substantially everywhere, although the increase was most obvious around Antwerp, in Holland, and in Flanders (Van der Wee 1993, 54).

### Sixteenth Century

During the sixteenth century the Low Countries became the dominant economic power in the west. Brabant, Holland, and Flanders led the way in growth. Antwerp in Flanders became Europe's leading commercial city. Urbanization proceeded apace, and the population grew rapidly. In both north and south the population grew by some 50 percent in the first sixty years of the sixteenth century (de Vries 1994, 12). In the provinces of Holland, Brabant, Flanders, Hainaut, Overijssel, and Gelderland, the urban population reached 30 to 55 percent of the total population (Van der Wee 1993, 55).

Such extensive urbanization depended on continuing agricultural development and increasing imports of grain. Progress in agriculture continued, particularly in Flanders. The fallow was abandoned, and its replacement with fodder crops ceased to be exceptional. Both clover and the turnip were increasingly used, particularly in the Waasland in Flanders. The horse had become the most common draft animal. Progress was particularly noticeable on farms of small or middling size (van Houtte 1977, 149–50). In northern and western Brabant and in Flanders hop growing and horticulture became widespread; in Flanders and Zeeland flax growing became very popular (Van der Wee 1993, 57). Further north in Frisia there was also agricultural progress, but it was more modest. For example, the Frisian farmer Hemmema left at most an eighth of his land fallow in the 1570s and probably followed a seven- or eight-year cycle. This region concentrated on pastoral specialties, particularly dairy production. In addition, Frisian horses were in great demand, especially for armies (van Houtte 1977, 152).

Agricultural specialization in the Low Countries was now supported by massive importation of grain via Holland (Van der Wee 1993, 57; de Vries and van der Woude 1997, 198). The primary port for this trade, Amsterdam, began to eclipse its old rival, Dordrecht. Expansion of trade was reflected in the beginning of canal building to supplement natural waterways (Pounds 1990, 245). In addition, more roads were built. The roadbook published in 1553 by Charles Estienne for France shows a dense road network in the southern Low Countries.

Agricultural growth continued throughout the sixteenth century and was noticeable everywhere, although in the eastern provinces (including Overijssel, Drenthe, Groningen) the increase was not in arable production but in the production of livestock for the market (de Vries and van der Woude 1997, 207–8). Only in parts of the south and east, where the communal system was fully developed, did development take a less favorable turn. There population increase was more rapid than the growth of gross production and income. In border regions of the south—Walloon-Brabant, Hesbaye, Cambrésis, and Picardy—output stabilized early (Van der Wee 1993, 56). The economic peak was reached in the early sixteenth century in Cambrai and was followed by a decline. The peak was reached even earlier in South Limburg. Like the communal regions of southwestern Germany and northern France, these areas maintained a monoculture of grain (Van der Wee 1993, 56; de Schepper 1994, 512). Unlike in the northwest, such as Limburg-on-the Vesder, Luxembourg, and the Walloon provinces, clergy and upper nobility were able to maintain their traditional power and authority (de Schepper 1994, 512).

On the foundations of general agricultural advance in most of the

Netherlands industry and trade flourished. In the period 1495–1520 trade was dominated by a revitalization of European trade. Long-distance trade changed from being exclusively a trade in small articles of high added value and now included large or heavy articles and bulk goods such as coal and oxen (Van der Wee 1993, 23). Most of this trade went through Antwerp, which was now the major commercial center of the Netherlands, replacing Bruges. Antwerp's commercial supremacy had come to rest on trade in three products: English woolens, South German metals, and Portuguese-Asian spices. The most important product was English cloth, most of which was dyed or dressed in Antwerp itself or adjacent towns (Munro 1994, 165–66). The ascendancy of Antwerp is reflected in its expansion. In 1374 it had barely five thousand inhabitants. By 1440 this number had increased to twenty thousand and by the sixteenth century to fifty thousand (de Vries 1984, 159; Pounds 1990, 193; see also Van der Wee 1993, 25).

Wars between the French Valois and the Spanish Habsburgs in the 1520s caused a serious breakdown in the transit trade of the Low Countries. Yet the growth of industry and agriculture more than made up for its decline. Everywhere population was rising rapidly, and real incomes actually rose. In the rural regions of the southern Netherlands it was primarily the use of more intensive methods of cultivation combined with increased employment in rural industries that maintained the prosperity of the growing population (Van der Wee 1993, 21, 22). An important group of nonagricultural skilled crafts also had developed in the countryside that provided special services to rural communities or towns—for example, fishing, peat digging, land reclamation, maintenance of dikes, construction and maintenance of windmills, and internal and maritime transportation.

Yet this prosperity in the southern Netherlands did not last. By the mid-sixteenth century Antwerp had received two setbacks to its commercial hegemony. Munro notes, "First, the flow of south German silver and copper lessened, as central European mines began to encounter diminishing returns, falling outputs, and rising costs, which made their silver uncompetitive when American bullion began to arrive at Seville. Moreover, Venice, whose spice trade had revived strongly, was attracting more of those metals to the Mediterranean. The second blow fell in 1548, when Portugal responded to these events by transferring her spice staple from Antwerp to Lisbon, closer to both the cheaper silver and the major spice markets of the Mediterranean" (1994, 176). At the same time, the English cloth trade was declining, partly because of the devaluation of the pound sterling during the debasements of the Tudor period.

Revolt against Spain

Economic growth was effectively halted in the southern Netherlands by the Revolt against Spain (1567), which caused the center of gravity of agrarian progress in the Low Countries to shift north. The south, located at the center of the revolt, was affected particularly badly by the fighting and unrest. The Antwerp money market never regained its earlier position as the dominant European money center (Van der Wee 1993, 28). The decline of Antwerp was exacerbated by Habsburg trade bans in 1563–65 and Alva's repression after 1566 (Munro 1994, 177–78).

Finally, the Eighty Years' War (1568–1648) following the Revolt from Spain practically destroyed the economy of the southern Netherlands. Misery, insecurity, and unrest dominated the region for many years. Population fell, and the southern Netherlands increasingly reverted to a rural economy (Van der Wee 1993, 30, 31). Warring was almost continuous in the south: the Dutch Revolt and the wars of Louis XIV occupied sixty-seven years of the seventeenth century. The wars at the end of Louis XIV's reign caused severe damage in the region, as from 1635 the country was prey to French invasion. Later, the Nine Years' War (1688–97) and the War of the Spanish Succession (1701–13) lasted longer and were waged on a much larger scale. In the southern provinces, which became the battlefield of Europe in the full sense of the term, any passage of troops left destruction and famine in its wake, and often epidemics followed (van Houtte 1977, 138, 227).

Much of the southern Netherlands became a depressed area at this time (Pounds 1990, 264; Van der Wee 1993, 259). In the second half of the seventeenth century there was a depression of agriculture in general and grain prices in particular (van Houtte 1977, 228). Tithe returns decreased all over the southern Netherlands, a trend that was apparent at the outbreak of the Thirty Years' War, in 1618. This decline was especially noticeable in the communal border regions. Near Maastricht and Liège tithe returns reached their lowest point soon after the middle of the century (Van der Wee 1993, 62).

The situation in the northern Netherlands (the United Provinces after 1579) was considerably more favorable, despite the fact that it was also frequently involved in warfare (t'Hart 1993, 32). Land productivity continued to rise until about 1650–70, especially in the coastal provinces (Van der Wee 1993, 32, 61, de Vries and van der Woude 1997, 210). Maritime trade in the north also boomed at this time. Herring, cod, and whale fishing became leading sectors, as did fish processing and shipbuilding. There was more extensive processing of colonial wares (particularly sugar). Specialized nonagrarian crafts continued to develop in the countryside: drainage of the polders, upkeep of dikes and waterways, maintenance of windmills, and services for nearby towns. The export industry in woolen and linen textiles expanded, and an urban luxury industry also developed, producing for export. The eastern parts of the United Provinces did not share in the economic boom to the same extent, although extensive livestock production for the market continued in the region (de Vries and van der Woude 1997, 205).

Population began to increase in both north and south in the first half of the seventeenth century. In the southern Netherlands this was due to recovery after the war, and in the United Provinces it was a result of the exceptional prosperity (van Houtte 1977, 137). Growth of population was most marked in the north and in the western, or maritime, provinces, where Amsterdam grew to be one of the largest cities in Europe, and the population of the province of Holland became more than half-urban. The population of the northern Netherlands rose from less than one million at the beginning of the sixteenth century to about two million at the beginning of the eighteenth, the fastest population growth in Europe in this period (de Vries 1994, 13). Growth was slower in the eastern parts of the United Provinces.

### Change in Farm Sizes

Agrarian change and increasing agricultural productivity were not accompanied by an increase in farm sizes in the Netherlands—quite the opposite was true: small farms proliferated all over the Low Countries throughout the late medieval and early modern periods. Furthermore, most innovative techniques and labor-intensive practices were used most commonly on smaller farms, not the larger farms. Large farms only developed in the far north, where they were associated with stock rearing, and in communal regions of the south and east. By and large they were not known for high productivity.

In the southern Netherlands a high population density had prompted the shift to smaller farms as early as the fourteenth century. Flanders in particular included many peasant proprietors, mainly on small farms. The number of small farms in Flanders increased over the period from 1329 to 1604. The typical farm went from an average of around 1.5 to 3.75 hectares to 0.15 to 1.5 hectares (Van der Wee, with Van Cauwenberghe 1993, 69–83).[3] As in the peasant revolts in eastern England some time later, these smallholders in Flanders played an important role in the peasant revolt of 1323–28. Out of almost three thousand rebel Flemish peasants whose property was confiscated after their defeat at Cassel in 1328,

1,632 had less than 4.4 hectares, and among these 1,183 had not even half of that. Smallholders also spearheaded the revolt of 1491–92 in Holland (van Houtte 1977, 76).

While small farms in the Low Countries had proliferated, large farms generally had declined. Since the later fifteenth century demesnes in the Low Countries had often been sold, often to nouveaux riches of the town. The shift of land into bourgeois hands was especially notable during the troubles of the late sixteenth century. In the sixteenth century townspeople's property predominated on the polders of Holland and made up a third of the region to the north of Namur and between Holland and Guelders (van Houtte 1977, 142, 145). Most of the land that townspeople acquired, however, they leased in small parcels for others to farm.

Only in the northern Netherlands and the communal regions of the south was there some trend toward larger farms in the early modern period in response to worsening economic conditions after about 1650. Particularly in Holland and Frisia and other coastal provinces, concentration of cultivated land became noticeable (Van der Wee 1993, 68; Van Deursen 1991; van Houtte 1977, 244; de Vries and van der Woude 1997, 219–20). This reflected the emphasis on pasture farming in this region, as generally pasture farms were larger than arable farms (van Houtte 1977, 246). In the eastern provinces there were some enclosures and a shift toward arable production and production of industrial crops, but there was no consequent rise in farm sizes (de Vries and van der Woude 1997, 220). Some large farms developed in the communal regions of the south and east, including the *censes* of the Walloon region. Such farms usually belonged to religious institutions or noble families. Unlike in midland England in the sixteenth and later seventeenth centuries, there was no enclosure movement associated with the development of such farms in the southern Netherlands.

This regional variation in farm sizes persisted until modern times. By 1800, in the region of today's Netherlands, arable farms had on average 16 hectares (about 40 acres), stock-raising farms about 60 (about 148 acres). In the old communal regions south of the Sambre and Meuse trench (parts of Liège and Limburg) the greater part of the cultivated land was occupied by large farms of between 40 and 160 hectares (about 100–400 acres [van Houtte 1977, 246]).

## Change in Labor Relations

Throughout the northern and southern Netherlands serfdom either disappeared early or had never existed. Contractual relations between owner and tenant were the rule by the early modern period. Sharecropping was uncommon. In sixteenth century Flanders and Holland, where *corvées* were maintained, they involved only insignificant obligations of cartage, that is, the obligation to fetch and carry for the lord (van Houtte 1977, 143).

Only in some of the more communal regions of the east and south, such as Namur, Ardennes, and Luxembourg, was the seigneurial system maintained more or less intact. Many manor houses remained in the possession of country squires, who were distinguished from larger farmers only by having a wall around their dwelling, barns, and stables, an imposing porch, and a chapel. They continued to exact rents and taxes and, as before, used *corvées* to mow or store their grain. Some of them possessed ironworks and made their villeins work there. Sharecropping, rare in the Netherlands and characteristic of a more backward agriculture, also persisted in this region (van Houtte 1977, 144, 145).

### Textile Industry

In addition to agricultural development, growth of the textile industry also contributed to the early prosperity and the trade of the Low Countries. The cloth industry remained the main basis of the region's trade until the nineteenth century (van Houtte 1977, 35). The development of the textile industry, however, was related to the growth of the agricultural economy in many ways, both direct and indirect. Many of the raw materials for the textile industry, particularly flax for linen, were produced locally. Further, rural prosperity promoted population growth, which provided an abundance of labor for the textile industry. The growing affluence of the rural population also provided a domestic market for the products of the textile industry, which fueled its expansion.

Cloth manufacture had a long history in the area, as Frisians were trading cloth as early as the ninth century. It is not known for sure where so-called Frisian cloths were made, but they may have been produced in the region later to be called Flanders. In the tenth and eleventh centuries the Frisians lost their trading preeminence, which was taken over by merchants of the Meuse and Scheldt valleys to the south. These merchants, with their urban traditions and age-old ties with the Continental interior, were better able than Frisians to establish a systematic trading link between northwestern Europe and the Mediterranean area. Their primary commercial offering was Flemish cloth. By the twelfth century this cloth was being exported to Africa, France, England, and Germany. In these places it often supplanted local production (Van der Wee 1993, 7; Munro 1994, 156 ).

By the thirteenth century the towns most associated with the production of cloth were the great *villes drapantes*—the towns of Ypres, Bruges, and Ghent in Flanders—although the cloth industry spread beyond those cities into northern France and to Brussels, Liège, and Aachen in the east (Pounds 1990, 173). Initially, wool for the textile industry had been produced locally. Later, English wool was used, especially for the best cloth. The first recorded export of English wool, bound for Flanders, dates to 1113, and it was common in Flanders by the end of the century. Imports came in mainly via the Zwin River, which was connected by waterway with the *villes drapantes*. Despite some production of fine cloths, at this time the most typical product of the industry was a heavy, well-fulled broadcloth. Germany was an important market for the cloth, although cloth was also exported to Paris, the Atlantic coast of France, and Spain. Some was sent to be further finished in Italy. Some went to the east as far as Constantinople (van Houtte 1977, 32–37).

After the fourteenth-century plague supplies of English wool began to dwindle, and its price increased. Competition from English and Tuscan ready-made woolens also increased. The broadcloth industry in the *villes drapantes* of Flanders began to decay, ending the golden era of the Flemish cloth towns. The decline became clear from the fourteenth century. This decline was compensated to some extent by a switch to the production of luxury woolens in Flanders and Brabant and other more specialized types of textile production, such as the making of carpets, rugs, and tapestry (van Houtte 1977, 80, 86). Most of this cloth was produced for the colder climes of northern Europe, especially the Baltic area (Munro 1994, 156). The luxury woolen industry also developed further north, in Holland. The cloth trade of Holland began to work English wool only at the end of the fourteenth century and quickly won a place in the European market. Its chief center, Leiden, one of Holland's first towns with a textile industry, produced nearly ten thousand cloths yearly around 1400 and almost twenty-five thousand a century later (van Houtte 1977, 82).

The southern Netherlands now saw the rise of *nouvelles draperies,* most of which were manufactured in rural areas (Munro 1994, 1560). These fabrics were short-staple woolen cloths that were lighter and cheaper than the broadcloths (Pounds 1990, 197; Van der Wee 1993, 8; Scott 1996, 17). By the late fourteenth century they were the latest fashion and in much demand. Now the cloth industry spread eastward into Brabant and westward into west Flanders and Artois (de Schepper 1994, 524). In the course of the later fourteenth century small towns like Ath, Lier, and Hondschoote also began to develop their own distinctive cloth industry, producing even lighter cloths (light woolens, serges, "bays" and "says") than *nouvelles draperies.* Hondschoote, in west Flanders, was typical of the new weaving centers; it specialized in such cloth from the late fourteenth century using cheaper wool, typically from Scotland, Lower Saxony, and Spain (van Houtte 1977, 158).

At this time the linen industry also expanded in response to growing demand. The cultivation of flax increased on peasant farms of Flanders, while its preparation and weaving were added to domestic crafts throughout the region (see van Houtte 1977, 68). Coutrai in west Flanders became a focus of the linen industry. Towns largely manufactured luxury linen goods for a clientele that was wealthy and able to support high production costs, but the rural linen industry also produced coarse goods, comparable with those of the wool industry and cheaper.

The new textile industries were largely free of the extensive regulation that had increased costs and reduced flexibility in the old broadcloth industry. As a result, the new centers could adapt easily to changes in fashion (van Houtte 1977, 83). This light-cloth industry grew to a considerable size, although it never became an urban industry. The competitiveness of Flemish linens was assisted by the decline of the French linen industry, which had been set back by the Black Death and the Hundred Years' War and the fact that German linens of the Rhineland, Westphalia, and Silesia were often excluded from the English market by the fifteenth century, due to conflicts between England and the Hanseatic League. This left the English market for linen almost entirely to the Flemings. The Mediterranean was also an important market for Flemish cloth, especially for the cheaper and lighter textiles (Munro 1994, 156, 176).

The sixteenth century saw the further development of textile villages in west Flanders and northern France. By mid-century the lightest cloths (serges and says) were becoming the major textile product of the Low Countries: Hondschoote, Armentières, Tourcoing, and Neuve-Englise all were noted for production of these cloths (Pounds 1990, 228). Thus, although the southern Netherlands had lost their supremacy in heavier woolens, they had gained a new industrial preeminence in less costly cloths. A substantial industry in finishing and re-exporting cloth also had developed. These activities were particularly important in Antwerp. In 1560 Italian silks and English woolens for refinishing accounted for 22 percent and 18 percent of total imports, respectively (55 percent of all textile products) (Munro 1994, 177).

By the late sixteenth century, however, the no-longer-new "new draperies" began to decline, while the broadcloth industry had became practically extinct in the cities of Flanders. Wars of the later sixteenth century hastened the end of the cloth industry in the villages of the southern Netherlands. All textile industries in the southern Netherlands were virtually extinguished in the Spanish wars and when the port of Antwerp was effectively closed (Pounds 1990, 286). Cloth production shifted to the northern Low Countries, where Leiden became an important center for the cloth industry, although the primary business of the United Provinces remained commerce rather than manufacturing. The influx of Protestant refugees from the south facilitated the shift to the north, as newcomers brought skills and methods necessary for manufacturing the new light cloths to Leiden and Haarlem in the northern Netherlands (Munro 1994, 177). Leiden took over where Hondschoote left off. The manufacture of light cloth had begun there by 1497 at the latest, but by 1664 Leiden was the most important manufacturing center for wool in Europe and perhaps in the world, as Ghent had once been with its wool industry three or four centuries previously (van Houtte 1977, 158).

## The Agricultural Revolution in the Netherlands

As we have seen, from the fourteenth to the seventeenth centuries the Low Countries showed precocious development in agriculture. As a result, the question of when precisely the agricultural revolution occurred in the Netherlands is vexed. Some claim an agricultural revolution occurred in the northern Netherlands with the high productivity of the sixteenth and early seventeenth centuries (Van der Wee 1993, 64). Exceptional levels of agricultural productivity declined in the northern Netherlands, however, during the late seventeenth and early eighteenth century, accompanying general economic decline (de Vries and van der Woude 1997, 210). The economy of the crown jewel of the United Provinces, Holland, stagnated after 1750 (van Houtte 1977, 230). Here is not the place to go into all the reasons that have been given for the general economic decline. Suffice it to say they may have included costs of empire and increasing taxation (see van Houtte 1977), rise of British maritime supremacy, rising wages, entrenched guild resistance to mechanization, and organizational rigidity (Van der Wee 1993, 33–41). In the late eighteenth century, however, the agricultural sector in the northern Netherlands rebounded and began to compensate for urban economic decline (de Vries and van der Woude 1997, 225). Intensive methods were readopted, and agricultural productivity rose. The decline had been less severe in the eastern parts of the United Provinces where grain production had increased since the 1660s. There small farmers also used horticultural methods to increase production of tobacco, flax, hops, and potatoes (de Vries and van der Woude 1997, 221). In this region, however, overall agricultural productivity remained lower than in the coastal provinces.

There was an increase in agricultural productivity in the southern (Austrian) Netherlands in the eighteenth century, and many have suggested this as the beginning of the true agricultural revolution in the Low Countries. Development in the Austrian Netherlands began in the eighteenth century and was disturbed there only once in 1701–13 by the War of the Austrian Succession. Recovery occurred first in the countryside with the revival of agricultural prices and the onset of peace (van Houtte 1977, 230). As a result of economic revival, population rose everywhere in the Austrian Netherlands. The population of Brabant rose overall from 1709 to 1755. Towns of the Austrian Netherlands also benefited from the clear economic improvement after the middle of the eighteenth century and made good their population losses (van Houtte 1977, 230).

Diversification of crops and the introduction of new crops (e.g., potatoes, vegetables) led the revival in the eighteenth century. Rural revival was accompanied by de-urbanization in Brabant (Van der Wee 1993, 66). Continuous working of the land became general in Flanders in the eighteenth century. In the Liège district of Hesbaye and among the alluvial lands of Zeeland and northern Brabant fallow periods were extended, so that fields henceforth were left fallow every six or nine years. Cultivation of potatoes, rape, or clover took the place of fallow periods. Increasingly, manure, peat ash, sewage, and rape cakes were used as fertilizer in Flanders. Tilling of the soil also was helped by improvement of agricultural implements. Early in the eighteenth century in Brabant the wheel of the plow was replaced by a mobile foot, the height of which could be regulated according to the desired depth of the furrow. It was the prototype of the modern plow throughout the West. A new type of harrow also was introduced (van Houtte 1977, 244). Such improved methods were most common on small farms, those directly farmed by their owners, or lands that belonged to various proprietors and from which rents and taxes were due, whether they were cultivated or not. On large farms taxes were proportional to the yield; they had less interest in improvement and were slower in adopting new methods of crop rotation and cultivation.

Once again, the more communal regions of the southern and eastern Netherlands lagged behind in this general progress. Only in parts of Walloon Flanders and in some communal regions of the two Limburgs and the eastern regions of the United Provinces were fallows continued and traditional techniques maintained (van Houtte 1977, 244).

Despite this impressive revival of agricultural productivity in the southern Netherlands, some scholars have claimed, on the basis of yield ratios of grain, that it should not be overrated, since the thirteenth- and fourteenth-century maxima were only just reached (Van der Wee 1993, 65). This time, however, agricultural development in the southern Netherlands was enough to create circumstances (rising per capita incomes, a surplus of foodstuffs) favorable for the first industrial revolution on the Continent, in what is now Belgium.

## Factors Specific to the Protonational Context

I have traced precocious agricultural and industrial development in much of the Netherlands to propitious local institutions and weak manorial control throughout the medieval and early modern period. These, however, were not the only factors responsible for early economic development in the Low Countries. As others have noted (e.g., North and Thomas 1973; Thoen 1990; Van der Wee 1993), continuing economic development in the Low Countries was made possible by, first, maintenance of political decentralization and some democracy in the Low Countries throughout the early modern period; second, comparatively stable monetary policies of the Burgundian and Habsburg rulers; and, third, development of a variety of legal and commercial institutions that protected property rights and facilitated trade. All these factors decreased transaction costs and promoted development in agriculture, trade, and industry. At the same time, periodic monetary instability, heavy taxation, warfare, and political upheavals increased transaction costs and disrupted development. These negative factors interrupted the long-term trend of economic development in the Low Countries in the late fifteenth centuries, the late sixteenth century, in the southern Netherlands in the seventeenth century, and then again in the northern Netherlands in the eighteenth century.

### Political Decentralization and Democracy in the Low Countries

An important component of the economic development of the Low Countries was the benign nature of the state and its policies (Thoen 1990; Van der Wee 1993, 9), beginning with the rule of the counts in the late medieval period and ending with the formation of the United Provinces in the late sixteenth century.

Over the medieval period a fragmented polity similar to that in Germany at the same time arose in the Low Countries. A division of power emerged, however, between towns, nobles, clergy, and counts that helped to guarantee stability and to limit heavy taxation and oppression (Thoen 1990, 36). Centralized imperial power had disappeared in the Low Countries with the death of Charlemagne in 811. It was replaced by a variety of secular and religious principalities, the borders of which were more or less fixed by the end of the thirteenth century.[4] Some principalities owed allegiance to the French king (e.g., Walloon Flanders, Tournai, Artois), while most of the rest owed allegiance to the German emperor. The Frisian areas had no sovereign authority. During the tenth and eleventh centuries each principality struggled to free itself from royal authority. Most managed to become more or less independent. By the second half of the twelfth century the sovereignty of the German emperor had become primarily symbolic. By contrast, in the French fiefs of French (Walloon) Flanders and Artois, French royal influence endured until at least the early fifteenth century and in legal affairs even longer. Tournai and the Tournaisis remained French until 1521 (de Schepper 1994, 499).

At the same time, the growth of towns posed a threat to the increasing powers of the local territorial rulers (Thoen 1990, 36). Many towns managed to gain independence from the local ruler. They developed their own governing board with members (*échevins*) and a leader (*écoutète*) who was appointed by the local ruler. Burghers, or major merchants, the town's patriciate, were responsible for town finances and defense. Towns fought for their financial freedoms, which they often were able to obtain, and for the ability to raise their own taxes and make their own laws. Each town in the Low Countries became a *communitas,* a legal corporate body. By and large town policies encouraged trade.

In response to the rise of the power of towns, counts became more like monarchs than feudal lords. Each count became, according to the fourteenth-century lawyer Phillip of Leiden, the *procurator rei publicae* (he who looks after the matters of the people). Counts supervised clearing and draining of the land toward the north. Contact with their subjects was through the estates and representatives from water boards, regional water boards, and representatives from towns and rural communities that were also legally corporate bodies. The counts also appointed their bailiffs as supreme judges within each region. This division of power between count and towns, and the benign rule and limited taxation it promoted, fostered early economic development in the Low Countries.

The rule of the counts was replaced by Burgundian rule in 1384, when Philip the Bold, duke of Burgundy, inherited through his wife, Margaret (heiress of the count of Flanders), the first territories of the Low Countries (Van der Wee 1993, 15; de Schepper 1994, 501). The Burgundians began the process of consolidating the Netherlands into a single state. This began when Philip the Bold's grandson, Philip the Good, purchased right of succession to the childless ruler of Namur. When he died, in 1429, Namur was added to the Burgundian realm. In 1430 Philip acquired Brabant through the extinction of the Burgundian house's younger line (Van der Wee 1993, 177). In 1433 he obtained the principalities of Holland, Zeeland, and

Hainaut. He also purchased right of succession to Luxembourg, which passed into his sovereignty in 1451 (de Schepper 1994, 501). In the late fifteenth century the House of Burgundy was integrated into the House of Habsburg, when Mary, daughter of the last Burgundian duke, Charles the Bold (r. 1467–77), married Maximilian of Habsburg (Van der Wee 1993, 25). When Mary died, in 1482, she was succeeded by her husband as regent. Consolidation of the Low Countries continued under the Habsburgs. Philip the Good's great-great-grandson, Charles of Ghent, became ruler (as Charles I) of the Spanish realms in 1516 and (as Charles V) of the Holy Roman Empire of the German Nation in 1519. He added the French fief of Tournai and the Tournaisis (1521), Friesland (1524) Overijssel and Utrecht (1528), Drenthe, and Groningen, and the Ommelanden (1536) into the Netherlands. With his conquest of Guelders-Zutphen in 1543, the unification of the seventeen provinces of the Netherlands was complete (de Schepper 1994, 502).

Burgundians and subsequently Habsburgs consolidated the Netherlands into a single state and centralized their control over it. Despite this, or perhaps because the process was a slow one, Burgundian-Habsburg rulers continued the policies of the counts toward their subjects. Significantly, they continued the counts' practice of providing a judiciary. A high level of popular democracy also endured in the Low Countries. The Burgundian dynasty's assumption of power was associated with the appearance of parliamentary assemblies in several provinces (late fourteenth century—although some assemblies predate this, e.g., Flanders [see Ertman 1997, 68]). These were typically made up of the three estates of the higher clergy, the upper nobility, and representatives of the cities.[5] The provincial estates were summoned by the Burgundian Habsburg ruler in order to hear his requests for taxation. From 1464 they were also asked to send representatives to the States-General (de Schepper 1994, 517).

Although the parliamentary assemblies never developed the right to approve legislation, they nevertheless managed to develop into quasi-permanent deliberative bodies for the enactment of rules of general import. They also were able to limit taxation, such that rulers had to be content with only occasional aides (direct taxes). As a response, Burgundian rulers (like the Tudor monarchs in England) reorganized government finances and upheld the notion that the prince should "live of his own," that is, from his own estates. Revenue from the ruler's domains remained an important part of Burgundian government revenues throughout the fifteenth century. The Burgundian dukes also borrowed from their stewards. In this way the dukes obtained greater freedom of action with respect to the provincial estates.

The regime of democratic institutions, benign rule, and comparatively low levels of taxation continued during the Habsburg period. State repression and taxation increased only after the religious troubles (the "breaking of the images") of 1566. At this time the Duke of Alva was sent to quell the disturbances, and he did so with great severity. Alva attempted to make royal authority less dependent on the vote of taxes by the States-General or the provincial estates by introducing permanent new taxes (van Houtte 1977, 188). At the same time, Phillip II intensified the activity of the Inquisition and reformed the bishoprics in the Low Countries. These moves were disliked bitterly and prompted widespread unrest and eventually revolt in the Netherlands of 1567 (t'Hart 1993, 19; de Schepper 1994, 526). William, prince of Orange, in fact had fled to organize resistance before Alva arrived. He organized guerrilla attacks on the Spaniards beginning as early as 1568. Within towns of Holland and Zeeland the guerrillas (called "sea beggars") were supported by Calvinist cells. With such support the sea beggars eventually came to control many major towns in Holland. The Spanish finally were defeated outside Alkmaar and Leiden (1573–74). In the latter instance the town opened the dikes and flooded the surrounding countryside to repel the besiegers. After Alva left, provinces of the Low Countries signed an agreement with Spain which was known later as the Pacification of Ghent (1576). Shortly thereafter, the northern provinces formed the Union of Utrecht (1579). This became the foundation of a new republic in the northern Netherlands, the United Provinces of the Netherlands, or, more succinctly, the Dutch Republic. The United Provinces was a union of the provinces of Holland, Zeeland, Utrecht, Guelders, Overijssel, Friesland, Drenthe, and Groningen (t'Hart 1993, 19).

Democracy persisted in the United Provinces (Downing 1992; de Schepper 1994, 527). Provinces were ruled by assemblies of provincial estates representing towns and landed nobility. Provincial estates also selected the *stadtholders* (who after a few years came to be drawn exclusively from the House of Orange). *Stadtholders'* power was augmented because they possessed important prerogatives in the selection of members of town governments, from which provincial assemblies ultimately derived their authority. Furthermore, *stadtholders* were the acknowledged military leaders of the republic. Officially, *stadtholders* were representatives of the king of Spain, who was still recognized as king in the United Provinces. Central power lay with the central assembly, or States-General, although in practice it was subordinated to provincial authority (t'Hart 1993, 19; de Schepper 1994, 527). In particular, the province of Holland, along with *stadtholders* of the House of Orange, became the predominant political force in the United Provinces. Holland was the wealthiest province in the union and contributed more than half of the revenues of the central government. Although it conducted the military and diplomatic work of the republic, the States-General never obtained effective rights of direct taxation (except for import and export duties assigned to the admiralties), and its major decisions were taken under the rule of unanimity.

Thus, it was largely through democratic means that levels of taxation were increased dramatically to pay for armies to protect the new republic. The costs of this warfare were tremendous, yet throughout the seventeenth century the wealthy United Provinces was able to bear the expense without undue harm to the economy (t'Hart 1993, 59–61, 86). This is in contrast to our expectation from hypothesis 6, in chapter 3, that high levels of taxation would inhibit economic development and suggests that it is not simply high levels of taxation that are detrimental to economic development but the context in which they occur.

In the southern Netherlands Spanish rule continued. Yet Spanish rulers largely gave up their efforts to increase state control, and the political situation reverted to a condition similar to that which had existed before the revolt (de Schepper 1994, 527). In the southern Netherlands, as in the northern Netherlands, political oppression remained light throughout the sixteenth and seventeenth centuries.

## Monetary Policy

Throughout this period monetary policy was erratic. Although such instability raised transaction costs, comparatively the currency was often more stable than many (e.g., the French). Occasional monetary instability was not enough to prevent Dutch economic growth.

Counts did not always ensure monetary stability. They frequently resorted to currency debasement when they needed extra money. Between 1318 and 1384 the fine weight of the Flemish silver groat fell from 4.55 to only 0.97 grams (van Houtte 1977, 50, 112). The Burgundians, and later the Habsburgs, generally pursued a stable monetary policy, although with significant lapses (Van der Wee 1993,14 ). For example, from the second decade of the fifteenth century onward the common Flemish silver groat, used as standard coin in both Brabant and Flanders, was subject to a series of debasements. Charles the Bold (Philip's son) and Maximilian of Austria financed their military activities chiefly with income derived from their mints (Van der Wee 1993, 180). Thus, by 1477 the weight of the Flemish silver groat had fallen to only 0.61 grams of silver (from 0.97 in 1384 [van Houtte 1977, 112]). By 1496 a more stable monetary policy was resumed, although devaluation of the groat occurred periodically. The weight of the silver groat fell from 0.40 grams in 1568 to 0.25 just before the Peace of Westphalia (1648). It was held at this level until the end of the eighteenth century (van Houtte 1977, 211–12).

In the new Dutch republic of the seventeenth century the disorder in monetary affairs continued. Throughout this period it was a prime concern for the government. It was largely to combat such troubles that Amsterdam instituted a public bank, the Bank of Amsterdam, in 1609. As changers still were suspected of taking good coins out of circulation, the town forbade private money changing and gave a monopoly of exchange to the new bank, which was to hand over to the mint all foreign coins it received. This monopoly did not cure the troubles of the money in circulation. If the bank did not entirely succeed in reforming the coinage, it played an important part in the development of paper money and commercial credit (van Houtte 1977, 214). All payments were made through the Bank of Amsterdam using bills of exchange, and it became a deposit bank for safe settling of accounts. The Bank of Amsterdam also introduced a stable money of account, the guilder, based on a fixed amount of silver. By the end of the seventeenth century the success of this money had made the guilder of Holland the dominant currency of the world (Van der Wee 1993, 146, 148, 33).

### Legal and Financial Institutions

Burgundian-Habsburg rulers centralized and rationalized the system of law in place under the counts. That is, they systematized a relatively impartial legal system, which protected property rights and facilitated the introduction of innovative methods of finance and credit—specifically, assignment, endorsement, and negotiability for bills of exchange and promissory notes. The legal system served to enforce all contracts and maintain confidence in complex systems of credit. All of this reduced transaction costs and facilitated trade.

While courts of the former principalities continued to function under Burgundian rule, their personnel changed dramatically. Initially, they were staffed by nobles and aristocrats, few of whom had legal training. This changed, however, as dukes of Burgundy and their Habsburg successors preferred to hire people with formal training in Roman and canon law. In the provinces of Brabant, Holland, Flanders, and Zeeland, the older elites, feudal nobles, and prelates had disappeared from the courts by 1530 and had been replaced by jurists of bourgeois or noble background. Increasing use of learned law and increasing professionalization of the administration of justice tended to create a growing legal uniformity (de Schepper 1994, 509).

Furthermore, provincial courts had begun to evolve into provincial councils that functioned as lower-level courts in the sovereign's judicial system. Decisions of lower courts, or of any other traditional court of law such as those held by urban and rural aldermen or by local and regional authorities, were subject to appeal to higher courts, where they could be modified or canceled (de Schepper 1994, 506–7, 509). At the top of this system were the jurists in the Grand Council of the king. After 1440 these jurists began to form a separate and more or less permanent structure within the Grand Council called the "Council of Justice," a body modeled on the *Parlement* of Paris. From 1469 on, this body functioned as the highest court of appeal in civil cases in all the lands of the duke of Burgundy (although its decisions could be overturned by the king's council itself). In 1501 the Council of Justice became fully separate from the king's council.[6]

This centralization of judicial functions led to the establishment of a relatively impartial system of justice in the Netherlands. The new central courts provided a higher degree of professionalism, faster settlement of lawsuits, wider legal validity of verdicts, and were seen as fairer and more impartial than other courts. As a result, they became very popular. Litigants increasingly resorted to these courts, especially in the sixteenth century, as trade relations across local, regional, and even national borders became more common (de Schepper 1994, 513) .

There was also increasing legislative centralization during the Burgundian-Habsburg period, which also promoted legal uniformity. Before the end of the fifteenth century the political functions of provincial councils were taken over by central bodies. After 1517 the Privy Council (part of the king's council) helped to issue general regulations valid for all provinces. Finally, in 1531 Charles V issued an ordinance requiring systematic recording of local and regional customs in the whole country in order to create greater legal security by means of a written common law. The ordinance also limited the privilege of interpreting legal customs to his councils (de Schepper 1994, 510, 511.)

These developments were restricted to urbanized provinces in the west, while the sovereign's jurisdiction expanded very little in communal regions of the Walloon and eastern provinces. Here public authority remained fragmented and was largely in the hands of feudal nobles, abbeys, and other large landowners. Not only did local and regional courts continue to function as courts of appeal in feudal, civil, and criminal cases, but the feudal and customary courts of these territories continued to operate much as they had before they were incorporated into Burgundian-Habsburg lands (de Schepper 1994, 515).

In more urbanized provinces, however, standardized written law and the development of a relatively impartial judicial system under the Burgundian-Habsburg rulers led to a continuation of protection of property rights in the Netherlands. This promoted financial stability, which in turn facilitated the introduction of innovative financial techniques in the Low Countries. The first Bourse, or stock market, was created in 1531 in Antwerp (Munro 1994, 174; van Houtte 1977, 113). Financing in Antwerp came to be arranged by bills of exchange or promissory notes containing the clause "to bearer" (van Houtte 1977, 215). Bills of exchange worked by means of a principal agent system involving four parties: two principals in one city where the funds were advanced, and two agents who effected (re) payment in another city. Bills of exchange provided considerable economies in trade by allowing merchants to conduct transactions without having to accompany their goods or funds and by obviating the very risky transport of specie, since payments always were made in the local currency (Munro 1994, 152). Promissory notes, on the other hand, were a statement of a debt obligation.

Some bearers of bills of exchange or promissory notes would transfer them to their own creditors for settlement and some would note this assignment at the foot or on the back. A royal edict of 1541 stipulated that the acceptance of the assignment must remain optional and that, if the final debtor defaulted, the earlier ones were held responsible (Munro 1994, 173). This provision, which protected the recipients of a bill of exchange or promissory note, prompted widespread use of assignation. By 1585 it was the normal method of settling commercial debts in Antwerp. Furthermore, soon the practice of endorsement, that is, noting assignment on the back of the bill of exchange title, became customary. Endorsement enabled easy identification of successive assignors, although the practice was not widespread until the seventeenth century. The principles of assignment and endorsement established the negotiability of bills of exchange and promissory notes, which made possible a huge increase in the transfer of paper (van Houtte 1977, 216; Van der Wee 1993, 26).

In 1541 the Habsburg government also legalized interest payments on loans up to 12 percent. This made possible the discounting of negotiable bills, since previously the amount so discounted had represented usury, as foregone interest. At the same time, there were also improvements in public finance. Provincial governments throughout the Netherlands were now engaged in short-term borrowing through letters obligatory (promissory notes). Even more important in public finance, however, was the now negotiable *rente,* or *censo,* an annuity dating from the medieval period. The Netherlands, especially Antwerp after the establishment of its Bourse in 1531, became sixteenth-century Europe's most rapidly growing market for such *rentes* (Munro 1994, 173).

All these practices were continued in the United Provinces, formed after 1579, as the constitution of the new republic gave special emphasis to both the rule of law and the protection of property rights.[7] Other innovations further decreased transaction costs in the United Provinces. Public notaries established offices near the marketplace, where they witnessed and recorded contracts and helped to resolve commercial disputes. This was a more efficient method of enforcing contracts than the former method of using local magistrates (North and Thomas 1973, 136). Should conditions of a contract be violated, the merchant involved could sue the offending party in the law courts conveniently located near the market. A decision by such a court could not be ignored if the merchant involved wished to continue to do business in the Amsterdam market.

### The Marketplaces of Europe (Bruges— Antwerp—Amsterdam)

Despite some inconsistencies, all these factors—low levels of political oppression, legal centralization and stability, and widespread use of innovative practices in banking and finance—lowered transaction costs throughout the Low Countries. Individuals and companies could invest and transfer capital with the assurance that their money was safe. This stimulated both production and exchange. First Bruges then Antwerp then Amsterdam successfully became the principal marketplaces of Europe.

In the fourteenth century Bruges became perhaps the most active exchange and money market outside of Italy. The scene of such transactions was the public square, called the *Beurze* or *Bourse,* after an inn of the same name run by the van der Beurze family, near where most of the Italian merchants usually met at certain times of day to discuss affairs.[8] This inn was later to lend its name to the first stockmarket in Antwerp: the Bourse. By the sixteenth century Antwerp had succeeded Bruges in its role as world market, although in many ways Antwerp had a greater foreign trade than Bruges ever had. Its cosmopolitan character perhaps made it appropriate that it was in Antwerp that Thomas More sited his meeting with the man who revealed to him the mysteries of Utopia (van Houtte 1977, 114, 183).

After the fall of Antwerp, Amsterdam became the marketplace of Europe. The entire seventeenth century was a golden age for the Dutch Republic, in trade, industry, the arts, and agriculture. Heckscher (1954, 104) notes that "only a few decades earlier the Netherlands was a small and powerless country engaged in a seemingly hopeless struggle with Spain, Europe's strongest power. Now it was the master of Europe's mercantile and military navigation, of colonial trade and of the most valuable colonial territories."

**Conclusion**

By 1700 the Netherlands had been the preeminent commercial region of Europe for at least two hundred years. This in turn was dependent on high levels of agricultural development, which had been promoted by less-communal agricultural systems and weak manorialization throughout most of the Netherlands. This was particularly true of Flanders in the southern Netherlands, where records show innovative agricultural techniques and high cereal yields as early as the ninth century and where feudal labor relations had largely disappeared at an early date. In the late medieval period agricultural improvements and innovation spread throughout the southern Netherlands and, a little later, in the northern Netherlands as well. Most of the Netherlands weathered the crises of the fourteenth century better than most regions of Europe. Economic growth continued, with only a minor setback in the late fifteenth century. In the sixteenth century rural development set the stage for the commercial development centered at Antwerp. Rural development in the northern Netherlands also preceded its emergence as a Europe's preeminent economic center after the troubles of the late sixteenth and early seventeenth centuries.

As expected from the hypotheses in chapter 3, in the border regions of more communal agriculture to the south and east there was little agricultural progress. Feudal regimes persisted here through the early modern period. These regions did not participate in the growth of agricultural productivity, urbanization, industry, or the general prosperity that characterized the rest of the Netherlands throughout most of the period discussed here. As late as the eighteenth century, these regions did not participate in the agricultural revolution taking place in the southern Netherlands at that time.

As in England, it was not just less-communal agricultural systems that promoted agrarian development and change in most of the Netherlands. Continuing agricultural and economic development was made possible by benign rule and the maintenance of some democracy during the rule of first the counts, later the Burgundian and Habsburg rulers, and in the United Provinces. Taxation itself was shown to be not necessarily detrimental to development, as the United Provinces sustained extremely high taxes during the seventeenth century, during the time of its greatest prosperity.

Also important was the development of a relatively impartial, centralized legal system that served to protect property rights. The central authorities also provided comparatively stable (if erratic) monetary policies. Both of these factors facilitated the ease with which paper could be used to settle accounts and generally decreased costs of commercial transactions. Town governments in the Netherlands also developed novel ways of financing government through development of public debt. All these policies were continued by the government of the United Provinces, after the ousting of the Spanish Habsburg rulers in the late sixteenth century.

Thus, despite nearly constant warfare and other political vicissitudes, economic development continued in the Low Countries throughout the late medieval and early modern periods. While the sixteenth century was the golden age of the southern Netherlands, the seventeenth century saw the golden age of the United Provinces in the north. Both regions were to decline in later years, but by European standards they remained highly developed economies into the modern period. Furthermore, the southern Netherlands saw an agricultural revival in the eighteenth century and subsequently became home to the first Continental industrial revolution.

CHAPTER 6

# Rural Institutions and Agrarian Change in France

Pour néant plante qui ne clost.

[He who does not enclose plants for nought.]
—Old French proverb

Li paisan et li villein
Cil des bocages et cil des plain.

[The peasant and the villein;
the one of the *bocage* and the other of the open country.]
—Wace, twelfth-century poet

France is the first negative case examined so far. Despite being a country endowed with much fine agricultural land, nevertheless its long-term agricultural performance was poor. France displays more variation in local field systems than the Netherlands and thus provides a more useful case for examining their effects. Here, however, the political context was different again. Unlike the weak central rule characteristic of England and the Netherlands, in France there arose in this time period a centralized government, often considered the archetypical "absolutist state."

As in England, France in the late medieval and early modern periods may be divided into regions of more communal and less-communal agricultural systems. The former were the *champagne* regions of the north and north east and the latter the *bocages* and less-communal open fields of the south and west (de Planhol and Claval 1994, 134). Yet, although the course of agrarian change followed a regional pattern as it did in England, Le Roy Ladurie (1987) has claimed that this pattern was the reverse of that found in England. He writes for the seventeenth century: "it is not the least of the paradoxes of the ancien régime that the *bocage* became more and more synonymous with archaism in theory and in fact, whereas in England, the enclosures, twin of the *bocage,* remained faithful to its old progressive vocation and became one with the imperative of agricultural progress. For the open fields, it was exactly the reverse. The open fields were economically reactionary in England, whereas they engendered high agricultural productivity in the Île-de-France and Picardy" (340). This would appear to directly contradict hypothesis 1 in chapter 3.

Yet on closer inspection we see that French evidence does not contradict our hypotheses. First, the "productivity" of northern France must be seen in comparative perspective. The only area of France where agricultural yields approached contemporary English yields were those less-communal areas of French Flanders and Artois in the far north (see map 9).[1] Second, as Le Roy Ladurie himself has shown using tithe data, even in the seventeenth century areas of most rapid agricultural growth in France tended to be less-communal areas, including Normandy, Provence, and parts of the west.[2] Third, other factors, in particular a rich soil and proximity to Paris and the urban markets of the Low Countries, can help explain the productivity of the north of France at the end of the period examined here. A poor and mountainous ecology, distance from urban markets, and political disadvantages can explain the lower productivity of many places in the south and west at the same time. Thus, even in France we find support for our hypotheses, despite the fact that other factors created a more complex outcome. In what follows I examine the regional differences in ecology, demography, market access, and rural organization in France and their effects on agrarian change. I also note the role played by national political factors in determining outcomes.

### Ecology, Population, and Markets

Ecology in France is most favorable for agriculture in the north. All the deposits of loess, or *limon*—rich loam soil or clay—are in the north (de Planhol 1988, 165; Prince 1977, 142). Indeed, the plains of northern France are considered some of the best agricultural land in all of Europe. Not only is the soil rich, but rainfall is plentiful and the climate generally temperate. In the south, in contrast, the ecology is much less favorable for agriculture. The whole region is mountainous and rocky, the soil poor, rainfall low; drought was often a problem in the south of France. The most common rock is limestone, and, as a result, soil tends to be alkaline (Pounds 1990, 19). It has been estimated that only about 29 percent of land in the south of France is cultivable, compared to 71 percent in the north (Price 1983, 21). Low rainfall makes spring sowing of cereal impossible. This meant that only one cereal crop could be grown per year, unlike in the north, where a spring and a winter sowing on different parts of village land

**Map 9. The French provinces**

was the rule. Brittany, in the west, also has poorer, rockier soil than the northern plains and is a comparatively inferior place for agriculture (de Planhol and Claval 1994, 140).

Along with a rich ecology, the north was the most densely populated region in France. In the late medieval period population densities reached 75 people per square mile in this region. This was much higher than contemporary English population densities and much higher than densities in the south of France. This regional distribution of population persisted after the crises of the fourteenth century (Pounds 1990, 149, 192). The major town of northern France, Paris, was the largest town in western Europe by the fourteenth century, and it held this position until the late seventeenth century, when it was overtaken by the city of London (de Planhol and Claval 1994, 259). Despite the large size of Paris, France as a whole remained a comparatively unurbanized region throughout the period discussed here. Besides Paris, there were few large cities. As late as

1700, less than 10 percent of the population lived in cities of 10,000 people or more, compared to about 13 percent in England and Wales at the same time and nearly 34 percent in the Netherlands (de Vries 1984, 39).

The north also had better access to water routes than the south. Rivers north of the Alps are mostly well suited to river traffic. They are deep, and their flow is regular. Problems such as low water and ice rarely interrupt navigation for more than short periods. It was partly because of the rivers that the Champagne fairs developed where they did in northern France. These fairs reached the height of their importance and prosperity in the thirteenth century (Pounds 1990, 139). Here traders could travel down from the north along the Meuse and Scheldt, from the Atlantic in the west along the Seine and the Marne, and from the south and the Mediterranean via the Rhône.

In the south, in contrast, navigable rivers are fewer. All the rivers that flow to the Mediterranean are unsuited to river traffic, as most drop steeply to the sea. In winter they often flood; in summer many are not much more than trickle. Only the Rhône is navigable year round, a factor that can account for the early commercial importance of Lyon (Pounds 1990, 20).

### Field Systems in Late Medieval France (c. 1200–1500)

Communal Open Field Systems

In late medieval France the communal open field system was found in its most developed form in the fertile northeastern plains of France: Champagne, Lorraine, Burgundy, and Picardy (see map 10). Bloch states that it "reigned supreme in the whole of France north of the Loire, except in the tablelands of Caux and the enclosed areas of the west, and was equally dominant in both Burgundies" (1966a, 48; see also de Planhold and Claval 1994, 140). In this region the system was physically similar to that in England. Fields were open and unenclosed, and villages were large and compact, although villages were more likely to be surrounded by a wall or some other fortification than they were in England (Bloch 1971 [1913], 83; de Planhol and Claval 1994, 135). Each cultivator had his or her share of land regularly scattered throughout the two or three large open fields of the village. Crops grown in each field were rotated from year to year, with one field always carrying the winter crop of wheat (or other cereal), one field carrying the spring crop (often barley or oats), and one field lying fallow. The village grazed all its animals on the fallow field each year and on newly harvested fields before the next sowing. In addition to these com-

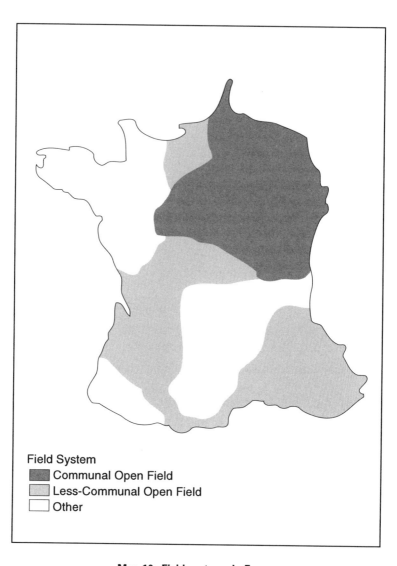

Field System

Communal Open Field

Less-Communal Open Field

Other

**Map 10. Field systems in France**

mon rights on village arable land, villagers also possessed common pasture rights to wastes and meadows of the village, if any existed—the true "commons." As in England, cropping, harvesting, and grazing on arable fields and in the commons were controlled by village laws. Penalties were imposed on those who did not obey them.

As in England, areas of communal open fields in northern France also tended to be areas with strong manorial control (Bloch 1966c, 239; Goubert 1973), although open field villages in France were more likely to have several lords than those in England (Bloch 1966c, 242; Slicher van Bath 1963b). The lord of the manor drew much of his income and supplies from the demesne—a compact block of land attached to a manor house—as well as from land interspersed with peasants' land in the open fields. In addition, the lord drew income from his rights of usage in forests and wastes as well as from fees (*banalités*) paid by peasants for use of various facilities of the manor—the mill, ponds, ovens, and so on. Levels of land rent and labor services were generally customary and could be changed only with difficulty, although labor services (*corvée*) were becoming rare in France by the fourteenth century. Exceptions were Burgundy and Franche Comté, where serfs existed to the end of the ancien régime and remained subject to heavy feudal dues and labor services (Goubert 1973). The seigneurs also received money payment, or *cens,* which was paid by tenants for use of the land, a practice that continued after the decline of labor services. They did not "rent" the land in the strictest sense, as typically they had hereditary rights to the land. (Although peasants may also have rented other land, customary or otherwise, from the manorial lord, as necessary.) In addition, peasants often had to pay a *champart,* a kind of seigneurial tithe generally amounting to between one-ninth and one-third of every crop, to which there was no direct English equivalent. As in England, the lord almost always collected dues when land or goods were transferred through sale or inheritance ("saisine, relief, lods, et ventes"). Seigneurial rents and fees differed slightly from region to region and could be heavier or lighter as the case may be.

As in England, the seigneur (or his representative) presided over the manorial court, in which were judged many affairs and conflicts of the village. According to the custom of the area, the seigneur judged peasant disputes over boundaries and grazing or those arising out of drunken brawling and ruled on matters of inheritance, minority, and guardianship (Goubert 1973). With the development of royal courts, however, in the late medieval period and after (later than the equivalent English development), seigneurial courts gradually lost most of their jurisdiction over criminal cases, although they retained jurisdiction over civil cases (Bloch 1966a). Lesser criminal cases could also remain in the hands of the seigneurial courts, although this varied greatly from place to place. (These rights were retained into the eighteenth century [see Markoff 1996, 115, 549].)[3] In the early modern period royal courts themselves became subject to the appeal jurisdiction of regional *parlements* (Major 1994).

Perhaps because by 1300 labor services (usually attached to landholdings) were little utilized by feudal landlords, the rule of primogeniture was not enforced in northern France in the late Middle Ages, although it was followed in some areas. In most communal open field regions inheritances were divided among sons. Thus, with population growth the fragmentation of land was pushed to a much higher level in open field regions of northern France than in the midlands areas of England. This caused some breakdown in the regularity of the open field system, although it retained the basic characteristics of strict community control over cropping, grazing, and use of the commons. By the late medieval period, however, areas of waste, woodlands, and meadow had dwindled, and large areas of commons had become rare in northern France.

Corresponding to the communal open field system were strong communities. People lived in compact villages and the communalism of living and work arrangements was reflected in village mores. Such a degree of communitarianism has impressed itself on many generations of French agrarian historians, who have been convinced that such *mentalités* were important factors in the lack of agrarian progress in the plains of northern France (e.g., Bloch 1966a; Neveux 1980). Changes of the sixteenth century and after, however, were to place considerable strain on the communities of the north.

### Regions of Less-Communal Open Fields and Enclosures

As one moved south, west, and north in France, the communal open field system became less regular and much less communal (see map 10). The far north of France—northern Artois, French Flanders, and eastern Normandy—were characterized by such less-communal open field systems (Plaisse 1961; Bloch 1966a, 48; Sivery 1977–79; de Planhol and Claval 1994, 140). Systems of open fields with scattered strips of arable land, yet not organized into a communal two- or three-field system, were also found in many areas of southern France, including Poitou, Berry, Provence, Languedoc, and the Garonne Valley (Bloch 1966a, 48; de Planhol and Claval 1994, 140). Unlike in the north, however, fields in the south were often larger and square shaped, rather than formed in long strips. As in England, in these regions of less-communal open fields, open fields could be found, but rotations of crops were based not on the great fields but, rather, on cropping shifts that could vary from year to year (Juillard et al.

1957; Plaisse 1961; de Planhol 1988, 140, 167). In the north a triennial rotation of crops was typical and, in the south, a biennial rotation of crops (Bloch 1966a, 31), mostly because of the impossibility of a spring crop. Also as in England, communal regulation of agriculture in these regions was usually slight (Bloch 1966a, 49; de Planhol and Claval 1994, 148).

Communal regulation of agriculture was also usually absent or slight in regions of enclosures, or *bocage,* including western Normandy, Maine, Perche, parts of Poitou and the Vendée, Bugey, and the Pays de Gex (near Lyon), throughout Brittany (apart from the region of Pontchâteau near the Loire), as well as in the southern mountainous regions of the Massif Central and the Basque lands of the extreme southwest (Bloch 1966a, 59). In the far north enclosures were also characteristic of parts of Artois and French Flanders. As in England, in regions of bocage or less-communal open fields houses were more likely to be scattered across the landscape or at most grouped into small hamlets, rather than collected into one large village (de Planhold and Claval 1994, 141).[4]

Communities were often weaker in regions of less-communal fields and enclosures than they were in areas of communal agriculture in the north, at least in the fifteenth century. The former regions were known for their individualism (Bloch 1966a, 57, 59). This statement has to be modified in light of two important phenomena—first, the existence of strong village governments governing local communities in Mediterranean France, and, second, the development of strong communities centered around the parish in western France and parts of the Massif Central (Markoff 1985, 774–75). In southern France the development of local self-government centered on large villages or towns may be traced to the continuation of the Roman legacy in this part of France (de Planhol and Claval 1994, 143). The development of parish-centered communities in Brittany was particularly a phenomenon of the eighteenth century, at which time these communities became the organizational basis for the counterrevolution in this area.

In addition, seigneurial exactions tended to be fewer in areas of *bocage* and less- communal open fields (with the exception of Brittany) than in areas of grouped villages and communal open fields. For example, among northern regions Normandy was distinguished by the absence of a classic manorial system. Serfdom had disappeared very early, if in fact it ever existed there (Delisle 1903; Sion 1909, 156; Bloch 1966a, 90; de Boüard 1987, 166). In the south, home of written (Roman) law, seigneurs had to prove their title to land by producing a written document. In the north custom was enough to establish the authority of the seigneur over the land and peasantry. (Hence the saying: "In the north, no land without lord, in the south, no land without title.") The relative difficulty of proving lordship meant that in the south there were many *allodial* (freehold) tenures, that is, tenures that were free from most seigneurial obligations. Such freeholds were practically absent in communal open field regions of the north. For example, in Basse Auvergne in the south about 30 percent of the land was *allodial* and not subject to seigneurial rule. Important exceptions to this rule were Brittany and some parts of central France, such as Marche, where serfs (*mainmortables*) existed nearly to the end of the ancien régime (Goubert 1973, 84, 111, 85).

In sum, as map 10 shows, the regions of communal agriculture were found in the north of France, while most of the west, south, and (in the far north) the region of Artois and Flanders were characterized by less-communal systems of agriculture.

### The Regional Pattern of Agrarian Change in Late Medieval and Early Modern France

In France these field systems shaped the course of agrarian change as they did in England and the Netherlands. Yet, whereas in southeast England and the southern Netherlands in particular all conditions tended to favor growth, in France such a coincidence of favorable factors was absent. In the north ecology and market access favored growth, while local institutions inhibited it. Conversely, in the south a poor ecology and more limited access to markets inhibited growth, while local institutions promoted it. Added to high levels of state oppression and taxation, the result (by about 1700) was comparatively low levels of agricultural productivity throughout France.

#### Late Medieval Period

The limited available evidence shows that, as we might expect, northern France was a rich agricultural region and a major grain producer in the late medieval period. At the same time, within the north it was in less-communal regions, in Normandy, parts of Artois and French Flanders, that agricultural productivity equaled that in the southern Netherlands and often surpassed the levels seen in eastern England at the same time.

In the less-communal regions of the far north, Artois and French Flanders, there had been a tradition of highly productive agriculture since the ninth century or even before. Agricultural practices in these regions were very similar to those in the adjacent southern Netherlands (Slicher van Bath 1963b; Fussell 1983, 147). In these regions very high yields of grain were recorded as well as use of intensive and innovative agricultural techniques such as complex rotations and the growing of legumes at an early date (Slicher van Bath 1963b; Pounds 1990; Thoen 1993). For example, average seed/yield ratios as high as 15 to 1 (for wheat) were recorded in the early fourteenth century in Artois (Slicher van Bath 1963a, 38; Le Roy Ladurie 1987, 110; Fourquin 1990, 125).

Normandy was another area of less-communal fields and enclosures in northern France known for its agricultural productivity in the late medieval period (Delisle 1903; Parain 1941), although it probably never achieved the levels of the far north (Sion 1909, 157; Bloch 1966a, 206, 207; Bois 1984, 194; de Boüard 1987, 161). The first application of a four-course rotation appeared in Normandy at the end of the thirteenth century (Ganshof and Verhulst 1966, 297). Other innovative agricultural techniques also were introduced at an early date in Normandy, for instance, use of horses (de Boüard 1987, 161), growing of forage crops (Sion 1909, 142), and deep plowing over the fallow field (Bloch 1966a, 206). In the west of the province there was profitable pasture farming providing butter, beef, and mutton to Rouen, and the province was an exporter of wheat (Sion 1909, 143, 147).

In contrast, areas of communal agriculture in the north and northeast, although sharing the same ecological advantages as these less-communal regions, showed comparatively lower yields. Seed/yield ratios for wheat were perhaps a little over 5 to 1 in the early fourteenth century. This was still high by medieval standards. It was also higher than cereal yields in the south at the same time, which averaged less than 5 to 1 (Le Roy Ladurie 1987, 111–13). Communal regions of the north produced a substantial quantity of grain for export (e.g., Picardy [see Fossier 1988, 124a, 214]). The Ile-de-France, the region around Paris, in particular had a reputation as a productive agricultural area at this time (Fourquin 1990, 126; Parain 1941). This productivity, however, was not a result of innovation in technique, as most of this area was characterized by a uniform three-course rotation of wheat-oats-fallow, with none of the innovative and more intensive techniques common in less-communal areas of the north (Bloch 1971 [1913], 113).

Given its ecological disadvantages, we might expect little development in the south. For example, because of its poor soil and low rainfall, it was never a major producer of cereals. Cereal yields were generally lower than in the north and may have averaged 4 or 5 to 1 (Le Roy Ladurie 1987, 113). Yet other crops were produced very successfully. By the thirteenth century parts of the Midi (all of southern France) were producing for both local and overseas consumption (Lewis 1984, 67). An intensive market garden agriculture grew olives, fruit, and vegetables to provide for urban markets, as this area was as urbanized as the Low Countries and northern and central Italy at this time (Bloch 1966b, 216; Clout 1977; Blockmans 1994, 231). In the southwest a prosperous, export-oriented wine industry flourished in Bordeaux by 1300 (Postan 1973; Le Roy Ladurie and Goy 1982, 139). Poitou, Gascony, and (communal) Burgundy and the Moselle were all major wine producers for the international market (especially the English market) by the thirteenth century (Postan 1952, 172).

### After the Fourteenth Century

Due to the Black Death population density probably halved in northern France (Pounds 1990, 218; Bois 1984). The south also lost a large percentage of its population during the plagues of the fourteenth century. The fourteenth-century crisis ushered in an economic recession throughout France. By the fifteenth century recovery was clear everywhere, and by about 1500 the population of northern France probably had regained pre-plague levels. Yet, as in England, recovery followed a regional pattern. Trends toward crop specialization and diversification were most characteristic of less-communal regions, while a monoculture of grain continued to characterize communal regions.

In the north tithe receipts show that grain production recovered in the middle of the fifteenth century (Robisheaux 1994, 87). By the late fifteenth century, however, the availability of cheap grain from the Baltic countries meant the Low Countries became less dependent on the traditional granaries of northern France. The quantity of grain exported from Picardy diminished in the late fifteenth century, from a peak attained between 1460 and 1470 (Fossier 1988, 215). In response to the fall in demand for grain there was some diversification in crops. In particular, viticulture flourished at this time, and flax cultivation developed in the valley of the Moselle (Neveux 1975, 113; Goubert 1973; Fourquin 1990, 280). Alsace also saw the beginnings of a prosperous polyculture (de Planhol and Claval 1994, 224). Such crop specialization, however, constituted only a small part of the total acreage devoted to agriculture in these regions. Vines, flax, and other specialized crops were grown mostly in gardens and other plots of private land. They were not a feature of the arable fields, where grain growing remained the predominant activity. Two-thirds to four-fifths of the land was reserved for cereal-growing purposes (Jacquart 1975, 217; Goubert 1986, 10; Fossier 1988, 262; de Planhol and Claval 1994, 216). Here cereal yields were not high, and even in the most fertile regions they remained well below contemporary yields in the less-communal area of French Flanders (Fossier 1988, 263).

In contrast, the new industrial crops (flax, woad, etc.) became comparatively more important in less-communal regions in the late fifteenth

century. In the northern regions of Artois and Flanders flax growing predominated. In the west and Brittany it was hemp; in the south, woad (Yun
1994, 116); and in Languedoc, olives. Toulouse and Albi became important centers for the commercial production of woad (de Planhol and
Claval 1994, 225). There was also a resurgence of viticulture along the
Atlantic coast, in the Bordeaux region. After 1420 grain production also
began to increase in the south and west. Tithe receipts—a rough indicator
of total grain production—reached bottom around 1420 and then
increased rapidly in the 1430s in the south and west (Robisheaux 1994, 87).
All the less-communal areas, in the south in Toulouse and Aix-en-
Provence and in Brittany showed rapid economic growth at this time. The
fairs of Lyon also continued to prosper (Yun 1994, 117, 123–24).

### Sixteenth Century

The sixteenth century saw a rapid growth of population and an expansion
of trade in France. In the north Paris emerged as France's preeminent city,
while the urban system of the south declined. Urbanization did not
increase greatly in France at this time, unlike contemporary developments
in England and the Netherlands (de Vries 1984, 39, 160–67). The trend
toward diversification of agriculture in less-communal areas of France
continued, while communal areas continued to focus primarily on cereal
growing. At the same time, there was a concentration of land and buildup
of large estates in most of northern France. Compared to contemporary
trends in England and the Netherlands, however, agricultural progress
was limited everywhere.

In northern France population growth encouraged partitioning farms
into smaller and smaller lots. At the same time, communal areas of northern France saw a buildup of large estates and a dispossession of the peasantry similar to that which occurred in midland England at the same time.
The trend toward large estates was promoted by increasing state oppression of the peasantry. The *taille,* or direct tax, began to increase in the sixteenth century (Jacquart 1975, 162). The *gabelle,* or salt tax (really a state
monopoly on the sale of salt), and other indirect taxes also became heavier at this time. These taxes exacerbated peasant debt and hastened expropriation of many small peasant proprietors. Furthermore, unlike in England and the Netherlands, the peasantry had no relatively impartial third
party to which to turn for legal support, as local courts, or *parlements* (the
highest court of appeal), were dominated by local elites. Thus, they were
no doubt often disinclined to rule in peasants' favor in court matters. Peasant land gradually was consolidated into the large estates owned by the
church, bourgeoisie, or government officials, who subsequently leased it

back to peasant cultivators to farm. By the late eighteenth century non-peasant proprietors possessed two-thirds to four-fifths of the land in northern France (Cooper 1978; Goubert 1986; Goldstone 1988), although peasants themselves worked all the land.

Unlike in midland England, however, few large *farms* actually emerged in northern France; thus, there were few efficiency gains from the concentration of landholdings. High population densities meant that landlords could earn higher rents by leasing out small plots of land to a number of peasant families to cultivate rather than by leasing out the entire estate to one or two farmers. Thus, large estates tended to be leased out as numerous small parcels. For example, the estates of L'Hotel Dieu near Amiens in the early seventeenth century were divided into 5 large farms, 6 smaller pieces of land that were divided between several farmers, and a remaining 40 percent of the land that was divided into yet smaller properties, dispersed over forty-one villages in more than 350 parcels of land. Such division of estates into many tiny farms was maintained in part by the tendency of lessees to stay on their rented plots of land over several generations. It became very difficult to evict lessees, as the farming community often made it impossible for anyone to take over another's land by terrorizing the new lessee (Deyon n.d., 67). Furthermore, some village communities openly tried to prevent the growth of large peasant farms (Duby 1968, 340). Thus, large estates remained a cluster of small peasant farms. These small farms offered no economies of scale and typically were farmed using traditional techniques.

There were some large farms in the communal regions of northern France, although they were a tiny minority of all farms. Each village in the north had at least one large farm (known as a *cense*), which could be as large as 100 hectares (247 acres) or more. There may have been also two or three other farms of 10–20 hectares (25–50 acres) operated by a single tenant farmer (Goubert 1986). These large farms usually were based on the seigneurial demesnes, although they could be the result of land consolidations by enterprising peasants. Such farmers (*censiers*) in Picardy, Cambrésis, eastern Normandy, and other areas farmed for the market in a rational way. Yet even on these large farms crop yields often were not high. The best wheat yields remained at about 8 or 9 to 1 (Deyon 1988b, 262; Le Roy Ladurie 1987, 111). Even in the best areas farms did not increase production to the extent necessary to keep pace with population growth (Neveux 1980).

The Parisian basin offers the most extreme example of all these processes. Here expropriation of peasants and land concentration was pushed to an extreme. Land was concentrated usually in the hands of rich merchants, politicians, or officeholders. By 1600 peasants owned as little as 21 percent of the land, and of these peasant landowners 83 percent had less than 1 hectare (about 2.5 acres) (Jacquart 1975, 266). At the same time, there were a number of large farms of about 50 to 100 hectares (123–247 acres), each of which was farmed by a single farmer. Most of these Parisian farms were not consolidated units, however, which lessened many of the economies of scale of a large farm. Consolidation was a process that was to await the late eighteenth and nineteenth centuries (de Planhol and Claval 1994, 265). Owners of large farms were prominent in the village; they were grain merchants, tax collectors, and syndics (representatives of the village assembly) (Jacquart 1975, 266). Thus, there was substantial class polarization between the rich and poor in this region. This entire phenomenon of the formation of large estates and class polarization in the villages was largely confined to the north (including part of eastern Normandy). The west and south of France never saw the development of large estates and farms as did northern France. Nor did the west and south see the contrast between rich and poor or the extreme poverty found in the north and the divisiveness these engendered in the rural community. In the south there was some dispossession of smallholders in the sixteenth and seventeenth centuries, but this primarily benefited some of the urban bourgeoisie, rather than the church, politicians, and officeholders, as in the north (Jacquart 1975, 267; Yun 1994, 133). There also remained a class of fairly substantial freeholding tenants in the south, farming about 40 hectares (about 100 acres) of land (Goubert 1986, 117).

One reason for the lack of peasant dispossession in the south and the continued existence of freeholding peasants was that the population was much less dense in the south than the north, so peasant farms were typically larger. Furthermore, overall taxation of farmers was less severe in the south than in the north and tended to be more equitable (Goubert 1973, 111). The whole of the Midi was well equipped for apportioning the tax burden among residents of a community due to the existence of registers known as *cadastres,* or *livres terriers.* These registers listed the description, dimension, and tax assessment of every plot of land. They had been in existence since the fifteenth century and earlier and were kept up to date and periodically renewed. They ensured that the tax burden was spread out equitably. In addition, in the south nobles were not exempt from taxation as in the north; only noble estates were. To prove that an estate was "noble" required production of authentic documentation. The existence of the *cadastres* meant that such documentation was difficult to forge, and, therefore, nobles were less able to avoid taxation than in the north. Further, in the south there was a history of loose seigneurial control over cultivators. The only tenants required to pay any seigneurial dues at all were those on noble estates. Thus, the peasantry had to pay fewer of the customary dues and taxes that they had to pay in the north, which reduced absolute levels of taxation in the south (Bloch 1966c; Goubert 1973, 85–91).

The situation in the north was very different. There all the land was firmly under seigneurial control. Taxes tended to be assessed on the basis of persons rather than property. Whole communities were given the tax bill to pay as best they could. The tax burden was supposed to fall mostly on the richest farmers, but the most powerful and best-connected farmers often could avoid paying any taxes at all. The nobility were exempt from all taxation. All of this meant that, in general, in the north taxes fell disproportionately on those least able to pay.

Perhaps as a result, peasant prosperity was most notable in the south and other less-communal regions of France at this time. In these regions specialization and diversification in crops and agricultural products was notable. Maize and buckwheat were introduced into southern, western, and central France at this time and became important subsistence crops (Le Roy Ladurie and Goy 1982, 143, 150; Braudel 1990, 268). In Aquitaine the cultivation of maize accompanied the abandonment of the fallow, and a highly productive wheat-maize cycle was established. This cycle became the basis of a prosperous agricultural sector in Aquitaine by the seventeenth century (de Planhol and Claval 1994, 218). The Bordeaux wine industry also flourished in the sixteenth century, while sheep and olive oil were important to the agricultural economy in the Midi (Le Roy Ladurie and Goy 1982, 139, 143). At this time transhumance gained in importance in much of southern France, and long-distance migrations were developing between Provence and the French Alps. The animals were mainly sheep, whose purpose was to produce wool. Cultivation of the mulberry and rearing of silkworms was spreading in southern France (Pounds 1990, 233, 231). In less-communal Normandy and parts of central France pasture farming began to expand.

In many less-communal regions there is evidence that agricultural productivity was increasing during the sixteenth century. This was most notable in Brittany, Normandy, Provence, and the far north. It was also notable in the Parisian basin, home to communal farming systems, although this was an exceptional region on any count. In the south Slicher van Bath (1963a, 42) found areas of very high yield agriculture in Provence in 1540 (seed/yield ratios of between 7 and 10 to 1 for wheat), although Le Roy Ladurie suggests that these figures are unrepresentative of Provence as a whole (see Le Roy Ladurie 1987, 111). Yet new evidence from estimates of total factor productivity (an estimate of agricultural productivity based on information from rents and prices) growth rates show that periods in which growth rates rivaled English rates may be found in the sixteenth and seventeenth centuries in the Île-de-France (Parisian basin), Normandy, the west country (including Brittany), and Provence (Hoffman 1991; see also 1996, 133). With the exception of the Île-de-France, these were all less-communal regions. Similarly, evidence from tithe data shows that by the seventeenth century agricultural production was rising in Normandy (based on stock raising), in the Parisian basin, in the far north in Artois (based on wheat), and in the south in Bordeaux, Languedoc (wine), the Basque country, and the area around Toulouse (maize) (Le Roy Ladurie and Goy 1982, 143). As before, with the exception of the Parisian region, these were all less-communal regions of France.

This evidence of greater agricultural development in less-communal parts of the country is matched by more qualitative evidence. In the north Normandy was known as one of the most prosperous agricultural regions in France by the sixteenth century (Sion 1909, 223; Bourde 1958; Bloch 1966a; Plaisse 1961). Normandy was one of the first provinces to use artificial meadows to grow feed for animals (i.e., convertible husbandry [Sion 1909, 222]) and one of the first to eliminate fallow lands. The prosperity of Normandy in the sixteenth century is also indicated by the disproportionate amounts it contributed to the Crown's coffers. By this time Normandy provided a quarter of French royal revenues, although it only accounted for about one-seventh of the land of the kingdom. Taxes in Normandy tripled from 1500 to 1600 (Bardet et al. 1987a, 273). Furthermore, Goubert (1973, 110; 1986, 21, 96) notes that Normandy, the west country, and the Midi (all less-communal regions) were more immune to the famines and epidemics of the seventeenth century than the communal, cereal-growing plains of the north.

Regional Differences in Enclosure

As in England, enclosure facilitated increases in agricultural productivity. Also as in England, enclosure occurred without difficulty in most of the less-communal areas of Brittany, Normandy, and the far north. Already in the fourteenth century Artois and French Flanders mostly were enclosed. Enclosure also occurred largely without difficulty in other parts of the far north, beginning in the sixteenth century (Sivery 1977–79, 507). Enclosure was permissible in Normandy as early as the sixteenth century. By this time Norman law had been changed to allow any peasant to enclose his or her lands (Sion 1909, 223). Enclosure for pasture farming was particularly noticeable in Normandy in the seventeenth and eighteenth centuries, where stock breeding for the Parisian market developed

(Le Roy Ladurie and Goy 1982, 142). Especially in eastern Normandy, however, enclosures also were used for arable farming along English lines (Bloch 1966a, 207).

In the south in Provence communal grazing practices disappeared at an early date, although actual enclosure was rare. Bloch notes that, as early as 1469, the Estates of Provence petitioned the king for the right to enclose (1966a, 198). They wrote:

> Since all possessions belonging to individuals should be for their own advantage and not that of others, the Estates pray that all meadows, vineyards, closes and other possessions, whatever they may be, which can be so treated shall be put in defence (i.e., shut other users out) throughout the year, under severe penalty and notwithstanding all customs to the contrary running in the places dependent on the king.

The king agreed to this. Although not generally implemented at the time, Bloch notes that it demonstrates the "less-communal" attitude present in Provence. By 1789 few areas of collective grazing were left in Provence, although few actual enclosures were erected, and there was no amalgamation of plots into large farms (Bloch 1966a, 205). Languedoc was slower to abandon collective grazing, as was Berry, although Dion (1934, 14–33) considered that it was not because they lacked the freedom to enclose.

The process of enclosure and the reduction of collective practices met with greater resistance in the champion lands of the north and northeast. In the north the emergence of richer, commercially oriented peasants within the village community gave impetus to changes such as enclosure. Over time, especially as the marketing of agricultural products became more profitable, many large farmers (whose landholdings were incorporated in the communal open field system) wanted to enclose and consolidate land in order to improve their methods of production. Many were influenced by writings of English agronomists of the eighteenth century. Yet, at the same time, population growth meant more and more poor and landless peasants who depended on common rights in the open arable fields for their livelihood. They greatly resisted enclosure and any abandoning of collective practices. Opposition also came from smallholders whose farms were so little that consolidating and enclosing them would have meant they were no longer viable as farms (Dion 1934). These very small farms depended on communal rights to supplement their grazing resources. In addition, the scattering of plots of land protected smallholders from the full impact of certain problems such as ice or parasites, which rarely afflicted all strips of land of a holding at the same time. Thus, for both the landless and smallholders consolidation, enclosure, and the end of collective grazing could be disastrous.

It was not just the landless and land-poor who opposed consolidation and enclosure of farms. Sometimes seigeneurs and large farmers themselves also benefited from communal rights and thus were reluctant to change them. For example, large farmers often benefited disproportionately from communal grazing on fallows and wastes. Since their farms were the largest, they often had the right to put more animals in the village herd (Root 1987; Markoff 1996, 172, 252). In addition, many seigneurs and landlords, and later intendants, were hesitant to advocate rural change, as they were fearful of revolt and of disrupting the collection of taxes and dues (Dewald 1987). Hence, a variety of interests helped maintain the status quo.

### Regional Differences in Labor Relations

The shift away from customary tenure was notable in France from about the sixteenth century and also followed a regional pattern. Leasing increased in the north, while sharecropping contracts (*métayage*) spread in the south. These trends, however, were not associated with significant improvements in agricultural practices—quite the opposite; they were associated with the beginning of agricultural stagnation, as promising developments we have seen (particularly in the south and west) were not sustained.

In the north, as noted earlier, as large estates grew, so did the practice of leasing them out to many tenants for periods of years. Until the sixteenth century leases were often odd contracts that ran for as many as ninety-nine years. By the end of the seventeenth century (perhaps reflecting population growth) the nine-year lease was most common (Goubert 1986, 33) and remains so in northern France to this day. Despite the spread of leasing and growth of large estates, however, peasants did retain hereditary rights to some land. For example, in Picardy peasants remained in control of about 40 percent of the land in the seventeenth century (Deyon 1988b, 263). In addition, as noted, lessees often had virtual hereditary rights to the land they farmed. Thus, despite the growth of leasing, farms remained very small, with the typical farm being in the two- to three-hectare range.

Leasing also became particularly widespread in Normandy, particularly after 1600. In fact, eastern Normandy almost saw the demise of peasant hereditary rights at this time. By 1800 most land in Normandy was leased, and seven-eighths of the land in eastern Normandy was leased land (Sion 1909). Yet, despite extensive leasing, only in a few places in France did the equivalent of the English tenant farmer, working a large farm in a rationalistic manner, emerge. Nor did the equivalent of the highly productive, small-scale Flemish or Dutch lessee emerge. The change to leasing had few beneficial results, and the development of leasing accompanied the perpetuation of small-scale, subsistence farming and rural poverty in the north.[5]

While farms in the north of France began to be leased out, the south turned to a system of *métayage,* or sharecropping, as did Brittany at about the same time (Wallerstein 1974, 106, Sexauer 1976). Sharecropping also was introduced into parts of western Normandy. After about 1500 sharecropping was widespread through both southern France and Brittany—Poitou being a good example. Before 1450 sharecropping was rare in this region; after 1450 it increased markedly. In the period from 1630 to 1690 the number of sharecropping contracts in Poitou went from 30 to 90 percent of all contracts (Jacquart 1975, 230).[6] Sharecropping often has been blamed for the "economic backwardness" of much of southern France, yet it appears to have been more a symptom of the impoverishment of the peasantry than a cause, a point supported by the rapid spread of sharecropping after the Wars of Religion in the sixteenth century (Yun 1994, 134). An increase in the power of local lords after the wars of religion may also have enabled them to introduce sharecropping regimes where none had existed before, in order to reduce the transaction costs involved in land management on land they may previously have not farmed or had leased (Emigh 1997). That is, the increasing peasant impoverishment and powerlessness in the south created by warfare (coupled with increasing state demands) was responsible for both low agricultural productivity in the south and a shift to sharecropping. The availability of prospective tenants meant that landlords could change terms on sharecroppers with impunity. As in the north, the result was widespread small-scale subsistence farming and rural poverty.

## Rural Industry

For poor rural dwellers working in the textile industry was an alternative method for increasing incomes and was performed during seasonal lulls in agricultural work. Although never as extensive as the contemporary English or Dutch industries, the French textile industry flourished in many regions, particularly after the sixteenth century. As in England, it was most prominent in less-communal regions.

A textile industry had developed in northern France as early as the thirteenth century, at which time it had been primarily an urban phenomenon. The cities of Rheims, Amiens, Saint-Quentin, and Rouen were all important manufacturing centers (Pounds 1990, 173; see also Munro 1994, 156). Cities of the north and of Champagne benefited from the decline of the Flemish industry after the fourteenth century. Rheims, in particular, grew into an important cloth-working center. By the sixteenth century, however, partly because of increasingly restrictive guild practices in the towns and partly as a result of the growing impoverishment of many rural dwellers, manufacturers were attracted by the availability of low-cost labor in rural areas. Parts of the textile industry began to shift to the countryside, to be performed in numerous small rural cottages. As was true throughout the southern Netherlands, the "new draperies" and lighter cloths were manufactured most commonly in rural parts of Artois and French Flanders (Le Roy Ladurie 1987, 341). This cottage industry provided an important alternate source of employment for many landless or land-poor rural dwellers.

Growth of the textile industry was not confined to the far north. The lower Seine Valley and southern France were important cloth-working areas. Some of the industry was urban, but most was carried on in rural cottages as part-time industry supplementing income from agriculture. Of the less-communal areas of the north, west, and south, by the sixteenth century regions in Normandy, Brittany, Touraine, Poitou, and Languedoc were most notable for the rise of the textile industry (Zeller 1970, 130; *Rand McNally Atlas of World History,* 1984, map 46; Le Roy Ladurie 1987, 341). Rouen particularly saw an expansion of textile production in the sixteenth century (Yun 1994, 128). The textiles of Brittany help account for the wealth that it brought to France when it was incorporated into the French kingdom in 1491 (Goubert 1986). By the sixteenth century Lyon had developed the silk industry it retains to this day (Pounds 1990, 236; Yun 1994, 128).

In sum, population, ecology, and market access all favored the north of France. Yet within the north it was only less-communal regions that, by the sixteenth century, saw levels of agricultural productivity to rival that found in England. Parts of the less-communal west and south also showed promising development in the sixteenth and seventeenth centuries. High growth rates, however, were not sustained for any length of time. Long-term growth rates throughout France were much less than those found in England during the same period of the sixteenth and seventeenth centuries (Hoffman 1991). With the exception of the far north, yields were variable, and even in some regions that had shown promising developments, such as Normandy or the west, little long-term progress was forthcoming.

Agricultural productivity for France as a whole remained comparatively low throughout the late medieval and early modern periods. In the

1670s, on the richest soil of northern France, Goubert found average wheat yields of 5.5, 6, and 5 to 1 (Slicher van Bath 1963a, 48). At about the same time average yields for all England and the Netherlands were around 6 to 1 (Pounds 1990, 279), although there was much variability from place to place. For example, in seventeenth-century England wheat yields ranged from 11.6 at Harwell, Berkshire; to 4 in Gloucestershire (Slicher van Bath 1963a, 48). In the seventeenth-century Netherlands wheat yields ranged from 14.1 to 4.8 in Friesland.

Nor did agriculture in France produce enough to feed the entire population. As a result, the seventeenth century in France saw catastrophic epidemics, famines, and, according to one estimate, about a thousand peasant revolts (Goubert 1986, 205). This was in contrast to England, where famines ceased in the seventeenth century (Overton 1996, 141), and of course the United Provinces in the Netherlands, which were enjoying their greatest prosperity. In France as a whole subsistence crises did not end until after 1740 (Le Roy Ladurie and Goy 1982, 104). Low agricultural productivity no doubt also inhibited urbanization, which did not increase greatly in France at this time, unlike contemporary developments in England and the Netherlands (de Vries 1984, 39).

## The Agricultural Revolution in France

The agricultural revolution was slow in coming to France. Agricultural production probably did not begin to rise significantly until about 1750. This date heralds the end of true famines in France. At this point the French population outgrew its old limit of about twenty million, probably attaining twenty-eight million by 1789 (Le Roy Ladurie 1987, 402). Michel Morineau, in his study of data from tithes and agricultural yields, suggests that yields did not start to increase in France until the first third of the nineteenth century (Morineau 1970; see also Le Roy Ladurie and Goy 1982, 5, Braudel 1990, 410). As late as 1850, 50 percent or more of the French population were engaged in agriculture (Dovring 1965, 604).

In many ways the English development catalyzed change in France. Agricultural and economic development in England gave the English state a competitive edge over its old rival France. To keep up, the French state was now anxious to promote both agricultural and economic development at home. By the eighteenth century the French state began actively to promote agricultural development along English lines (Slicher van Bath 1963b, 322, Bloch 1966a; Braudel 1990). Widely distributed pamphlets, agricultural societies, and agronomists encouraged growth of fallow crops, enclosure, extensive manuring, and other intensive agricultural practices. To help enclosers and improvers the Crown passed edicts allowing enclosure of the open fields and common land. As we may expect, such pressures produced different results in different regions. By and large, less-communal areas were more responsive than communal areas. Thus, as in England, it was less-communal regions that led the way in the French agricultural revolution.

In communal lands of the northeast pressures for agricultural change were often ignored. Individual *Parlements* of various provinces also passed decrees to enclose and rearrange the arable fields of a village, but the decrees were not obeyed (Dion 1934, 62). Seigneurs and others who could buy their way around communal rights had some success at consolidation and enclosure, but this was an expensive undertaking and for this reason did not occur often (Hoffman 1988). As a result, enclosures of village plow land for pasture farming or division of the village common lands were uncommon in champion lands of northeastern France. Although there was a great expansion of cereal culture around Paris and in the traditional grain-growing plains of the north at this time, adoption of innovative techniques, such as convertible husbandry, the growing of fallow crops, and complex rotations, was rare (Bloch 1971 [1913], 113). This suppressed yields and productivity.

In these regions of northern France tensions between the few well-off farmers of large farms, who often wanted to enclose and improve the land, and all others increased. These tensions became acute in the seventeenth and eighteenth centuries and finally helped fuel the French revolution. The *Cahiers de doléances* of the revolutionary period show the resentment many villagers felt toward rich peasants who were attempting to engross and enclose their holdings (Deyon n.d.; Deyon 1988b, 266; 1988c, 320), although other issues loomed larger. Yet even the revolution and the subsequent division of the commons and seigneurial demesnes did not break down the communal farming system. Medieval agricultural practices continued largely unchanged in many of these areas. As late as the 1920s, Marc Bloch wrote: "Springtime on the plateaux of Lorraine and in the plains of Alsace and Burgundy is still marked in the fields by the appearance of the three contrasting hues, corresponding to the three 'courses'" (1966a, 240). Complete change did not come to the champion lands of the northeast until after the devastation of World War II.

In the north most change occurred in the less-communal regions. Improvements in agricultural techniques and increases in production were particularly evident in Normandy, Artois, and French Flanders. Artois and French Flanders saw the further development of an intensive, highly productive agriculture producing wheat, barley, and oats as well as more specialized market crops such as potatoes and flax. By the early nineteenth century wheat yields in this region nearly reached the English high of over 22 hectoliters per hectare (see map 11; Morineau 1970, 179; Le Roy Ladurie 1975, 114; Braudel 1990, 408). Normandy was another advanced region. By the early eighteenth century it was an important wheat producer (Bardet et al. 1987b, 302). Pasture farming expanded in Normandy at the same time. By 1815, in terms of average income per hectare, Calvados (in western Normandy) was the richest rural department in France. Only two of the communal regions of northern France, the Beauce and the Île-de-France, both close to Paris, compared to Normandy and the far north at this time (Braudel 1990, 289, 285).

In the west, in the Vendée, there was notable improvement in agricultural innovation after the end of the eighteenth century. In Brittany tenant farming began to take over from sharecropping at the same time (de Planhol and Claval 1994, 344, 153). In the south in some regions there was improvement in agricultural productivity. There was a further shift away from cereal production toward viticulture, orchard growing, and horticulture. Other crops besides cereals (fruits, vegetables, grapes, olives) were grown using very intensive techniques and showed very high yields. This was particularly notable in areas of commercial agriculture such as in the valleys of the Garonne and Tarn. In Aquitaine a productive rural sector based on a maize-wheat cycle continued to flourish. In the maize region in the late eighteenth century Arthur Young contrasted the "good" rural economy of the south, where the fallow had disappeared, with the "poor" rural economy of the north, where fallows continued (qtd. in de Planhol and Claval 1994, 219).

Much of the south and west, however, became further impoverished. Compared to the north, by the middle of the nineteenth century agricultural performance was generally poor in the south and, to a lesser extent, the west. Labor and land productivity were both higher in the north of France than in the south and west at this time (Pautard 1965; de Planhol and Claval 1994, 157). By this time the height of male conscripts from the northeast was on average 5 to 6 centimeters greater than in the south and west, testifying to better standards of living in the northeast (de Planhol and Claval 1994, 155). Cereal yields remained low in the south at less than 12 hectoliters per hectare. This was lower than most other areas of France at this time (from the 1840 census [see map 11]).

The south and west were now the bastion of the smallholder in France (Pautard 1965; Juillard, Meynier, de Planhol, and Sautter 1957; Sexauer 1976, 504). In 1787, in Limousin, 58 percent of holdings were less than 1.7 hectares. In Laonnais 75 percent and Loiret 81 percent were less than 3.4 hectares (Slicher van Bath 1963b, 321). Françoise Quesnay, in Diderot's *Encyclopédie* of the eighteenth century, noted that "large-scale agriculture

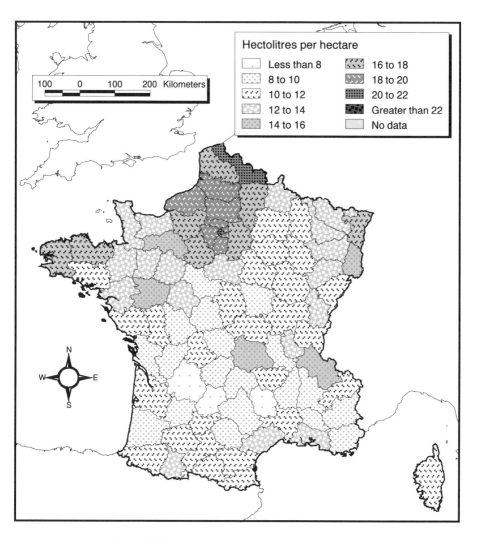

Map 11. Wheat yields in France, 1840. (Adapted from Morineau 1970.)

is confined to about 6 million acres of land, made up for the most part by the provinces of Normandy, the Beauce, the Île-de-France, Picardy, French Flanders, Hainaut and a few others" (qtd. in Le Roy Ladurie 1987, 339). The regional difference in farm sizes was still visible in 1862 (see map 12). In fact, to this day farms are smaller in the south and west than in the north.

Despite improvements in parts of France, by English and Dutch standards nineteenth-century French agricultural techniques remained backward and productivity low. The vigorous advocacy of new agricultural techniques by the Crown in the late eighteenth century had few effects, as the root crops and leguminous grasses that had successfully transformed much of English agriculture were utilized in only a few areas in France. As late as 1861, lucerne, sainfoin, and clover accounted for only about half the area of natural grassland in France (Braudel 1990, 282, 407). French agriculture continued to have a poor reputation in general (Fussell 1983, 146). As a comparison to England, in 1815–24 output per agricultural worker in England has been estimated at 45.6 (value added per hectare in pounds sterling), while in France the estimate is 37.6 (O'Brien and Heath 1982, 735). Wheat yields per acre were also higher in England than they were in France, with an average of about 12–18 bushels per acre in France at the beginning of the nineteenth century as against about 22–24 bushels per acre for England at the same time (Bennett 1935; Allen and O'Grada 1988, 103, 111). Only in French Flanders did French yields rival contemporary English yields. To this day French farms are small and agriculture is inefficient by world standards.

**Factors Specific to the Protonational Context**

Regional factors cannot explain fully the overall poor agricultural performance of France in the early modern period. To do this we must turn to protonational factors that stifled agrarian change. These included periodic warfare and, partly as a result of this warfare, the growth of an unwieldy and inefficient royal state bureaucracy. While this bureaucracy did little to protect property rights of ordinary farmers, it penalized production, stifled trade, and royal policies (often unintentionally) worked to prevent agrarian change and perpetuate communal farming systems. All these factors increased transaction costs and discouraged agrarian change in France.

Warfare

Both the north and south of France saw periodic warfare, clustered into three major periods: the Hundred Years' War, from about 1335 to 1450;

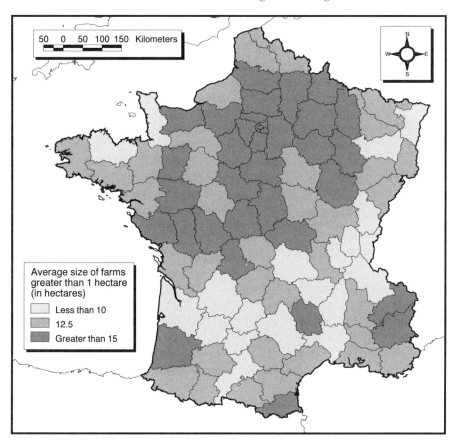

**Map 12. Average farm sizes in France, 1862. (Adapted from Pautard 1965.)**

the Wars of Religion of the sixteenth century (c. 1562–98); and the Frondes of the seventeenth century (c. 1648–52) (Chevalier 1994, 369).

The Hundred Years' War took place mainly in the north, where it affected primarily Normandy, Picardy, and Flanders, although some battles occurred in the south (e.g., Poitiers in 1356). This was a foreign war, primarily between England and France, although other states were involved periodically. The Wars of Religion (1562–98) were a series of conflicts between the monarch and princes. Ostensibly over religious issues, they were nearly as much struggles between the old nobility and the new class of royal officials over royal patronage (Major 1994, 108). The Wars of Religion spared few provinces (Jacquart 1975, 194), although the Parisian region and parts of the south were particularly badly affected.

The Frondes were a series of conflicts between the monarch and aristocracy combined with conflicts within the aristocracy (between the old nobility and royal officials) over royal patronage. They also involved peasant revolts. At first the Frondes primarily affected the Paris region. Subsequently, they were concentrated in Normandy, Anjou (central), Burgundy (central east), and Guyenne (southwest). During the Fronde, French intervention in the Thirty Years' War also caused problems. The Thirty Years' War (1618–48) was waged largely outside of France, but troop movements still caused damage in northern and central France. After the seventeenth century no major wars were waged on French soil until the Franco-Prussian war of 1870, by which France lost control of Alsace and Lorraine to Germany.[7]

Warfare did untold damage to agricultural capital, animals, equipment, and buildings. It physically disrupted the various tasks of the agricultural year, and it also hurt agriculture by disrupting the normal process of exchange and trade. Hoffman (1991) has demonstrated how periods of war were associated with dramatic drops in agricultural production in the Parisian basin in particular, although rural regions often recovered fairly quickly. War also hastened the impoverishment and expropriation of the peasantry, pushed rural communities into debt, and forced the sale of common land (Yun 1994, 134). Furthermore, the outcomes of these wars subjected the south of France more securely than ever to domination by the north, which was no doubt an important factor contributing to the decline in the southern economy.

### State Taxation and Policies

Taxes (both direct and indirect on sales and export goods) to support war activities also sapped the countryside. They may have had a more negative effect on the rural economy than the actual warfare. War taxes often persisted beyond the war itself and created a disincentive for agricultural production.

The original French direct tax, the *taille,* was implemented initially during the Hundred Years' War. Until the fourteenth century direct taxation had been rare in France. During the Hundred Years' War, however, the first permanent direct tax, or *fouage,* the *taille,* was established. It was granted to Charles VII by the Estates-General at Orléans in 1439 as the culmination of a long process in which the king had tried to raise money necessary to evict the English (see Ardant 1971, 239; Wolfe 1972, 26–40; Allmand 1989). The direct tax became the largest source of Crown revenue. It was borne primarily by the rural populace; the nobility was largely exempt. In England, in contrast, regular direct taxation did not begin until the nineteenth century.

After the fifteenth century levels of taxation crept up inexorably, although with momentary lulls. For example, it is estimated that fiscal pressure on agrarian production in France decreased from 1482 to 1547 (Yun 1994, 125). Between the end of Henry IV's reign (1610) and the death of Mazarin (1661), however, taxes rose faster than in the previous eighty years. After 1660, when farming incomes began to fall, this became a greater proportion of farming income. Contemporaries complained bitterly about the severity of taxation.

Pierre Goubert, in his study of agriculture in the Beauvais district north of Paris in the early seventeenth century, estimated charges on a smallholding of under 8 hectares (often only 4–5 hectares). The *taillage* alone claimed the entire production of 1.5 hectares and together with other taxes claimed 20 percent of the gross yield. To this was added the tithe and other ecclesiastical charges, amounting to a further 12 percent and the tenant's rent amounting to about 20 percent. Altogether, about 52 percent of the total yield went to rent and taxes (Goubert 1960, 180f.; Abel 1978b, 164). Quesnay, in the 1750s, estimated that of the total yield of French cereal farming about 70 percent went to farming expenses, while 13 percent went to the landowner as rent and to the treasury in tax, leaving barely 4 percent to the tenant (Abel 1978b, 163).

In France in addition to direct taxes there were also indirect taxes on the rural populace. These included taxes on traded goods and the forced government monopoly on salt as well as debasement (Spufford 1965; Sussman 1993). Debasement of the coinage (either in quantity or in quality of metal used in minting), the oldest form of taxation in France, had been a lucrative way for French monarchs to raise money for centuries. In France, unlike in the rest of western Europe, the French Crown had absolute control over the coinage by the fourteenth century and retained it thereafter. Debasement became a regularly used method of imposing additional taxes on the populace. For example, Philip the Fair (IV) obtained about 58 percent of his revenues in 1298 from coinage manipulation (Spufford 1965; Fryde 1991, 260). At the beginning of the Hundred Years' War, in the fourteenth century, Philip VI debased the value of the *livre* such that by 1343 it was only one-fifth of what it had been in 1336 (Spufford 1965, 124). In 1349 he reportedly received 70 percent of his income from the feudal fee from minting (Munro 1972, 22; see also Sussman 1993). Debasement played havoc with trade and may have discouraged production for the market. It also undermined seigneurial authorities, who received their rents in coin, typically fixed at customary levels.

After the debasements of the late medieval period, seigneurs often received rents that were almost worthless.

The French Crown also used sales taxes, taxes on exports and other trade goods, and the salt tax (*gabelle*) intermittently from the late thirteenth through the fourteenth centuries. Over the fifteenth and sixteenth centuries these indirect taxes, like the direct taxes, increased. Roads and rivers became crowded with tolls and customs. For example, after the Religious Wars the trading corridor of the Rhône below Lyon became laden with tolls that deterred traders (Yun 1994, 134). The *gabelle* in particular became one of the more important sources of royal revenue (Dupont-Ferrier 1976). These indirect taxes helped prevent development of a national market in France, which raised costs for producers and traders.

By the early seventeenth century royal taxation in France was much more oppressive than royal taxation in England. As a comparison of taxation in both countries (excluding debasement), in 1628, Louis XIII derived revenues from Normandy alone equal to Charles I's total fiscal income from all England (Stone 1960, 32), although the English population was higher than that of Normandy. Such taxation not only absorbed the surplus produced by the peasantry; it also helped discourage greater production (North and Thomas 1973; Braudel 1984). In England, in contrast, the state was less able to tax the populace. Thus, taxes on farmers remained relatively unchanged over the same period (from about 1381 to the early 1600s) and in consequence formed an increasingly smaller proportion of a farmer's total income (Fryde 1991).

Another means by which the French state indirectly penalized grain producers in France was through state control of grain prices. In England, on the other hand, the state did not attempt to control grain prices to the same extent, and, when it did, prices typically aided the cereal growers, rather than disadvantaging them as in France. Cities in northern France, particularly Paris, were home to a large urban proletariat who were in danger of starvation in times of high bread prices or economic downturns in the textile industry. This urban population would riot; it even would send roving gangs out into the countryside that hunted for stores of grain and raided the homes of and killed rich peasants accused of speculating in grain. To keep the peace, urban officials would regulate prices of basic agricultural commodities such as cereals and bread. Control of grain prices was also a policy consistently pursued by the central state, not the least for fear of the Parisian proletariat. Keeping the price of bread low was always a priority for the French monarchs. Trade in cereals itself was frequently forbidden (Usher 1913, 223–39; de Planhol 1988, 227; de Planhol and Claval 1994, 241), as authorities feared that a free market in grain would create grain shortages in urban areas. Regulation of grain prices and control of the grain trade served to lower profits for farmers, which reduced their incentives to produce cereals, which in turn exacerbated the grain shortages that had prompted the price controls in the first place.

In short, high levels of taxation, debasement, indirect taxes on trade, and controls on the market in agricultural products increased costs faced by producers, discouraged trade, and retarded the process of agrarian change throughout France.

## Rise of Royal Bureaucracy

Tax increases not only discouraged improvements in agricultural productivity; they also funded the growth of a huge and corrupt royal bureaucracy, which itself ultimately helped to discourage economic growth in France. In addition, the justice supplied by this bureaucracy often did little to protect property rights of common people.

Dupont-Ferrier (1976) documents large numbers of officials at all levels who emerged from the late fourteenth through the fifteenth century in France. Their number never ceased to rise, despite the fact they were abolished periodically by popularity-seeking monarchs (mostly in earlier years). In the *pays d'élection*[8] the basic fiscal unit was the *élection,* which had as its head an *élu.* Beneath *élus* were all sorts of lesser officials: the *élu's* lieutenants, clerks, tax collectors, procurers, and lawyers. A number of officials were responsible for the salt tax and were in charge of the salt storage sites—the *grenetiers* (chief salt officials), inspectors, measurers, and lieutenants. Still others were in charge of customs and export taxes. At the top were the *generaux des finances.* To have one of these positions was considered the crowning point of a career in royal office. The positions of tax collector–general and inspector-general were also highly desirable, if somewhat less prestigious than the *generaux des finances.*

After 1467 all these officials enjoyed an almost irrevocable tenure of office. After about 1521 the officeholder became the legal owner of his office. All these offices could be sold or occupied in conjunction with another royal office (Chevalier 1994, 381). There were many opportunities for venality, which often was considered a legitimate benefit of office. The king made little effort to check it. Nepotism was also rife. From 1388 to 1416 many families of *élus* and other officials installed their children, brothers, nephews, and cousins in positions in the same *élections.* The king's blindness to all this may be accounted for by the fact that he expected to borrow from his officers and often did. The profitability of royal offices in turn accounts for their popularity. Offices were coveted with "scarcely disguised savagery" (Dupont-Ferrier 1976, 85, 195, 194). As time went on, the system became more and more unmanageable, until little of the king's taxes actually found their way to the king (Mettam 1988, 209). Such a vast, complex, corrupt, and inefficient apparatus increased uncertainty in fiscal affairs and raised transaction costs throughout France.

The royal bureaucracy also provided a legal system. Yet, unlike in England and the Netherlands, this system did not provide relatively impartial central courts to which individuals could turn against impositions on their property or rights. One reason is the generally high levels of corruption that prevailed throughout the French bureaucracy. In addition, there was the increasing localization of the French legal system. In the late medieval period the king of France had offered an institution somewhat similar to the English common law courts in the form of the *grand jours*. These were temporary sovereign courts set up in distant provinces, staffed almost entirely by members of the *Parlement* of Paris (Major 1994, 19). Yet this changed, starting in the fifteenth century, as provinces were given their own *parlements*. Decisions of the royal courts became subject to appeal to these bodies. The first such parlement was in Toulouse in 1420, followed by Grenoble in 1453, Burgundy 1484, Normandy in 1499, Provence in 1501, and Brittany and Savoy in 1523, and a parlement was created to serve Béarn, Navarre, and Soule in 1620 (Major 1994, 20–28, 105; Chevalier 1994, 385). Parlements were dominated by local elites who received little or no supervision from above. Nor was there any centralization of law codes, which remained highly local and varied greatly from place to place (de Planhol and Claval 1994, 188; Blockmans 1996, 244). Thus, unlike in England or the Netherlands, courts were less likely to serve as an impartial third party when judging property or other disputes. Ultimately, it was peasants and other small landowners whose rights suffered most as a result.[9]

### Crown Policy and the Survival of Communal Agriculture

The peasantry often looked to the Crown as their protector against local oppression. By this means royal policy itself inadvertently played a major role in the survival of communal agriculture in northern France (Hoffman 1988). Legal recognition by royal authorities, which had begun to tax communities as corporate bodies, strengthened the rural community all over France over the years 1330 to 1560. The fifteenth century saw the introduction of the post of *syndic* in communal open field regions, the representative of the village community to royal authorities. As time went on, royal recognition of and protection for the village community increased, along with taxes the community was required to pay.

The seventeenth century saw continued attempts to rationalize royal finances, that is, to sidestep the royal fiscal bureaucracy and ensure that the kings revenues actually made it to the king. The most important step taken was the creation of the post of *intendant*. He was the king's representative in the provinces. His main duty was to ensure the king's interests, that is, mostly to make sure royal taxes were paid. In order to do this, a major task for the intendants was to ensure that the main taxpayers, peasants, were able to make their payments. Especially in the land of *taille personelle,* the north, this involved protecting the village community, which continued to pay taxes in common. To ensure peasants' continued ability to pay, the Crown prohibited confiscation of peasant livestock for payment of debts. There were also attempts made to reclaim communal properties (woods, wastelands, and meadows) that had been alienated in the past to pay debts, as the loss of these properties made it difficult for the community to pay its taxes.

Root (1987) documents this process in particular for Burgundy, a province dominated by communal open field systems, in the eighteenth century. In eighteenth-century Burgundy intendants enforced *contrainte solidaire,* which meant that richer members of the community were responsible for taxes due if others did not or could not make payments. The intendants also fought domination of the village assemblies by "councils of notables," that is, well-to-do peasants in the community. Such policies had the effect of discouraging agrarian change, as it was these well-to-do peasants who were most interested in bringing it about. Last, the intendant's policies also helped protect communal agriculture by resisting agricultural reforms such as the implementation of enclosure laws, which would have assisted the privatization of land. Intendants wanted to avoid the social upheaval such reforms would create, which also would jeopardize the flow of royal revenue.

Royal policies thus inadvertently helped maintain communal agriculture and prevented any long-term agricultural development and change. Ironically, this result was quite counter to the Crown's own interests. Here the contrast with England could not be more apparent, as parliamentary policies often worked in favor of agricultural improvement and change.

## Conclusion

In France local institutions (in conjunction with other factors) influenced the regional course of agrarian change. Ecological and market conditions were most favorable for economic growth in the north. Yet in much of this region agrarian change was hindered by communal agricultural systems, although there is evidence of highly productive activity outside of the communal cereal fields, on private gardens. Unlike in England, the emergence of large farms in the communal regions was not associated with a highly productive agriculture. Large farms were typically leased to many small farmers, and, unlike in the Netherlands, these small farms remained comparatively unproductive and subsistence oriented. Throughout the late medieval and early modern period it was in less-communal regions of northern France (Artois and French Flanders, Normandy) that agricultural change and improvement were most evident. These regions also became important centers of the French textile industry. Later, it was these regions that led the way in the agricultural revolution of the nineteenth century.

Market and ecological conditions were much less favorable in the less-communal south and west. Nevertheless, especially in areas with decent farming conditions and access to markets, such as the Rhône Valley and in Guyenne, there was a prosperous rural economy based on a variety of crops. As in less-communal regions in the north, they were also regions where textile industries tended to develop. A diversity of economic activities throughout the south and west meant that these regions, although often subsistence oriented, did not experience the famines and subsistence crises of the seventeenth century to the same extent as the communal regions of the north. Nor did they experience the polarization between rich and poor common in the north at this time. There were periods of high growth in many of these regions, yet they were not sustained. By the nineteenth century much of the south and west had become impoverished.

National conditions contributed to the generally poor performance of agriculture and the rural economy in both the north and south of France. Periodic warfare was detrimental to the rural economy. A growing state apparatus, through heavy taxation, periodic debasement of the coinage, control of grain prices and the grain trade, and general corruption, increased transaction costs and penalized producers throughout the period examined here. Protection for property rights was uncertain, because of the high levels of corruption and because a localized court system evolved over the early modern period. Laws and their enforcement differed greatly from place to place. Superimposed over this was state protection for peasant rights, which often served to protect communal agricultural systems and thus contributed to the lack of agricultural development and change.

By the nineteenth century only the far north of France (spared from French royal rule for at least two centuries) had wheat yields to rival those found in most of England and the Netherlands at the same time. To this day France bears the legacy of its delayed agricultural revolution with a high percentage of the population still engaged in agriculture and small average farm sizes.[10]

## CHAPTER 7

# Rural Institutions and Agrarian Change in the German Lands

Ce n'est donc ni à l'esprit, ni au génie de la nation qu'il
faut attribuer le peu de progrès que nous avons fait, mais
nous ne devons nous en prendre qu'à une suite de conjunctures fâcheuses, à un enchaînement de guerres qui
nous ont ruinés et appauvris autant d'hommes que
d'argent.

[It is then neither to the spirit nor to the genius of the
nation that it is necessary to attribute the small amount
of progress we have made, but we need only take it from
a series of harmful conjunctures, a sequence of wars that
have ruined us and deprived us of men as much as of
money.]
  —Frederick the Great, *De la littérature allemande*

The German lands—that is, much of what made up the Holy Roman
Empire in 1500—or what we may loosely call Germany, present another
negative case of agrarian change. The configuration of other important
factors, notably, state structures, class relations, and almost continual
warfare, was quite different from France. In place of the growing state
consolidation and centralization characteristic of early modern France, we
see increasing state decentralization in early modern Germany as the ties
holding the empire together gradually weakened. Thus, this case allows us
to gauge the effects of local institutions on agrarian change in a very different political context than what we have seen hitherto: a loose federation
of semi-independent principalities and states.

  Even in this different political context at the national level, however,
regional structures shaped the pattern of agrarian change in Germany. In
the late medieval period the regions that emerged as the most important
producers of both cereals and animal products for the market were those
of less-communal farming systems, in the northwest, north, and east. As in
England, these regions were home to prosperous, productive peasant
economies and a well-off peasantry. Along the north coast and in the
northwest this peasant economy survived through the early modern

period. In eastern Germany, however, political developments were quite different. Here the early modern period saw not an improvement of the conditions of peasants and workers, but a reimposition of feudal-like labor dues and restrictions on a peasantry that had once been one of the freest in Europe. This, along with the disasters of war and the growth of Prussian absolutism after the seventeenth century, helped to stifle agrarian development in eastern Germany. In what follows I trace the pattern of agricultural development and agrarian change in Germany and the role played by ecology, population, market access, agrarian structures, and political factors in determining regional outcomes.

### Ecology, Population, and Markets

Ecologically, southwestern Germany (including Württemberg, the Palatinate, Nassau, Hesse, Kalenberg, Ansbach, and part of Wolfenbuttel, Bavaria, and Saxony [see map 13]) is the best endowed agricultural region in Germany. Most of the deposits of loess soil (rich, easy-to-cultivate loam soil) are here in this region of gently rolling hills (Pounds 1990, 19; Fulbrook 1990, 3). In the northwest the North Sea coasts are often marshy. Further inland the land becomes hillier with a few deposits of loess (Pounds 1990, 19). Much of the rest of the north and east of the German lands, including coasts bordering on the Baltic Sea, is a flat region of notoriously poor soil, the "sandbox" of the Holy Roman Empire. All this area had been covered by ice sheets during the glacial period (Samsonowicz and Maczak 1985, 7). As these ice sheets melted, they left behind clay, sand, and gravel, none of which was easy to farm. The sands in particular were congenial only to heaths, pine, and scrubby trees (Pounds 1990, 14). Below and to the west of this heathy plain is the hilly region of central Germany (the Harz mountains, or the Erzgebirge). Further south still lie the Alps. In terms of climate the north and west tend to be wet and mild, while the east and south tend to have a more continental climate and are drier, with greater extremes of temperature (Fulbrook 1990, 3).

In the late medieval period population density followed ecology, as it was densest in the more fertile west. Much is unknown about population densities throughout Germany, however, as for this period there are few population records in Germany equivalent to the hearth lists of France and the tax returns of England. The area of densest population (more than twenty persons per square kilometer or about thirty-two persons per square mile) was in the northwest. It stretched from the southern Low Countries to the Rhine near Cologne. The upper Rhine area in southwestern Germany had a similar density (Samsonowicz and Maczak 1985, 8;

**Map 13. The German lands, c. 1550**

Pounds 1990, 163, 191), as did the area beyond the Rhine toward Soest, Paderborn, and Brunswick. West Germany was also the most urbanized region, although, unlike in England, the Netherlands, and France, continued political fragmentation in Germany meant that cities everywhere were comparatively small in the early fourteenth century. None reached the size of London (30,000), Paris (50,000), or Bruges (50,000) at the same time (Pounds 1990, 161, 164, 224; Fulbrook 1990, 22). Cologne, the largest city, did have over 25,000 people. In the east, in contrast, population density was low, with perhaps eight to fifteen people per square kilometer (Samsonowicz and Maczak 1985, 8; Pounds 1990, 149). It was also much less urbanized. Cities were fewer and generally much smaller than cities in the west, with ten to twenty-five thousand people at most (Pounds 1990, 164; Fulbrook 1990, 22).

An intricate network of navigable rivers, the most important being the Rhine, meant that all of western Germany had easy access to major markets, first at the fairs in Champagne to the west, later in cities of the Low Countries. In the Middle Ages the fairs of Champagne constituted the major market center of Europe. At these fairs arrangements were made for exchange of all items of trade, particularly cloth, spices, and salt but also bulky goods such as grain. These fairs declined in the fourteenth century, largely because of prolonged warfare (Munro 1994, 154), and were replaced by a new system of fairs in Switzerland and southern Germany. The most popular of these new fairs were held at Geneva and Zurzach in Switzerland and at Nördlingen and Frankfurt in Germany, although there were others (Pounds 1990, 179, 203; Yun 1994, 117). These new fairs were never as large as the Champagne fairs, partly because much trade had moved to the cities of the Low Countries, first to Bruges and then to Antwerp (Postan 1952, 184).

As with the Champagne fairs, these cities were easily accessible by river and by sea, particularly from western Germany. From the Rhineland it was possible to reach Antwerp by way of the waterways of the Rhine delta, at that time a great deal wider and deeper than they became in modern times. The major problems with river transport in the west were not natural but man-made. Rivers were encumbered with man-made obstacles such as mills, fish weirs, and, above all, tolls. The Rhine was probably the most heavily encumbered with tolls. Besides waterways, there was a dense road network in the Rhineland and western Germany, as shown in the roadbook published in 1553 by Charles Estienne for France (Pounds 1990, 208, 244, 245).

In contrast, in the late medieval period the east had much less easy access to markets and fairs of the west and was in general less urbanized and commercialized. Smaller fairs were established late here—at Leipzig, Pozna, and Gniezno—which endured throughout the Middle Ages (Pounds 1990, 203). After the fourteenth-century crisis Leipzig became a major fair and was one of the two cities through which English textiles entered Germany by the second quarter of the fourteenth century (Yun 1994, 117). In the East there were fewer rivers and only three of any importance for shipping: the Elbe, Oder, and Vistula. Grain and other products for export to the west had to be taken by road to a river, from where it was shipped to a port, and then it was taken by sea to its final destination, typically a major city in the west.

**Field Systems in Late Medieval Germany (c. 1200–1500)**

East and west Germany also differed in the nature of local land-use systems. Land-use systems in Germany showed considerable complexity, but they can be reduced to a few simple types, following Huppertz (1939) and Abel (1978, 74). These types can be arranged on a more communal to less-communal continuum.

Communal Open Field Systems

Much of southwestern and central Germany west of the Elbe was characterized by the same kind of communal open field system found in central England (Huppertz 1939, 125; Du Boulay 1983, 170; Cameron 1993, 112). That is, the system featured two or three large open fields (*Zelgen* or *Schläge*) divided into segments called furlongs (*Felder* or *Gewänne*), long strip fields, communal rotations, and common grazing. Separate from the arable land (*Äcker*) was meadowland (*Wiese*), gardens (*Kraut, Flachs, und Hanfland*), and sometimes land devoted to viticulture (*Weingärten*) (Sabean 1990, 52 [these names are from the eighteenth century, but I assume they did not change]). Communal open field regions in southern Germany were, like their English counterparts, regions of compact, nucleated villages (*Haufendörfer*), which ranged in size from the large villages typical of Franconia to the smaller nucleated villages typical of the region of Hohenlohe (Robisheaux 1989, 23). Unlike in England, in Germany the residential area of the village was typically surrounded by a wattle fence called an *Etter* or a hedge to protect the village from raids (Du Boulay 1983, 170; Rösener 1992, 159), reflecting the more volatile and dangerous situation in the German lands, a point to which I will return later.

As in northern France and midland England, these regions of Germany were characterized by personal dependence of the peasant on the feudal lord. Feudal relations also extended above the local level, as these regions remained the heart of the Holy Roman Empire until the sixteenth century (Press 1994, 440). All the great ruling families of the German lands—Zähringer, Hohenstaufen, Habsburg, and Hohenzollern—had their origin in this region (Du Boulay 1983, 95).

In the high Middle Ages a small proportion of the land of the manor made up the demesne farm (*villa,* or *curtis dominica*), which was cultivated by slaves and dependent tenants. The rest of the land was divided among peasant tenants. Each tenant occupied a *Hufe,* equivalent to an English *hide* or French *manse.* These tenants, known as *Hufebauern,* were required to provide labor services for the lord and to pay rent. Yet, as in France and the Low Countries, the gradual deterioration of the manorial system from the tenth to the thirteenth centuries saw a decline in demesne farming and a reduction of labor services required of the peasantry (Ganshof and Verhulst 1966; Rösener 1992, 27, 140). The decline in demesne farming also was associated with a decline in manorial intervention in economic affairs of the village. By the thirteenth century cultivation of the village land was not directed wholly by manorial agents; typically, the village community supervised cultivation itself (Blickle 1992, 155).

Despite the decline in labor services, however, peasants still were burdened with dues that had to be paid (in kind or in money) to lords of the manor, personal lords, and judicial authorities. These dues were not light. They varied greatly from manor to manor but could include rents; personal dues; tithes; bailiff charges; merchets and heriots; fees for use of such manorial monopolies as mills, communal ovens, and breweries; and taxes. The entire burden, however, may have been lighter than in England, perhaps reflecting the continuation of direct farming by lords in England at that time. Evidence from the Rhineland and the Moselle region suggests that German peasant dues in the high Middle Ages amounted to about one-third of the gross proceeds from grain produced by peasant tenants. In comparison, the dependent peasantry in England often had to hand over up to one-half of their gross proceeds from grain (Rösener 1992, 140).[1]

Inheritance practices are often obscure in the medieval period in Germany, although in later years the regional distribution of inheritance practices became clear. In the late Middle Ages feudal lords generally favored impartible inheritance, because it facilitated administration of the estate (Bloch 1966b, 61; Pounds 1990, 331). We may infer that this means that impartible inheritance was not uncommon in the heavily manorialized, open field regions of southwestern Germany. With the weakening of manorial control over the later Middle Ages, land became more likely to be inherited partibly, although in those regions where manorial or princely control remained strong impartible inheritance remained the rule (Sabean 1990, 15; Rösener 1992, 189; Robisheaux 1989, 81). In general, however, partible inheritance became the most common custom in southwestern Germany by the early modern period (Robisheaux 1989, 81).

Although the manor had declined as an economic center, it often retained its importance as the legal center in the later Middle Ages. The village court continued to be held in the old manorial center. Manorial officials were often the important officials within the village community organization. The *Schultheiss,* or village mayor, was typically the representative of the lord and was often also the judge or *Richter* (Blickle 1992, 161).[2] He worked with a local group of substantial older villagers called jurors, or *Schöffen.* If the judge was exercising high jurisdiction delegated by the king or prince, he might be called a *Vogt,* or steward (Du Boulay 1983; Robisheaux 1989, 33). Unlike England, the Netherlands, and France, centrally supplied justice did not emerge in Germany in the late medieval period, reflecting greater political decentralization in the German lands.

Furthermore, some old manorial laws left traces in village laws of the high and late Middle Ages (Rösener 1992, 55). These village laws were recorded in village *Weistümer,* in the Rhine and Moselle region and the extreme southwest (Blickle 1992, 159; Rösener 1992, 159), or *Dinghofrodeln,* in the upper Rhine Valley. These customals documented the *Zwing und Bann,* meaning the right to command and prohibit within the bounds of the village. Laws dictated the timing of cropping, harvesting, grazing, the use of commons and woods, and so forth. They were enforced by the village community organizations and court. The village council of all fully entitled members of the village community was the most important organ of peasant administration. It met at least once a year on certain set days. In early times it met under the linden tree, in the churchyard, or in the village green at the center of the village. In later times the council preferred the village parlor (*Gemeindestube*) or the house of the mayor. Attendance was mandatory for male members of the community. Wives or children were not allowed to represent them. The main tasks of the village council consisted of control of the village budget, regulation of crop rotation within the framework of the three-field system, promulgation of the village laws, and election of village officials (Blickle 1992, 155–56; Rösener 1992, 165). It also held its own courts (Robisheaux 1989, 34). It appears also that the well-developed village community of the late Middle Ages in western Germany, particularly in Swabia and Franconia, was as closely knit as its English and French cousins (Aubin 1966, 469; Blickle 1981, 82; 1992, 156; Rösener 1992, 155; Scribner 1996, 306).

### Less-Communal Open Field Systems and Enclosures

Land-use systems in the east were established during German colonization of the Slav lands in the thirteenth and fourteenth centuries. By the early years of the fourteenth century Germany's frontier states were Pomerania, Brandenburg, and the province of Silesia. Further east, the German fighting orders, the Teutonic knights and the Brethren of the Sword, had settled along the east Baltic coast and inland from the lower Vistula to the Gulf of Finland (Pounds 1990, 145). Most villages and fields in these colonial regions appear to have been specially planned and laid out by the new settlers, often under the guidance of a person hired for the purpose—the *Lokatur* (Aubin 1966, 462; Mayhew 1973, 47, Abel 1978a, 36; also see chap. 2). They often took a highly regular form. We know much about them, not from customals, as in the west, but by the deed of foundation, the *Handfeste*. All *Handfesten* were based on the German town law of Kulm, on the River Vistula south of Danzig (Du Boulay 1983, 176). In all these new settlements communal use of land was much less prevalent than in old Germany of the southwest (Rösener 1992, 152).

Two main village forms were adopted: the *Strassendorf* (street village) and the *Angerdorf* (green village). These resembled villages in old Germany (southwest) in that they were compact villages surrounded by open fields. In addition, as in villages in the west, they usually were fenced, for defensive purposes. Instead of being concentrated in a central compact village, however, houses of the village were typically aligned along a road (street village) or along the sides of the rectangular village green (green village). Each house had at least some private fields right behind it. As in the west, each village also was typically associated with three open fields, where each field had one or more *Gewänne* (furlongs), and each *Hufe* or holding had strips in each *Gewänne* (Aubin 1966, 464).

Yet this open field system differed in significant ways from the communal open field system of the southwest. First, the open arable fields of the village were laid out more regularly, in fewer and larger strips. Each individual holding was larger than in the west and ranged from about 24 hectares to about 33 hectares (59 to 82 acres) or more (Abel 1978a, 77). Partly because of the size of each strip, there was a tendency for a consolidation of each cultivator's landholdings in the open fields (Barraclough 1962, 276). Often this resulted in *Gelänge* fields, in which the strips were consolidated in a large block and the farmhouse was connected directly with its land (Huppertz 1939, 126; Aubin 1966, 465). This type became more common as colonization progressed eastward. Such *Gelänge* fields were farmed entirely on an individual basis. Second, there was usually no appreciable area of common land (*Allmende*), other than a small village green. Communal grazing of several villages on wasteland, which was common in the west, was unknown in the east (Aubin 1966, 469).

Extreme variants of this row village type were the *Waldhufen, Hagenhufen,* or *Marschhufen* villages, in which the farmhouse was located in the middle of farmland, which extended in a long strip on either side of the farmhouse (Huppertz 1939, 126; Aubin 1966, 465; Mayhew 1973, 73–77). Here the farm contained all its own land, meadows, pasture, and arable land as a self-contained unit. As with *Gelänge* fields, each farmer was free to farm his or her own long strip of land as he wished (Barraclough 1962, 276; Pounds 1990, 168). These systems were found particularly in eastern Germany in Silesia, Bohemia, the Erz Mountains to the north and northwest of Bohemia, parts of southern Saxony, the mouth of the Weser and the Elbe, the North Sea marshes, in Brandenburg, and around the Vistula River in East Prussia (Huppertz 1939, 126). This type also could be found in some newly settled places in the West—in the forest of Thuringia, for example.

Another types of settlement was the small defensive village called a *Rundling*. *Rundling*, like the *Weiler* (hamlets), were quite small; they usually had less than a dozen houses in total. A *Rundling* was similar to a small green village, in which houses were tightly arranged around a small open space, or green. *Rundling* villages were concentrated in a north to south line along what had been the boundary between east and west Germany. These were the districts most fought over as Germans moved east (Aubin 1966, 463). The mostly closed fields spread out in a fan-shaped form on all sides of the central village and typically were not farmed in common (Huppertz 1939, 125).

Village government associations grew up in the newly colonized areas from the twelfth century. Unlike in the southwest, however, their functions were likely to be primarily legal and administrative rather than economic, such that most peasants were free to cultivate their own land as they wished (Pounds 1990, 168). In these regions there were few commons to supervise. Village governing bodies organized the daily life of all members and helped to maintain peace by enforcing law and order on everyone living within the boundaries of the village (Rösener 1992, 156–57). Most villages made up a minor judicial area and a separate parish (Aubin 1966, 469). Toward the end of the Middle Ages and in early modern times, however, the position of the village mayor and of the rural community in general deteriorated east of the Elbe and Saale. The decline of their power and independence was a result of the so-called refeudalization of this area.

The far south and the northwest were regions of many hamlets and independent farms. Like the *Rundling*, *Weiler* (hamlet) and *Einzelhöfe* (independent, isolated farms) were characterized by very few common rights in land. Hamlets were found in the south and northwest: in Westphalia, in the Upper Palatinate, parts of Württemberg, and parts of Bavaria (Huppertz 1939, 124; Du Boulay 1983, 170). In hamlets the landholdings of each peasant often were entirely enclosed or else only distributed in a few sections of the village land. Regions of scattered independent farmsteads were located in the northwest (including Westphalia and Holstein) and the far south as well as in East Prussia (Du Boulay 1983, 170). As in eastern Germany, communal and manorial control of economic life was minimal in these regions.

## Peasant Freedom in Regions of Less-Communal Open Fields and Enclosures

As in England, areas of few common rights were also often areas of a large free peasantry and limited manorial control in the late medieval period.

These areas included Westphalia (the northwest), part of Thuringia (central Germany), the North Sea coast, and Prussia (Moeller 1977, 30). In northwest Germany manorial control was minimal and villages were governed by cooperative peasant associations called *Bauerschaften* (Rösener 1992, 155; Scribner 1996, 306), under the supervision of a peasant master and a peasant judge. Members had to be holders of full-size holdings; usually, they farmed the oldest fields of the developed farmland in the area. The peasant court (*Burgericht*), known since the twelfth century, heard disputes between neighbors (although not economic grievances concerning land sales and transfers). In the area between the Weser and the Elbe (north central Germany) the *Bauerschaft* was usually an organization concerned with feuds and defense. It was the lowest-level unit in military levies (Rösener 1992, 156). Another community institution in such areas was the *Mark,* whose members were usually the owners of full-size peasant farms. Members of the *Mark* also belonged to both the *Bauerschaft* and (sometimes) to certain lordships with their respective courts.

In areas without manorial or princely control in addition to village policing, peasant feuds were common. Feuds and vendettas in a number of free peasant communities along the North Sea coast are known to have continued without any apparent interruption from the early to the late Middle Ages. Regions such as Frisia and the marshes north of the lower Elbe retained their frontier style of armed self defense and peasant law into the early modern period (Rösener 1992, 174 ).

In the east the close association between manorial and peasant economies that characterized the open fields of the west was absent. Many villages had no primary lord or manor (Barraclough 1962, 276; Pounds 1990, 168). On initial settlement the *Schulze,* or mayor,[3] was granted jurisdiction. The village looked to him for justice in all but the gravest matters. Members paid him their rents and in theory received supervision of their services. Typically, labor services were absent. There was also less mixing of the lands of lords, knights (military men), and peasants. Knights' and lords' demesne lands were often separate from peasant holdings. This situation was the rule in Mecklenburg and East Prussia, although intermixture predominated in East Holstein and was known in the New Mark (Aubin 1966, 477). Furthermore, demesnes of knights and lords were little different in size to those of the peasantry: The knight was the "peasant's neighbor" rather than his lord (Barraclough 1962, 278; Hagen 1985, 84). According to the land register of the *Mark* of Brandenburg from the year 1375, knights' farms were not much larger than large peasant farms. The majority were from 2 to 4 *Hufen.* According to one source, thirty-seven peasants had as many Hufen as the knights. The difference was in the extremes: there were no peasant farms over 40 hectares (99 acres) and no knights' farms under 4 hectares (10 acres). Knights' farms also differed from peasants farms' because they typically were free from any customary dues and service and had various privileges and legal rights (Barraclough 1962, 278; Abel 1978a, 77). Peasants owed their lords rents and sometimes services, but these tended to be low, at least initially (e.g., in Brandenburg [see Hagen 1985, 85]).

In the east peasant freedom was in part a result of clearing. By agreeing to clear and settle formerly wilderness areas of central and eastern Germany, the peasantry were able to obtain very favorable terms, low rents, secure property rights, and autonomy. Thus, many peasants were able to improve substantially their situation by settling in colonial regions. There was even a saying for it: "Rodung macht frei" (Clearing makes you free).

Yet another important reason for the freedom of the peasantry of the east and central Germany was the traditions many settlers brought with them. As we saw in chapter 2, the majority of settlers came not from the heavily manorialized southwest of Germany but from densely populated regions of northwestern Germany, the Low Countries, Westphalia, and eastern Saxony. As Rösener notes:

> The new villages in the east of Germany took as their model the legal rights of an independent peasantry which had been established in assarted areas west of the Elbe and in particular in the Dutch settlements along the marshes of the North Sea and its rivers. The strong participation of Flemish and Dutch peasants in the stream of east German settlement, especially in the Altmark, Mark Brandenburg and Saxony, meant that the legal rights of the settlers were determined by the long standing experience of these groups, and in some places there was even explicit mention of *ius fladricum* (Flemish law). The legal position of many of these settlers was characterized by minimal ties to the manor, better property rights and fewer feudal obligations than was the case elsewhere. (1992, 40; see also van Houtte 1977, 8)

The office of *Schulze,* or village mayor, characteristic of clearance settlements, may have been of Dutch origin. This Flemish and Dutch model served for centuries as a model for villages in the north and east of Germany. All were characterized by a large degree of self-administration and far-reaching autonomy (Rösener 1992, 156, 157).

In short, communal agricultural systems were located mostly in the central and southwestern parts of Germany. These were also the most heavily manorialized regions of Germany, where the majority of peasants

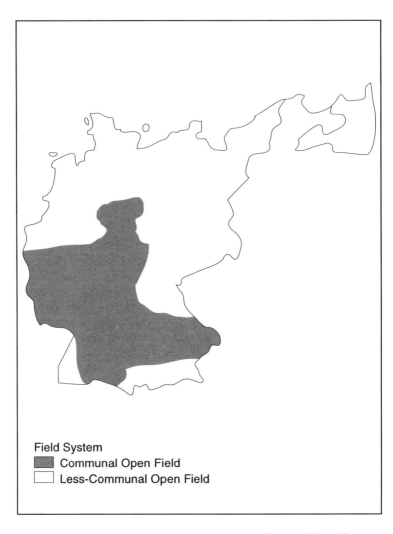

Field System

■ Communal Open Field

□ Less-Communal Open Field

Map 14. Field systems in the German lands. (Adapted from Huppertz 1939.)

were unfree. Areas of predominantly individual rights to land were concentrated in the east, northwest, north, and far south of Germany (see map 14).[4] In the late medieval period these were also regions where manorial control was light and the majority of the peasantry were free, a situation that in the east was a legacy of the colonial past.

## The Regional Pattern of Agrarian Change in Late Medieval and Early Modern Germany

### Late Medieval Period

The central hypothesis, from chapter 3, is that agricultural development is most likely in regions of less-communal farming systems. I also hypothesized that agricultural development is most likely in regions with state support for property rights, little political oppression, a dense population, or access to markets. In Germany, as in France, these factors interacted to produce complex regional outcomes. Nevertheless, there is support for the central hypothesis. Western Germany, like northern France, had the richest soil, was the most densely populated region of Germany, and had the greatest access to urban markets. Yet within western Germany it was less-communal areas to the north that were the most agriculturally productive and innovative throughout the late medieval and early modern periods. Eastern Germany lacked many advantages of the west; it was remote, sparsely populated, and the soil is sandy and poor. Nevertheless, less-communal regions of eastern Germany, such as Mecklenburg and Pomerania, and areas along the North Sea coast were productive agricultural regions at an early date.

Given its advantages in terms of population, ecology, and market access, we might expect that agricultural development and agrarian change would occur first in the west rather than the east. Evidence suggests that it did. In all of the west there was substantial production for the market in the late medieval period. This promoted improvement in agricultural production in both north and south. Within the west, however, both improvements in agricultural productivity and agrarian change predominated in less-communal regions. The most productive and innovative regions of late medieval Germany were the less-communal regions of the northwest and the lower Rhineland (Robisheaux 1994, 83; Scott 1996, 8). Here there was an intensive culture of cereals and other crops using innovative techniques. In this region, already by the thirteenth century fodder crops, peas, and lentils were being sown on the fallow. Abel gives two examples from different monasteries in Cologne for 1251 and 1277 (1978a,

97). That was the start of the "improved" three-course rotation that was to make such great advances in the sixteenth and eighteenth centuries. The benefit to be derived from combined arable and pastoral husbandry was discovered early here. While animals provided manure for soil and so improved yields, fodder crops provided food for animals.

Constant cultivation of fields also was not unknown in this area at this time. The so-called one-field system (*Einfeldwirtschaft*) was a regional peculiarity. Under this system a single crop was cultivated year after year on the same field, using intensive techniques (extensive manuring, weeding, etc.) to keep the soil fertile. The northwest of Germany was known also for its continuous cultivation of rye in a special type of field, the *Eschboden* (Abel 1978a, 87; Rösener 1992, 128).[5] A number of villages in this region continued to use the technique until the introduction of artificial fertilizer in the nineteenth century (Mayhew 1973, 20; Rösener 1992, 128–29). The system was found as far east as Mecklenburg (Mayhew 1973, 85; Abel 1978a, 87) and as far west as the eastern Netherlands. As in eastern England at the same time, horses were in widespread use in these northwestern regions and were a sign of a prosperous peasant economy (Rösener 1992, 113). Specialized crops also were grown. In some regions hops were an important crop. For example, as early as the end of the thirteenth century, the town of Lübeck on the Baltic coast let out farmland on the provision that every year a certain amount of it was to be planted with hops (Abel 1978b, 72). There was also substantial pasture farming in this area. Frisian marshes were particularly famous for their cattle, which provided not only meat but also butter, milk, and cheese (Rösener 1992, 134).

The same market demands that promoted agricultural production in the northwest also promoted production in the communal regions of southwest Germany. Outside of the common fields, in gardens and other pieces of private land, agricultural productivity could be high. As in parts of northern France, gardens produced considerable yields of vegetables (cabbage, beets); hops, flax, and hemp (for textile making); and madder and woad (for dying) for the market. Wine production also became one of the most important sectors of the peasant economy along the Rivers Rhine, Moselle, Neckar, and Maine. Vines and industrial crops were grown using intensive, horticultural techniques. It is important to note, however, that (as in northern France) viticulture occurred in private gardens or other pieces of land *outside* of the communal field system and was "subject to the vine and vineyard law, which permitted the walling in of the vineyard grounds, the necessary nursing and harvest work, and the side-use of the viticulture land for grass, vegetables and fruit" (Abel 1978a, 97, 98).

Apart from private gardens and vineyards, communal agricultural systems hindered productivity and innovation in southwestern Germany. As in northern France, a monoculture of grain prevailed on the vast open fields (which occupied most of the land), on which there was little use of intensive agricultural techniques. In fact, in regions of viticulture a two-field rotation (in which half the land sits fallow each year) persisted through the spread of the three-field rotation in neighboring areas (Abel 1978a, 89; Rösener 1992, 119). It has even been argued that the rise of viti-culture encouraged the introduction of a two-field system in some areas, as tillage was succeeded by coppicing to provide tanbark and vine props for the vineyards (Scott 1996, 8). In this region the most common cereal crop was spelt (common wheat) for subsistence use (Sabean 1990, 1; Rösener 1992, 127), a hardy and frost-resistant cereal that dates back to the early Middle Ages (Robisheaux 1989, 25). Peasants clearly neglected grain fields to put their energies in their gardens and vineyards. As a result of such neglect, grain yields were low, and little was produced for export (Abel 1978a, 89; Rösener 1992, 119). Private garden land and vineyard became much more valuable than communal land. For example, in southwestern Germany in the later Middle Ages an acre of vineyard cost perhaps four times that of an acre of farmland (Abel 1978a, 129). In these regions oxen remained the typical draft animal. Unlike in northwestern Germany, there was no happy combination of arable and pasture farming. Cattle were few, as it was difficult to keep them through the winter given the scarcity of fod-der (Pounds 1990, 232).

Given its disadvantages, in terms of remoteness from major markets, poor soil, and low level of population, we might expect there to be little agricultural development and change in eastern Germany at this time. Yet this was not the case. In contrast to the agriculture of the communal southwest, the less-communal regions of eastern Germany produced a great surplus of grain in the late medieval period. By the end of the thir-teenth century all German lands east of the Elbe were major grain-pro-ducing regions (Mayhew 1973, 137; *Rand McNally Atlas of World History,* 28). Flemish towns and Friesland were importing grain from these regions before the end of the thirteenth century (Abel 1978b, 20). From the start of the thirteenth century Flemings imported grain from Lower Saxony and the Old Mark of Brandenburg through Hamburg (van Houtte 1977, 44). Since most farmers in these areas at this time were free peasants, this was peasant, not estate, production. There was, however, some estate agricul-ture in the region. The estates of the Teutonic order in East Prussia partic-ularly were oriented to producing grain for export in the late thirteenth and fourteenth centuries. The satires of Little Lucidarius, which date to the end of the thirteenth century, made fun of the Teutonic knights by picturing them at court discussing the price of wheat, cheese, eggs, and sucking pigs, the milk yield of their cows, or the falling off of their harvests (Abel 1978b, 6).

Information on yields for this period is scarce, so it is difficult to ascertain productivity fully at this early time. In eastern regions agricultural techniques were not as intensive as they were further west. The three-course rotation, leaving a third of the land fallow each year, was introduced in the late medieval period and was widespread by the fourteenth century (Mayhew 1973, 85; Pounds 1990, 335). There were, however, places of more intensive agriculture. More intensive forms of cultivation on the *Esch* were found in Mecklenburg; and a very intensive form of four-field system also was found in parts of Mecklenburg and Pomerania (Mayhew 1973, 85; Abel 1978a, 88). As in northwest Germany, horses had replaced cattle as the predominant draft animals in these regions by the thirteenth century. In southern Germany, by contrast, peasants continued to use oxen as draft animals in plowing even after the high Middle Ages (Rösener 1992, 113).

In sum, by the fourteenth century flexible farming systems and a comparatively free peasantry in the northwest promoted a productive agriculture and use of intensive methods of cultivation. In the southwest response to market demand was inhibited by the fact that so much of the land was incorporated into communal agricultural systems, although productivity was high in private gardens and vineyards. The less-communal east lagged behind the west in general in the adoption of intensive agricultural methods but was a major cereal producer by the thirteenth century, despite its poor natural endowments and remote location.

### Change after the Fourteenth Century

As everywhere in Europe, the middle of the fourteenth century saw a sharp decline in population levels throughout Germany. In 1348 and 1349 plague spread through all Germany. Plague did little, however, to alter the distribution of the population, which remained concentrated in western Germany. Cities remained comparatively small, although some grew over the late medieval period, notably Lübeck and Danzig—both deeply involved in the expanding Baltic trade (Pounds 1990, 193).

The Hanseatic League was formed at this time to deal with problems facing the east-west trade in grain and other commodities (wood, fur, honey; grain was not yet their major concern) (Yun 1994, 114–15). In 1356 representatives of a large number of north German and Baltic cities formed the Hanse of cities. This was really a union of three earlier, regional Hansas (Munro 1994). Its purposes were to obtain privileges and rights of passage through the Danish sound, to suppress piracy within the

Baltic, and to maintain secure places for Hanse merchandise in Flanders, England, and Russia. Membership in the Hanse extended from the lower Rhineland to Riga and Reval in the eastern Baltic and included not only the many small port cities of the Baltic but also a large number in Westphalia and lower Saxony. Those cities were members that sent representatives to the irregular meetings of their Hansetag, or Parliament. The formal head of the League was Lübeck. It was the natural leader of the Hanseatic League, as it dominated not only the salt trade but also the Baltic herring fisheries and the chief access routes between the Baltic and North Seas (Munro 1994, 161). The alliance, which remained informal, with the number of its members fluctuating between seventy and eighty, maintained its control over Baltic trade throughout the fourteenth and early fifteenth centuries (Brady 1996, 271).

As in other countries, the demographic decline of the mid-fourteenth century led to a decline in wheat prices, desertion of villages, and contraction of farming lands in many parts of Germany. As in England, the crisis may have afflicted communal regions somewhat more than less-communal regions. Village desertion was particularly common in central and southwestern Germany (Abel 1978b, 82), while it was often insignificant in the less-communal northwest. In much of eastern Germany the crisis of the mid-fourteenth century also appears to have been less severe (Yun 1994, 114–15).

As in France, contraction of cereal growing in the later fourteenth and fifteenth centuries led to greater crop specialization in most places in Germany. Cultivation of the grape, fruit, and industrial crops expanded, often on land that had been used for arable crops (Mayhew 1973, 102; Abel 1978a, 129; Yun 1994, 116). The great demand for wine in fifteenth-century Germany promoted viticulture especially (Robisheaux 1989, 27). Along the lower Rhine Valley vineyards spread as far as Xanten. Wine-growing reached north as far as Schleswig-Holstein. In the east vineyards appeared along the Oder and Vistula, around Torun, Tapian, Rastenburg, and Königsberg in East Prussia (Abel 1978b, 72). Cattle raising for meat and milk in north Germany also expanded at this time (Yun 1994, 116). Hop growing began to develop in Bavaria and further north, around Rostock, Kiel, and Cologne. In the southwest madder was grown in the Speyer district, and the flax of the Moselle region became famous. Another interesting development was the frequent construction of fish ponds at this time. The growing of specialized crops occurred in all regions, both communal and less communal, although viticulture spread most strongly in the communal regions of the southwest, mostly because this more southerly region was the most favorable ecology for vine growing (Abel 1978a, 130, 131, 129). Yet, in communal regions, once again, cultivation of these crops was confined to land outside the village field system. As before, cereal agriculture on the common fields often was neglected. It has been estimated that subsistence crises in southern Germany occurred every eleven years or so in the fifteenth century (Robisheaux 1989, 43).

The growing of specialized crops in Germany at this time was stimulated by the simultaneous growth of trade. Besides its involvement in the Baltic trade, Germany lay at the heart of two trade corridors that began to grow in importance, one from east to west and one from north to south following the Rhine Valley. Along the east-west route large numbers of cattle were driven from Hungary and Galicia and other parts of eastern Europe (Abel 1978a, 178; Samsonowicz and Maczak 1985, 18). Along the north-south route the traffic of textiles from Flanders and England along the Rhine grew. At the same time, in addition to an older linen industry, towns in the south of Germany began to develop a new textile industry producing fustians (see later discussion; also Munro 1994, 159). Augsburg and Nuremberg grew into important manufacturing centers based on metallurgy and fustian weaving. The growth of this trade promoted the development of several important new fairs in the fifteenth century, in addition to those at Nördlingen and Frankfurt in Germany. These included new fairs at Nuremberg, Vienna, and Krakow.

In the Baltic the Hanse continued its trade, but by the fifteenth century its control of Baltic trade was declining. Territorial states, particularly Sweden, Russia, and Poland, increased their power over Hanseatic cities, and trade itself suffered from war, which was more or less continuous, in the eastern Baltic region. Member cities declined in number until only a few small towns of the Mecklenburg coast remained obedient to Lübeck (Kirby 1990, 6). Finally, the Dutch and English began to intrude into what had previously been the closed trading sphere of the German Hanse (Pounds 1990, 206). The Hanse, however, was by no means a completely spent force. Its ships still sold Baltic wood, wheat, and dried and salted fish at Antwerp in the sixteenth century (Kirby 1990, 7; Yun 1994, 127).

## Sixteenth Century

The population of Germany only recovered fully by the early sixteenth century, an economic boom time throughout western Europe. In western and eastern Germany the demand of urban markets of the west helped to stimulate economic growth (Samsonowicz and Maczak 1985, 12; Yun 1994, 134). Not only did trade with the west develop, but internal trade within eastern Europe in general expanded, as demonstrated by the continued proliferation of regional fairs (Topolski 1985, 132). There was rapid population growth in both east and west at this time, such that the population of Germany may have reached fifteen million before the Thirty

Years' War (1618–48 [Pounds 1990, 264]). Population remained concentrated in western Germany, along the length of the Rhine Valley, and in south Germany; while it was less so in Thuringia, Saxony, and the northwest; and least east of the Elbe (Holborn 1959, 37).

Once again, agrarian development followed a regional pattern. It was most outstanding in the less-communal northwest. Northwestern Germany increased its production of cattle and dairy products (Abel 1978a, 181). Schleswig-Holstein began to establish a reputation for breeding horses (Mead 1981, 60). Wealthier peasants of Ditmarsch (at the mouth of the Elbe) became active in the livestock trade, fattening cattle in their meadows and exporting them to Holland and the East Frisian ports. Alongside the export of oxen and other livestock, an intensive dairy farming industry was developing in Ditmarsch in the marshlands of the North Sea coast and around the bay of Kiel. Butter and cheese were sent from there in great quantities to Amsterdam and Groningen as well as to Hamburg, Bremen, and further south into Germany (Kirby 1990, 159). The dairy trade was particularly important to peasants of Frisia and Ditmarsch. Frisian cattle were known at this time. In Frisia the dairy trade was the main cash product of the region (Abel 1978b, 113).

Production of cattle and animal products was based on permanent pastures provided by marshlands bordering the North Sea coast and western shores of the Baltic. As in earlier periods, it developed side by side with intensive farming methods (Scott 1996, 2). Convertible husbandry was introduced into this region at this time. The peasants of Ditmarsch developed an advanced system of convertible husbandry, in which land enriched by four years of grazing was used for cereal growing for two or three years (Kirby 1990, 20). On the west coast of Schleswig-Holstein a similar type of convertible husbandry called the enclosure system (*Koppelwirtschaft*) gained ground. Such methods enabled farmers to grow more corn to the acre because dung from grazing beasts was not wasted, while at the same time they improved and intensified stock raising. Fodder crops were becoming common in the area: rape, beans, peas, and vetches were all used as fodder crops. New crops such as lupine and lucerne were also used. There was increased use of fertilizer, complex crop rotations, the abandonment of fallow, and all the other indications of an advanced, intensive agriculture (Abel 1978a, 174–75; Scott 1996, 8). In these areas, notably the middle and lower Rhine, the coastal strip of Frisia and western Holstein (Eiderstedt, Ditmarsch), there were also changes in the nature of peasant land tenure. Revocable leases for fixed terms became common by 1500 (Scott 1996, 9) and were an indication of the commercialization of agriculture.

As a result of these developments, there was widespread prosperity among both large and small farmers in northwest Germany at this time (Mayhew 1973, 119). Wood carvings in churches of Ditmarsch and the two-storied brick country houses the farmers built themselves to this day bear witness to the standard of living farmers were able to enjoy. There is an old saying that in the countryside of Eiderstedt, just north of Ditmarsch, gold and silver were more common than iron and brass (Abel 1978b, 130; Kirby 1990, 20).

Southwest Germany also participated in the increase in production for the market. The Rhineland, along with Gascony and Burgundy, continued to supply all of northern Europe with wine. Yet wine prices were beginning to decline in Germany by the early sixteenth century (Robisheaux 1989, 27), and viticulture began to disappear from less-favorable growing areas, such as further north along the Rhine around Cologne (Pounds 1990, 231).

By the early seventeenth century the area devoted to viticulture was shrinking even in southwestern Germany. Rising grain prices in the later sixteenth century instead promoted the production of cereals, and peasants with the larger farms were able to take advantage of the high grain prices. Their prosperity was reflected, as in the northwest, in the size and comfort of their houses (Abel 1978a, 199). Prosperity was limited, however, to a small elite of villagers, no more than 5 or 10 percent of all households (c. 1581 [Robisheaux 1989, 153]). The majority of villagers did not participate in this new prosperity. In general, not enough cereal was produced locally for local needs. Robisheaux shows that in the district of Langenburg, in the county of Hohenlohe in southern Germany, in 1605 about half of all households could not produce enough grain to meet their own needs (1989, 155). The cities of the southern Rhineland were provisioned partly with grain was shipped from the East and then transported by river (Pounds 1990, 247). In the southwest agriculture was not known for innovative methods. It is perhaps telling that all German agricultural writers of the day were from regions outside of the communal southwest: Conrad Heresbach was a learned jurist and counsel of the duke of Cleve (on the lower Rhine); Martin Grosser was a parson in Silesia (in eastern Germany); and the most famous of them all, Johann Coler, was a parson who came from Silesia but lived a long time in Saxony and Brandenburg and died in Mecklenburg (Abel 1978a, 171).

In the less-communal east, in general, yields were much lower than in the northwest (Slicher van Bath 1963a, 15; for wheat, see 43). Cereal growing developed and prospered, however, along the whole north coast from Kiel to Lübeck, Stettin, and Danzig, up to Riga and far inland (Abel 1978b, 108). At this time some innovative techniques were introduced in the region. The beginning of a multicourse rotation also was taking hold on Fehmarn and inland of Lübeck. With this system the fallow was becomingly increasingly more uncommon. Further south, however, in part of Poland, Bohemia, Silesia, Saxony, and Lusatia the three-field fallow system remained the norm (Żytkowicz 1985, 69). East of this grain-growing region was a pastoral region that supplied central and western Germany with the produce of its animal husbandry, mostly cattle and sheep. This region included parts of Poland, Bohemia, Hungary, the Ukraine, Moldavia, and Wallachia. The demand for beef in many west German towns was supplied largely by oxen from Bohemia and other parts of eastern Europe. For example, 50,000 to 60,000 oxen were exported annually from Hungary to Vienna and south Germany in the second half of the sixteenth century until the Thirty Years' War (Topolski 1985, 138; Scott 1996, 2).

In sum, by the sixteenth century, while production for the market increased all over Germany, advanced agricultural practices (growing of fodder crops, fertilization, complex rotations) were most common along the lower Rhine and along the northern coasts to the Prussian-Polish east. These regions had in common access to the major markets of the west; they were also regions of less-communal agricultural systems.

## The "Refeudalization" of Eastern Germany

In eastern Germany, however, the sixteenth-century boom gave impetus to a trend that had already begun in the fifteenth century, the so-called refeudalization[6] of much of the area east of the Elbe. This had begun with the recession of the fifteenth century, although sometimes before this. The recession had weakened territorial rulers, and local lords were able to exploit this weakness to obtain jurisdictional rights over the peasantry (Carsten 1954, 94).

At first, only social and legal freedoms of the peasantry were threatened. Eventually, however, their economic freedom was curtailed also. In the sixteenth century the rising value of agricultural commodities led lords to expand direct farming of the demesne. To obtain cheap labor they began to use their legal rights over the peasantry to demand labor services. Thus, a large proportion of what had begun as one of the freest peasantries in Europe became obliged to labor like serfs on commercial estates producing grain for the world market. For example, in fifteenth-century Brandenburg demesne farms of the nobility were small. Slowly nobles were able to use their positions as both manorial and judicial lords to extend manorial rights over the peasantry, reduce their personal freedom, increase their labor obligations, and convert hereditary tenures into much less advantageous ones. Nobles also increased their landholdings at the expense of the peasantry. By the sixteenth century a landowning aristocracy farming very large estates had emerged in Brandenburg. In the last quarter of the sixteenth and the first of the seventeenth centuries the number of *Hufen* held in demesne in Brandenburg increased from 3,236.5 to 4,885.5, or by about 50 percent, while the number of peasant *Hufen* decreased from 21,889.5 to 20,240.5, or by 8 percent (Carsten 1954, 158).[7] At the same time the position of the village mayor and of the rural community in general deteriorated. This process culminated in the seventeenth and eighteenth centuries in a new kind of manorial system (*Gutscherrschaft*) in eastern Germany, characterized by large estates farmed by *corvée* labor, as opposed to *Grundherrschaft,* in which duties from tenants are collected mainly in rents.

The refeudalization of eastern Germany vastly reduced numbers of free peasants in this region, but peasants still farmed the majority of the land (Carsten 1954, 158; Abel 1978a, 224). For example, Hagen notes that for the Middle Mark of Brandenburg a 1624 census shows that the peasantry tilled about 77 percent of the 26,000 *Hufen* covered by the census (Hagen 1985, 108). In the Electorate of Prussia at the end of the eighteenth century (when the manorial system was at its most developed) state officials and nobles farmed only one-fifth and peasants four-fifths of the arable land (Berthold 1963; qtd. in Abel 1978a, 224). Furthermore, the emerging nobility of eastern Germany were most unlike their counterparts in other parts of Europe. Contrary to west German landowners, aristocratic landowners east of the Elbe always had been involved directly in farming the land themselves (Abel 1978b, 132; von Thadden 1987, 25). During the sixteenth-century price revolution, when farming grew more profitable, these landowners devoted themselves more than ever to cultivating their own land. Most were not particularly wealthy, and many appear to have been not much more than well-off free peasants (Carsten 1954, 164; Anderson 1974, 262; Melton 1988, 56). Hagen writes that, although there were real profits to be had from Junker manorial enterprises, production costs were very high (1985, 113; 1989, 308).

In general, in the east, where refeudalization was successful, many peasants were reduced to a level not much better than serfs. Of these people the Pomeranian chronicler Thomas Kantzow wrote in the 1530s that:

> They have no rights in their farms and must render their lords as much service as he demands. Sometimes these labours leave them no time for their own work, and so they grow poor and flee away. These same peasants have a saying that they "serve only six days a week; on the seventh they carry letters." Such farmers are no better than bondsmen, for their lords can send them away at will, but if the farmer or his children want to move elsewhere against their lord's

wishes, he can fetch them back as his own bondsmen. . . . And the children of this same peasant, whether sons or daughters, may not move away from the estate farms. It is not enough that their father's farm is occupied, but they must accept and cultivate some deserted holding of the lord's choice. So many flee or move secretly away that many a farm is left empty, and the owner must arrange for it to be occupied by another peasant. If the fugitive has left nothing behind to stock the farm, the landlord had to provide the new occupant with horses, cows, pigs, carts, plough, seed and other things, and perhaps forego his interest for a few years, until the place is in working order again. Then the new man and his children become as much his bondsmen as the other peasants. If he or his family move away, even with the lord's permission, they must leave behind them everything that was supplied at the beginning or its equivalent. And they may be sent away at the lightest pretext, or may flee away of their own accord. (Qtd. in Abel 1978b, 131)

Hagen has argued that the peasantry were not ruined by the increase in labor services and the tightening of manorial control to the extent implied by this passage. In Brandenburg, for example, he shows that increased labor services were accompanied by the freezing or lowering of rents in cash or kind. That is, there was some compensation for the increase in labor services, and he argues that most peasants found retaining their farms worth the increase in labor services they were now required to provide (Hagen 1985, 83, 116). In other areas the peasantry retained a fair degree of their former autonomy, as in the villages of East Pomerania in the sixteenth century. Here local government was in the hands of the peasant elite, in addition to the *Schulzen,* or mayors, and the *Schöppenbank,* which constituted the local court. This court met every quarter and dealt with questions of property and inheritance as well as the maintenance of order. These authorities maintained streets and bridges, built dams, provided a firefighting service, and even used funds to defend the village's privileges against noble impositions. They also arranged for the upkeep of priests and teachers. The relative absence of feudal lords and the maintenance of a strong peasant community committed to preserving its rights and liberties gave the peasantry a control over their own affairs not dissimilar to that enjoyed by the free peasantry of Ditmarsch (Abel 1978b, 131; Kirby 1990, 32). They also enjoyed a similar degree of affluence. The frequency with which sumptuary legislation was breached by the peasants of eastern Pomerania suggests that they were wealthy enough to buy forbidden velvet and satin (Kirby 1990, 159).

The decline in the legal position and freedoms of the peasant class in eastern Germany may have contributed to the decline of agricultural productivity in this area (Topolski 1985, 130). Intensive techniques such as convertible husbandry saw no further development in this region after this time, although the region continued to produce a large quantity of grain for export. Techniques remained primitive. The expansion of demesne estates was not accompanied by a rise in productivity. If anything, levels of output declined (at least in the seventeenth century [see Kirby 1990, 22]). Customs receipts on grain exports by the Brandenburg Junkers suggest a faltering of grain production for export between the years 1584 and 1624 (Hagen 1989, 313). Cereal yields throughout the Baltic region were poor. The yield in much of eastern Europe was around 3 to 1 (all grain [Kirby 1990, 21; Pounds 1990, 279]). Yields in the east tended to be higher on the remaining peasant farms. For example, in seventeenth century Estonia grain yields appear to have been higher on the poorer soils of north Estonia (an area of peasant agriculture) than in the south (an area of large estates) (Kirby 1990, 248).

Furthermore, despite manorialization, much of the total amount of grain produced in the East still came from peasant farms. For example, on the Oxenstierna estates in Livonia revenue from the peasantry was almost four times as great as that from the demesne in the period 1624–54 (Kirby 1990, 248). The same was true in Poland and Bohemia, where the peasantry were the principal grain producers for the market, at least until the late seventeenth century (Żytkowicz 1985, 69, 72). In east Germany, even where the landed nobility had large and well-managed enterprises, such as the jurisdiction of Tapiau in east Prussia, only scarcely half (45 percent) of the average grain revenue of the jurisdiction during the years 1550 to 1696 consisted of the harvest of the manorial proprietary enterprises. The remainder came from the grain tax of independent peasants (26 percent), mill dues (14 percent), and other taxes (Abel 1978a, 214).

Decreases in the productivity of grain production may have helped promote the seventeenth-century decline in the grain trade, as it reduced the competitiveness of Baltic grain on the western markets. Furthermore, cultivation of new crops such as rice and maize in southern Europe and improved agricultural methods increased self-sufficiency in western Europe and made it less dependent on Baltic grain (Samsonowicz and Maczak 1985, 22; Kirby 1990, 229–30). The average volume of grain shipped to Dutch ports in the first half of the eighteenth century was less than half of what it had been a hundred years previously. Shipments of grain from Danzig never again equaled those of the early seventeenth century, where as many as a hundred thousand lasts of rye and wheat may have been shipped to the west (Kirby 1990, 229–30).

In southwest Germany a similar tightening of manorial control occurred in the sixteenth century (Blickle 1981, 46). Many lords tried to strengthen ties of personal lordship over their peasants to prevent them from moving elsewhere (Du Boulay 1983, 181; Robisheaux 1989, 28, 35; Fulbrook 1990; Blickle 1992, 45). They also tried to compensate for their loss of income by demanding heavier dues. All of this helped provoke peasant unrest and, finally, the Peasants' War in 1525 (Blickle 1981, 188; Du Boulay 1983, 184; Robisheaux 1994, 86). Despite defeat of the peasants in the Peasants' War, in the long run refeudalization was less successful in the southwest than in eastern and central Germany. Feudal obligations and demands stayed far less onerous than they were in eastern Germany. Peasants were often able to obtain heritable land tenure and fixed and low customary rents, which, along with feudal ties, remained largely unchanged in this region until the eighteenth century (Du Boulay 1983, 178; Pounds 1990, 275; Robisheaux 1989, 66, 187; 1994, 82). In Württemberg, for example, serfdom and *corvée* labor were not abolished until 1836 (Sabean 1990, 47).

In the northwest of Germany, also, peasant freedom was suppressed somewhat during the sixteenth century. For example, in Schleswig-Holstein in 1524 the nobility were granted almost unlimited juridical rights over their peasants, whose right of appeal to Denmark was abolished. Peasants were not allowed to leave their holdings without the permission of their lord, who also could forbid them to marry (Kirby 1990, 43). In many places, however, the free peasantry managed to maintain many of its rights and autonomies throughout the early modern period (Rösener 1992). Notable among them were the peasants of Ditmarsch, who managed to defeat the heavily armored *Lansknechte* of King Hans of Denmark in 1500. They defended themselves in the Dutch fashion by cutting the dykes and flooding out the invaders (although they were finally subjugated and incorporated into the county of Holstein in 1559 [see Du Boulay 1983, 97]).

## Regional Differences in Farm Sizes

Refeudalization also had an impact on changes in farm sizes. A legacy of recent colonization in the east was that farm sizes were substantially larger east of the Elbe than they were in the west. The standard farm in the newly colonized areas consisted of two hides, or holdings, or approximately 33 hectares (about 82 acres) (Mayhew 1973, 5; Rösener 1992, 41). For example, from the land register (Landbuch) of the Mark of Brandenburg from the year 1375, of 154 old district peasant farms, 25.3 percent had many *Hufen,* 66.2 percent had a complete *Hufe,* and only 8.4 percent had a partial *Hufe*. That is, about 24 percent of all peasant farms were between 20 and 40 hectares, 70 percent between 5 and 20 hectares, and 6 percent between 0.5 and 5 hectares. According to the land register, knights' farms were not much larger than large peasant farms. The majority were from 2 to 4 *Hufen* (qtd. in Abel 1978a, 77).

Farms of both peasants and knights east of the Elbe, however, were at least twice the average farm size in the West (which was perhaps 20 or 30 acres). Population growth in the thirteenth century caused farm sizes to shrink in both east and west, but the regional discrepancy in farm sizes was maintained into the fifteenth century. The refeudalization of the sixteenth century was associated with a general increase in farm sizes in eastern Germany. Nobles expanded their demesnes at the expense of their peasants. Nobles typically farmed their estates directly using wage labor and the labor of their tenants and did not lease them out in many pieces to tenant farmers, as was the case in northern France and many other places in western Europe at that time. Thus, compared with northern France, farms in eastern Germany became very large. By the seventeenth century large estates were a feature of the agrarian economy east of the Elbe. Over half the estates in Mecklenburg, Pomerania, and parts of East Prussia were over 100 hectares (247 acres) in size, while the average size of a manorial demesne in Poland was even larger (Kirby 1990, 249).

Estate formation did not remain limited to regions east of the Elbe and Saale. In northwest Germany, also, kings and earls seized peasant farms during the sixteenth century, often to take advantage of the growing demand for pasture farming products. They farmed these estates themselves, mostly as smaller private enterprises but in several cases also as large enterprises. For example, the count of Oldenburg pursued cattle raising on a large scale, with around 4,000 hectares (about 10,000 acres) (Abel 1978a, 181). Unlike the great estates of the east, however, these great estates of west Germany later disintegrated when economic conditions changed (Abel 1978a, 168).

Laws were passed in the north and east that had the effect of keeping farms large. As manorial control strengthened in the later fifteenth century, lords and princes demanded impartible inheritance of holdings, and laws were passed requiring it. Impartibility, coupled with other regulations on inheritance, helped give rise to a relatively homogeneous and wealthy upper stratum (both nobles and peasants) possessing large and medium-size holdings in both the east and the northwest. Below the large farmers were many peasants possessing only little land or none at all who provided additional labor these farms required. In the southwest, in contrast, where refeudalization had been less successful, partible inheritance tended to prevail, and smallholdings were common (Sabean 1990, 15; Brady 1996, 263).

In this region state fiscal interests may have also fostered the establishment of partible inheritance. It was production of wine, vegetables, and industrial crops that created the most revenue not only for the peasants but for the state as well, and partible inheritance of arable land promoted these productive activities (Sabean 1990, 16). For example, in Württemberg a substantial part of state income was built on the tithes and excise taxes on wine (Sabean 1990, 43). Constant division of holdings over many generations meant that farms became very small in southwestern Germany—typically under 5 hectares (about 12 acres) in area (Mayhew 1973, 134; Fulbrook 1990, 82). This regional difference in farm sizes—small farms in the southwest, larger farms in the east and northwest—persisted into the twentieth century in Germany (Abel, 270; Pounds 1990, 332).

## Enclosure

There was no widespread enclosure movement in the early modern period in Germany as there was in England (Scott 1996, 9). Most German lands remained unenclosed. William Jacob, who toured Europe during the years following the Napoleonic Wars, wrote that in the "great part of France, a still . . . greater portion of Germany, and nearly the whole of Prussia. . . . The fields are almost universally unenclosed" (qtd. in Pounds 1990, 332).

Only in the northwest was enclosure extensive. Here permanent, enclosed pastures date back to the Middle Ages. In the sixteenth century on the west coast of Schleswig-Holstein a type of convertible husbandry involving enclosure (*Koppelwirtschaft*) became common. By the nineteenth century much of the northwest and some of the north coast region was enclosed (Pounds 1990, 335).

## Rural Industry

Germany never had a textile (or any other) industry to rival the English and Dutch cloth industries at their height. In Germany we see something of a regional pattern to the distribution of the cloth industry similar to that in England (and to a lesser extent France). The rural cloth industry was concentrated in less-communal regions. This, however, was not true of the more extensive urban manufacture, which was concentrated in the cities and towns of southwest Germany.

The linen industry in the towns of south Germany (notably Constance, St. Gallen, Lindau, and Kempten) dates at least to the early fourteenth century. By this date the region was known for its better-quality linen (Pounds 1990, 174; Scott 1996, 13). In the 1370s, when warfare disrupted the supply of Lombard fustians, various south German towns—

Ravensburg, Regensburg, Constance, Basel, Augsburg, and Ulm—converted their domestic linen industry to a fustians (cloth with a linen warp and a cotton weft) industry using cotton imported from the East, particularly Syria (Munro 1994, 159). Linen working also continued in this area, now more often in the smaller towns and villages. The major textile industry in Germany, the wool cloth industry, was also concentrated in the large towns of southern Germany. Only spinning was performed, part-time, by women in the countryside (Scott 1996, 17). By the mid-sixteenth century the leading textile cities of southern Germany began to switch to the lighter says and serges already common in Flanders.

In less-communal regions the textile industry was a rural industry. Linen manufacture was established on the plain of northern Europe and was especially important in Westphalia by the sixteenth century (Pounds 1990, 294; Scott 1996, 2, 15). By this time a third area that developed a linen industry of considerable size was Bohemia, Saxony (the Electorate), and neighboring Silesia, although it was widely considered inferior in quality to that produced in the west. Linen cloth was intended largely for export to the west, although some was sold locally or further east (Samsonowicz and Maczak 1985, 17). Woolen cloth was produced in Silesia, Bohemia-Moravia, and Greater Poland as well as in Saxony and Lusatia primarily for eastern markets. This woolen cloth, like the linen, was considered inferior in quality to western cloth. Polish customs registers from the 1580s indicate the importance of this eastern cloth industry. Estimates from these Polish registers give the annual import of Silesian textiles at 100,000 pieces; Saxon, Bohemian, and Moravian at a mere 13,000; and western, arriving by sea, at approximately 20,000 pieces (Samsonowicz and Maczak 1985, 17–18).

In addition to the cloth industry the metal industry was important in some regions, including the lower Rhineland and central and southern Germany (Pounds 1990, 175; Scott 1996, 4). Silver was discovered in Germany around 1460, which stimulated the mining industry. Iron and copper industries also expanded at this time (Yun 1994, 123–24). The mining boom in parts of Germany continued to flourish throughout the sixteenth century.

### The Thirty Years' War and Seventeenth-Century Decline

The seventeenth century was a period of crisis in German agriculture, in part because of the Thirty Years' War and in part because of a Europe-wide economic decline, which had begun in the late sixteenth century. It is estimated that about 40 percent of the rural population and 33 percent of the urban inhabitants of Germany fell victim to the Thirty Years' War (Abel 1978b,

155; see also Robisheaux 1989, 79). Indirect results of the war included famine, high corn prices, and an epidemic. The epidemic began in southeastern Germany in 1634 and from 1636 to 1640 spread over the greater part of central, west and south Germany with terrible results. In some villages and towns it claimed half the inhabitants or more as victims. As a result of war and sickness, farmhands became scarce and demanded high wages (Abel 1978b, 156; Hagen 1989, 327–28), which promoted a switch to pasture farming in some regions of Germany (Robisheaux 1989, 249).

Cereal prices stayed high until the middle of the century, when they began to fall. In east Prussia and Lithuania falling prices led farmers to feed grain to their cattle or leave it to rot in the fields. As noted earlier, after the mid-seventeenth century the grain export trade from east Germany and Poland petered out. Exports of grain from Danzig declined to a mere fraction of what had been sent westward a century earlier (Kirby 1990, 353). According to records, rent and tax arrears begin to multiply as early as the 1640s.

Economically, with the exception of parts of the northwest, all Germany stagnated (Fulbrook 1990, 65). Neither agriculture nor any other part of the economy flourished, and petty princely absolutisms consolidated their control. As trade and commerce declined, towns shrunk, especially in the east (Fulbrook 1990, 64). In east Germany there were further legislative attempts to reduce the peasants to abject servility (Barraclough 1962, 394)—although these were not always successfully enforced (Hagen 1989, 325). Yet, at the same time, to no small extent the oppressed condition of the east German peasant was due to the low prices of agricultural produce (Hagen 1989, 323). Landlords as well as peasants suffered from the unfavorable trade conditions of postwar decades. Many were deeply in debt (Abel 1978b, 179–81). Increasing tax demands by the growth of the absolutist state in Brandenburg at this time also sapped the resources of peasant and Junker alike (Hagen 1989, 334–35; see later discussion). Agriculture saw a slow decline. By about 1700 yields (of all grains) all over Germany were much lower than in England, the Low Countries, and even France at the same time. Yield ratios throughout Germany may have averaged only about 3 to 1, as opposed to an average of about 5 to 1 in France, and 6 to 1 and higher in England and the Low Countries (Pounds 1990, 279). Only in northwest Germany, which had escaped much of the devastation of the Thirty Years' War and incorporation into the Prussian kingdom and where peasant freedoms were still viable, were methods more innovative and yields higher. Schleswig-Holstein in particular still contributed grain regularly to the European market (Mead 1981, 80). This entire northwestern region was increasing in prosperity at a time of general decline everywhere else (Fulbrook 1990, 65).

In sum, given the distribution of farming systems in Germany and the hypotheses offered here, we would have expected the highest agricultural productivity and most agrarian change in the northwest and eastern regions, the regions of less-communal agriculture. To a certain extent this occurred. By 1700 agricultural productivity was highest in the northwest of Germany, where agricultural techniques were also innovative by European standards of the time. Yet agricultural productivity never became particularly notable in the East, despite periods in which much grain was produced for export. This was in part a result of the refeudalization of the early modern period and, later, the growth of state power—both processes facilitated in the seventeenth century by the Thirty Years' War.

### Eighteenth and Nineteenth Centuries: Comparative Agrarian Stagnation

In comparison to England and the Netherlands, by the early eighteenth century German agriculture was comparatively backward. With the exception of the northwest, by 1700 there was a general agricultural depression in Germany. Economic stagnation persisted into the next century, as Frederick the Great (King Frederick II [1740–86]) noted. In the east neglect of animal husbandry was the measure of agrarian backwardness. Grazing pastures were in short supply, only 5 percent on average of the landholding of the Prussian peasantry, for example. The inevitable consequence was inadequate manuring and poor grain yields from land (Kirby 1990, 354). In the southwest the land in gardens and vineyards was intensively cultivated and often highly productive, as in previous centuries (Mayhew 1973, 173; Sabean 1990, 20). Outside of the gardens and vineyards, however, arable agriculture remained underproductive. In many areas of the southwest an inefficient two-field system continued to be used for cereal agriculture (Smith 1967, 209; Mayhew 1973, 170).

As in France, rulers in eighteenth-century Germany were concerned about the low levels of agricultural productivity. England and the Low Countries had shown that a prosperous country required a productive and prosperous rural sector. Thus, both French and German rulers were keen to spread the English or Dutch example in their respective lands. In the northwest George III (of England) was interested in adopting the new methods on his lands in Hanover. In East Prussia Frederick William I (1713–40) embarked upon an ambitious resettlement program as a means of introducing improved farming methods into these areas. Resettlement and land reclamation helped revive the Prussian agrarian economy (Kirby

1990, 354). Frederick the Great (1740–86) approved of the new methods and sent young Prussian farmers to study them in England (see Pounds 1990, 286). Frederick the Great also promulgated enclosure laws and proclaimed himself an opponent of communal farming (Mayhew 1973, 178). He set up commissions to investigate farming systems that could suggest enclosure of various regions. Starting in 1763, there followed general directives, instructions of the courts of justice, and finally—first in Silesia, in 1771—a "permanent law" in which was set out that all communal property or mixing of landholdings that had constrained agriculture and free use of the fields and meadows would be dissolved entirely and split up. A similar concern with agricultural productivity by state and village officials also became apparent in the southwest in the eighteenth century (Sabean 1990, 28).

Reforming efforts showed most success in less-communal parts of Germany. For example, enclosure laws were most effective in the north, where existing landholding systems meant that consolidation and privatization of land was relatively easy and more likely to be seen as beneficial. Consolidation and enclosure was much more difficult in the south. It was not until the twentieth century that the highly fragmented open fields of the south and southwest were subject to large-scale consolidation and enclosure (Mayhew 1973, 187, 189).

There was also a regional pattern to the spread of new crops and rotations. These were most readily adopted in the northwest and parts of the east. Part of the reason for this was Brandenburg-Prussia's agrarian policy, which protected local production from foreign competition (Abel 1978b, 193; Kirby 1990, 354). In Holstein and parts of Mecklenburg a system based on complex rotations on enclosed land developed in the eighteenth century. In northern Germany along the coast of Friesland and in parts of the Rhineland and Westphalia, along the Baltic coast from eastern Schleswig through to East Prussia, and in Saxony, four-course and more rotations were found (Mayhew 1973, 170). Further south, in the industrial regions of Saxony a seven-field system is recorded. Convertible husbandry also spread in northern Germany from the North Sea coast toward the north and east (Abel 1978b, 208). Schleswig Holstein was one of the most advanced regions (Kirby 1990, 353). By 1800 this North Sea coastal region was still the chief exporter of cattle and animal products, as it had been in 1600. By this time the huge east-west cattle trade had declined sharply, for the reason that by this time Brandenburg, Prussia, Saxony, and the larger part of west Germany were practically self-sufficient in meat (Abel 1978b, 211).

In communal regions the three-field system remained, but the drive toward increased productivity and innovation showed itself in some places where there was change to an "improved" three-course rotation. For example, in central Germany the three-year system was retained, but crops were planted on part of the fallow. Roots, peas, vetch, buckwheat, clover, lupin, and sainfoin were grown as fallow crops more and more often during the last decade of the eighteenth century (Abel 1978b, 208, Sabean 1990, 53), and many villagers begged for the right to innovate in the field rotation (Sabean 1990, 28). In some areas a specialization in cattle raising was notable (e.g., Hohenlohe [see Robisheaux 1989, 254]). On the open arable fields, however, the monoculture of spelt in a three-field framework was maintained. For example, in the county of Hohenlohe (near Württemberg) spelt still made up about 66 percent of field crops found in inventories in the 1860s. As in France, continued concern by state and other officials with preserving revenues often posed obstacles to change. For example, in Württemberg the tax on wine was a substantial part of state income. Thus, the ducal officials forbade changing cultivation of land devoted to grape production into the nineteenth century. Other jurisdictions and institutions, similarly jealous of their tithe rights to various kinds of land, discouraged change in the use of the land. Nevertheless, to some extent market forces prevailed, and in Württemberg (and other areas in the southwest) the amount of arable land declined over the nineteenth century, and the amount of land devoted to pastoral purposes increased (Sabean 1990, 446, 44, 52, 449).

Further east and on poorer soil, the old three-course rotation still predominated, and in some remote regions even the three-course rotation had not yet been established (Abel 1978b, 208). There were pockets, however, of progressive agriculture. A seven-field system was used in East Prussia in which the rotation was frequently rye, barley, barley, oats, oats, peas, then fallow (Mayhew 1973, 169, 172). Estate agriculture, if not particularly notable for its high productivity, remained profitable in some regions as it produced quantities of grain for the market (Abel 1978b, 215).

The regions of innovative agriculture in the northwest and along the north coast were exceptional, as most of the German rural economy continued to stagnate. Generally slow progress in agriculture was reflected in the slow pace of industrialization and urbanization. At the beginning of the nineteenth century the total population of all free cities and university towns of Germany was scarcely the equivalent of the population of Paris (Barraclough 1962, 414). Agricultural productivity did not begin to rise throughout all the German lands until the second half of the nineteenth century. It was soon eclipsed by Germany's industrial revolution, "a product of conscious imitation and borrowing that lasted until about 1870," which was to propel Germany to the position of the most powerful industrial nation on the Continent on the eve of World War I (Cameron 1993, 243).

## Factors Specific to the Protonational Context

While local institutions influenced the course of agrarian change, to explain agrarian outcomes and the poor performance of agriculture in most of Germany fully the role of two other factors must be discussed. They were, first, legal decentralization, characteristic of late medieval and early modern Germany, and, second, warfare. Legal decentralization in the east led to the decline of legal support for the property rights of ordinary people during the boom years of the sixteenth century, making refeudalization possible. In the southwest legal decentralization had the opposite effect and promoted the blossoming of court systems and the growth of a highly litigious society. Neither of these developments promoted rural economic development. Warfare of the sixteenth and seventeenth centuries both ruined the rural economy and exacerbated the trend toward refeudalization in the east and also paved the way for the rise of Prussian autocracy, which had further negative effects on the rural economy in northern and eastern Germany.

### Legal Decentralization

Legal decentralization in the German lands dates back to the Middle Ages. The Holy Roman Empire had been a loose and sprawling entity. By the late fourteenth century the empire consisted of several parts: the emperor's dynastic lands; the electoral territories (seven), whose rulers' electoral function tied them closely to the monarchy; and several old zones of strong royal influence in the southwest, such as Franconia, Swabia, the Rhineland, and Thuringia. The lands of the north and northeast were incorporated into the empire only loosely and generally were far removed from royal influence (Barraclough 1962, 358; Press 1994, 440). Continued political decentralization meant that there was never any "Germany" as such. This meant that there was no common coinage used throughout the German lands. It also meant that there was no common body of law, let alone a central system of royal law, such as existed in England and in the Netherlands under the Burgundian-Habsburg rulers, and which was beginning to emerge in France. Both currency and law remained local in origin and regionally differentiated, mostly to the detriment of trade (Barraclough 1962, 411, 399).

The emperor had his own courts, but their use had declined in the thirteenth century as princes took over high territorial justice. Complete freedom from royal jurisdiction was given to the electors in the Golden Bull of 1356 and subsequently was demanded successfully by other imperial princes, most imperial towns, and many church foundations.[8] Instead of central justice, the emperor attempted to bring order to the empire by means of the Public Peace, or *Landfriede.* This was most evident in the west. In the north and northeast royal power was largely absent and public order was administered either through princely courts or through ad hoc courts set up by leagues of nobles and towns (Du Boulay 1983, 85, 76, 80).

In western Germany the Public Peace was neither an imperial law nor a permanent system of courts but an ad hoc agreement between varying combinations of princes, lords, and towns within a given region to keep the peace and to suppress certain types of serious violence for a set period of time. It was typically initiated by the emperor. A Public Peace was proclaimed at a certain place for a certain length of time and was intended to operate by means of officials appointed for the occasion by the contracting parties. Normally there was an official committee under a captain with responsibility for a particular area. The captain was usually an imperial official and called *Hauptmann,* or *Obmann.* Reporting to the captain were officials, provided by local lords, who sealed the document of Peace. The public was warned not to commit violent crimes or else suffer the consequences. When necessary, officials would seize offenders and bring them before special judges.

Besides the Public Peace, another less-common attempt—also in the west—to impose law and order on late medieval Germany was the *Veme* or *Feme,* the Vehmic courts of Westphalia. For about a century a number of minor court holders calling themselves "free counts" endeavored to administer justice in the emperor's name all over the German lands in cases of serious crime or where justice in civil cases had not been provided by other courts. In 1353 the archbishop of Cologne claimed that he had the right to supervise these free counts. The counts themselves, who took their titles mostly from small villages in the area of Dortmund in southeastern Westphalia, claimed to have received authority from the emperor. Before long the emperor indeed had granted the archbishop of Cologne the right to create and supervise them. By 1392 the courts were known everywhere as the Westphalian courts. Their jurisdiction was practiced sporadically all over the west German lands, even against nobles and towns. The organization was deliberately secret and operated through undercover members, not unlike a Mafia. The Vehmic courts declined after 1430, when German cities began to resist them and their decisions. Ultimately,    the emperor himself (Frederick III) called for an end to the Westphalian jurisdictions (Du Boulay 1983, 83–85).

Below this level there were local legal systems. West of the Elbe these legal systems were a legacy of Carolingian rulers. They had created a network of counties in which the count exercised high and low jurisdiction on behalf of the emperor. The failure of royal power and the process of decentralization resulted in countships being granted to intermediate lords. Local divisions in Germany went under different names and were liable to change as lordships changed, but they included divisions (equivalent to the English hundred and wapentake) of *Gau, Zent,* or *Hundert.* The jurisdiction exercised in these divisions might belong to a great lord or a minor one. In rural areas lesser courts were administered by the lord's agents in cooperation with leading villagers. Records of local customs that survive show great variation in details of relationships, obligations, and privileges. Judicial courts typically met thrice yearly (Du Boulay 1983, 87). East of the Elbe, in early days, peasants had held their land under the prince, with the local mayor as judge. Later, as noted earlier, the powers of the mayor declined, and local lords eroded the rights of local citizenry.

Decentralization of the empire gathered pace after the fourteenth century, and the power of the emperor dwindled. The fifteenth century saw the consolidation of princely power in the west (Holborn 1959; Barraclough 1962, 321). These princes typically obtained complete jurisdictional rights within their territories (although their power at the local level should not be exaggerated [Robisheaux 1989, 36]). This coincided with the introduction of Roman law in the west. Procedures were changed as old-fashioned judges and juries were replaced by jurists trained in universities.[9]

At the same time, representative bodies developed everywhere in Germany, most of them representing the nobility and towns in dealings with territorial princes (Carsten 1959, 425; Fulbrook 1990, 34). By the end of the fifteenth century there were essentially two tiers to German politics in the west: the Imperial Diets, attended by emperor, princes, heads of ecclesiastical territories, independent knights, and representatives of the imperial towns; and at the local level there were territorial assemblies in which the prince typically met with representatives of the privileged classes (Fulbrook 1990, 27). Yet (unlike in England) development of representative government did not reinforce rights of the common people. In fact, quite the reverse was true. Princes attempted to reduce the powers of the representative bodies often by compensating the nobility at the expense of peasants, that is, by recognizing the subjection of the peasantry to the nobility and conferring new rights on the latter. Thus, the *Landtage* (estates) themselves became instruments for attacking rights of the peasantry (Barraclough 1962, 393).

With the rise of territorial states the institution of the Public Peace declined. The Public Peace was opposed particularly by the nobilities, who feared loss of wealth and jurisdiction. They preferred the arbitrament of war. There was a remarkable amount of warfare between princes themselves. Problems of imperial jurisdiction remained unsettled, and the Public Peace movement never flourished again (Du Boulay 1983, 81–83).

In the sixteenth century there was something of a revitalization of royal justice. Maximilian I (r. 1493–1519) succeeded his father as emperor in 1493. Maximilian implemented various reforms, including abolition of the right of feud and establishment of a law of public peace (*Landfriede*). An Imperial Chamber Court (*Kammergericht*) was also established. It came to be influenced, however, primarily by electors and princes (Fulbrook 1990, 34; Press 1994, 446). In addition, the Imperial Council (*Reichshofrat*) developed into a court that competed with the Imperial Chamber Court. Perhaps as a result, the power of the emperor did not vanish entirely. By the second half of the sixteenth century, in the west, the Habsburg de facto monarch of the empire was able to consolidate his control, in part by conceding compromises with the Protestants in the religious settlement of 1555. Ferdinand of Austria was recognized as emperor in 1558, and Habsburg rule was stabilized (Press 1994, 447, 457).

The primary effect of the survival of imperial courts was to maintain the hundreds of tiny principalities in western Germany after the sixteenth century. They successfully resisted incorporation into larger units by appeals to the emperor (Fulbrook 1990, 70). Imperial courts had most influence on relations between the principalities and had little or no influence within the principalities themselves. Peasants and townspeople within individual principalities had to rely on justice supplied locally, by the village itself, or the prince or other territorial lord. By 1500 princes were beginning to develop more common courts and administrations, with a concomitant growth of officials (Fulbrook 1990, 34; Robisheaux 1989, 123). The Thirty Years' War reinforced the trend toward princely absolutism and the proliferation of hundreds of independent principalities in western Germany.

As a result of these processes in the west the court system became exceptionally densely developed. The courts provided forums for the endless negotiation of communal rights. Although the peasantry had access to legal protection for their property rights as a result; in this case transaction costs were increased because of the constant litigation over property rights. One positive outcome was that peasants were often able to use the court system to resist the tightening of manorial control over the village commune in the west at this time. As a result, in the west and the southwest conditions for the peasantry never became as severe as in the east. Heritable tenure continued, and taxation rates often remained low (Robisheaux 1989, 123, 227, 242). Communal agricultural systems and state restrictions on land use, however, continued to keep agricultural productivity low in this region.

Outcomes were very different in the east. Perhaps because of the region's loose incorporation into the Holy Roman Empire, there was not the same splintering of political units in the east as in the west. Nor was there the proliferation of courts. Instead, local lords retained and consolidated their power over the peasantry after the fifteenth century. They were also able to exploit their jurisdictional privileges to increase labor services required of the peasantry (Mayhew 1973; Hagen 1985, 93). The Thirty Years' War accelerated the trend toward subjugation of the peasantry in the east (Barraclough 1962, 396). War also promoted the rise of absolutism in northeastern Germany. The Elector of Brandenburg was able to take over a region severely weakened by the Thirty Years' War and the war with Poland of 1655–60 (Carsten 1954, 275; Fulbrook 1990, 77) and was able to use the threat of war to obtain funds from the Estates for a modest army. With the support of his army, the Elector was now able to ignore the Estates and levy taxes without its approval and thus consolidate his control over Brandenburg, Pomerania, and, by 1674, Prussia. This autocracy helped to maintain an oppressive and unproductive agrarian regime throughout eastern Germany (Fulbrook 1990, 80).

## Warfare

As a landlocked area, surrounded by potentially hostile peoples, the German lands were constantly at war. Unlike England and France, where a central monarchy was able to preserve peace to some extent, in Germany the weakness of central authority promoted anarchy. Constant warfare promoted the development of an aristocratic warrior class and a militaristic culture by the thirteenth century (Fulbrook 1990, 21). It also increased uncertainty, raised transaction costs, and thus discouraged economic growth.

The colonization of the east was born in warfare. One of the first settlements was by the religious Knights of the Teutonic Order, whose express purpose was to conquer the heathen Slavs. The constant danger present in these regions is noticeable in the office of the mayor, or *Schulz,* whose primary responsibility was defense of the village. Warfare was no less prevalent in the southwest. Here the many princes and territorial lords were constantly at war with one another. Private war was more frequent in this region than in any other. The disappearance of the Hohenstaufen Dynasty, the Interregnum, and the rivalry of Habsburg, Wittelsbach, and Luxemburg Dynasties left many areas unsubjected, or not yet subjected, to higher nobility, with the consequence that there were innumerable occasions for dispute. The constant turmoil that prevailed particularly after the end of Hohenstaufen rule in the mid-thirteenth century is reflected in the castle-building boom, when it is estimated that some 10,000 castles were built. Large numbers of German knights and their followers spent much of their time fighting. Knights with too little to occupy them even could become *Raubritter* (knightly bandits) (Du Boulay 1983, 79, 73).

In the fifteenth century there was a series of minor wars between princes all over Germany. Most notable were conflicts between Brandenburg, Bavaria, the Palatinate, and their subjects and neighbors. The later sixteenth century saw the most intense conflicts. Northern Europe was embroiled in almost continuous war from 1561 to 1658 as Sweden struggled with Denmark, Russia, Poland, and Brandenburg for control of the Baltic and its important trade. Hostilities culminated in the Thirty Years' War (1618–48), a war that devastated much of northeastern, central, and southern Germany in particular. It disrupted agriculture and destroyed the dynamic network of international fairs that had flourished in eastern Germany and other places in eastern Europe (Topolski 1985, 138). Effects of the war may have reduced the population overall by 30 to 40 percent (Pounds 1990, 256; Robisheaux 1989, 79). Losses in southwestern Germany as well as in the northeastern provinces, devastated by the Swedish armies, were 50 percent and more (Sabean 1984, 8; Kirby 1990, 245). The high levels of taxation during and after the war did even more to slow the growth of rural economies (Sabean 1984, 9; Hagen 1989, 335).

Wars continued to decimate the population and to disrupt trade and agriculture long after the Thirty Years' War ended in 1648. The northeast witnessed war with Poland from 1655–60 (Carsten 1954, 275). Following the Peace of Westphalia in 1648, French encroachments on German territory, culminated in the Wars of the Palatinate (1688–97) and of the Spanish Succession (1701–14) (Barraclough 1962, 386; Pounds 1990, 256). It was not until the eighteenth century that population decline in Germany ceased and a recovery took place. The northeast in particular remained depopulated until well into the eighteenth century (Pounds 1990, 264).

## Conclusion

In this chapter we have seen that in southwestern Germany, as in northern France, communal agricultural systems hindered agricultural development and agrarian change, despite the region's many advantages in terms of access to markets and ecology. In the communal southwest agricultural productivity tended to be low, except on private gardens, which were often devoted to market-oriented specialties such as viticulture. Productivity was generally higher and agricultural techniques were more innovative in the less-communal north and northwest. All regions experienced an increase in agricultural productivity during the prosperity of the sixteenth century, although once again this was most notable in the less-communal regions of the north and northwest. Once again, productivity increases in the south were confined to private gardens, while most land remained devoted to a relatively unproductive monoculture of grain.

In terms of yields and the use of intensive agricultural techniques, the less-communal east tended to lag behind most of western Germany. Yet it was home to a productive export agriculture in the late medieval period, and grain from this region became essential for the maintenance of urban populations in places such as the Netherlands in the early modern period. Refeudalization, however, helped suppress agricultural productivity in this region after the sixteenth century.

German agriculture in all regions suffered two major setbacks over the period examined here. First, the political decentralization of the German lands allowed the refeudalization of eastern Germany in the sixteenth century, as there was no central government to support rights of the peasantry against those of powerful local lords. As in France, a balance of power between nobles and monarch never developed, and peasant rights suffered as a result (Moore 1966). In southwestern Germany political decentralization promoted the proliferation of court systems and an increasingly litigious society, which also raised transaction costs associated with the protection of common property rights. Neither outcome promoted rural economic development.

The second setback was warfare, as noted by Frederick the Great. This was always a problem in centrally located Germany, and it was highly destructive of the rural economy. The Thirty Years' War of the seventeenth century practically destroyed rural Germany. Perhaps even worse than the devastation warfare caused directly were its long-term effects: consolidation of princely absolutisms in the west and the rise of autocracy in Brandenburg in the north. These changes promoted an unproductive rural sector. As a result, an agricultural revolution was slow in coming to Germany. Yet, as we have seen in England and France, when innovative techniques were introduced, they were most readily accepted in the same areas that had been agriculturally progressive in the Middle Ages—particularly the northwest and the north coast area.

CHAPTER 8

# Rural Institutions and
# Agrarian Change in Sweden

Of corn I sow ten parts,
And then I nine do reap;
A tenth I give to the priest,
And am happy the rest to keep.
—Old Swedish rhyme

Agrarian outcomes in Sweden place it with Germany and France. As with these countries, agricultural production in Sweden did not begin to rise significantly until the eighteenth century. At the same time, the case of Sweden makes it possible to examine the effects of local field systems independent of local class relations, as, contrary to what we have seen in England, the Netherlands, France, and Germany, in Sweden communal open field systems coexisted with weak manorial overlordship at the local level. At the national level the rising Swedish absolutism of the early modern period was more reminiscent of the situation in France than of the situation in England, the Netherlands, or Germany.

In the early fourteenth century the territory of Sweden occupied much of the current area of modern Sweden, although the most southerly region of the peninsula (the provinces of Blekinge, Halland, and Skåne [see map 15]) and the northwestern provinces (Jämtland and Härjedalen) were then part of Denmark-Norway. In addition, Sweden included part of what is now Finland (Mead 1981, 4; Metcalf 1995, 522). The Swedish state was only just beginning to develop and was focused in the central region around Lake Mälaren. Here the silting up of the entrance of the lake forced the port city onto the island of Stockholm (Pounds 1990, 146), which by the late Middle Ages was an important center of the copper and iron trade (Gissel 1981b, 190). At this time all of Sweden was sparsely populated, heavily forested, and barely cultivated. In the early fourteenth century, at a time when the population of France numbered a little less than 20 million (Le Roy Ladurie 1987, 23; Braudel 1990, 137), Sweden had perhaps 700,000 people (Sawyer and Sawyer 1993, 42). In 1500 there were still fewer than 1 million people in Sweden (Kirby 1990, 16).

**Map 15. Sweden**

Settlement followed a pattern familiar from other regions of Europe: in most of the east of central Sweden and in the south of the peninsula (then Denmark) there were open fields and compact villages (by Swedish standards); to the west and north there were scattered farms and smaller hamlets. Unlike the Continent, manorialization was fairly weak all over the Swedish peninsula, with the exception of the Danish south. Unfortunately, the lack of overlordship in many areas means recorded information on agrarian matters is even more scarce than usual. Agrarian expansion in Sweden dates to the mid-eighteenth century (Isacson 1979, 183; Magnusson 1996, 45). As in France, the configuration of factors was inauspicious for change: the best land—in the central plains and to the south—was characterized by communal farming systems, which inhibited change, while less-communal systems were located in the more remote and ecologically marginal regions of northern and western Sweden. Furthermore, early developments in less-communal areas were inhibited by encroaching state control in the sixteenth century and after.

### Ecology, Population, and Markets

Although much of Sweden has a temperate climate, ecology put strict limits on agriculture in some regions of Sweden. This was true in the northwest, where the Keel chain of mountains forms part of the boundary between Norway and Sweden. It was also true in the far north, where the climate is subarctic. North of the 58 degree latitude (which runs to the north of the city of Göteborg), even stock rearing is difficult, since cattle have to be kept indoors for many months, consuming large quantities of fodder (Kirby 1990, 15). North of the line where deciduous trees give way completely to coniferous forest (about the 60 degree latitude—called the *limes norrlandicus* by the Swedes), much of the land is uninhabitable (*Rand McNally Atlas of World History* 1983, 96; Sawyer and Sawyer 1993, 30, 3; Mead 1981, 11).

To the east of the Keel Mountains there is a wide, uneven plateau with plains, mountains, hills, and rivers that flow southeast into the Gulf of Bothnia. In central Sweden there is an extensive area of plains. Here there are many large lakes, including Vänern, the third largest lake in Europe. Just to the south of this plain, between the Kattegat and the Baltic Seas, there is a high central region that rises to almost 1,300 feet (400 m) above sea level (Mead 1981, 14; Sawyer and Sawyer 1993, 27). The rest of southern Sweden is lower in elevation although hilly in places. This is the best agricultural region of Sweden, with the soil and climate most suited for agriculture (Mead 1981, 20).

A high latitude means the vegetative season in Sweden is short compared with that in other parts of Europe, and such ecological conditions helped keep population densities low in Sweden. Urban development was limited, and settlement was concentrated around the seaboard (Mead 1981, 10, 20, 12). In the later Middle Ages Sweden was still a land of forests: deciduous forests south of the *limes norrlandicus,* coniferous forests to the north. These forests were an important part of the rural economy as Swedes depended on what they collected and gathered in them—berries, nuts, fungi, and so forth—to supplement their diets. Hunting and fishing were also important. As a result, the diet of Swedes included much more meat and fish than diets of other Europeans at the same time (Mead 1981, 39; Sawyer and Sawyer 1993, 31).

This ecological setting and sparse population meant that Sweden was somewhat peripheral to European trade and commercial activities (Mead 1981, 10; Hecksher 1954, 59–60). In trade and commerce, however, Sweden had two important advantages. First, its peninsula location and many rivers gave Sweden easy access to water routes. In the winter communications were enhanced by the frozen conditions: people and goods could be transported everywhere by sled. Second, Sweden lay adjacent to the Baltic Sea, an important trading area in Europe. Both factors facilitated communications and trade both within Sweden and between Sweden and Europe.

In the late Middle Ages water routes and the sea trade in general from Sweden to Europe were controlled by the Hanseatic League. With League outposts in all main ports, it managed to gain a monopoly of most seagoing trade (Mead 1981, 57; Sawyer and Sawyer 1993, 161). The trade involved an exchange of grain from the Baltic, salt from Lüneburg, and cloth from England and Flanders for Swedish products—herring (in Danish Skåne), dairy products, and metals—mostly iron and copper (Metcalf 1995, 526). Much of this trade passed through Lübeck, making an examination of the commodity composition of trade between Stockholm and Lübeck in 1368 instructive. Exports from Sweden included butter (44.6 percent), iron (20.1 percent), copper (17.5 percent), and furs and hides (16 percent). Imports were cloth (51.3 percent), salt (22.9 percent), and miscellaneous goods (25.8 percent) (Heckscher 1954, 48). Dried or salted fish was also an important export at this time, particularly from the Danish Scanian market (Sawyer and Sawyer 1993, 161; Gissel 1981b, 190).

### Field Systems in Late Medieval Sweden (c. 1200–1500)

Communal Open Field Systems

The ecologically hospitable plains of eastern Sweden and the Danish provinces in the south were home to communal, open field farming systems similar to those in midland England, northern France, and southern Germany (see map 16). As elsewhere, villages tended to be large and compact in these regions (Österberg 1991, 7), at least by Swedish standards—which means about five farms per village (Teitsson 1981, 185; Sawyer and Sawyer 1993, 46). This field system in Sweden is revealed in the Provincial Codes, which date from the thirteenth and fourteenth centuries; and from the large number of land maps prepared by government surveyors beginning in the last decades of the seventeenth century (Heckscher 1954; Göransson 1961).

In some respects the Swedish communal open field system resembled those of England and the Continent. It was characterized by farms made up of strips scattered regularly through large open fields, communal cropping, and communal grazing. Yet, unlike other communal open field systems in the rest of Europe, in late medieval Sweden there was no fallowing or rotation at all. The most typical system was an extensive, one-field, one-course system (*ensäde*), whereby the same crop was planted on the same land year in and year out (Heckscher 1954, 28; Söderberg 1996, 26). When the soil became exhausted and the yields began to decline precipitously, parts of the arable were simply abandoned and turned into pasture. This one-course system was made possible by the abundance of land relative to population in Sweden and was found in both communal and less-communal regions alike. In more infertile areas of eastern Sweden there was even a more extensive slash-and-burn type of agriculture (*svedjebruk*). Under this system swathes of forest or uncultivated land were burned then cropped for a few years, often with a year or two of rye (typical on burned land) and then a year or two of turnips or cabbages. The land then might be grazed for a while before being allowed to revert to woodland. After twenty or thirty years the process would be repeated (Sawyer and Sawyer 1993, 32; Magnusson 1996, 54–55).

In places where the population was denser there were systematic rotations (*växelbruk*). The Provincial Codes show the existence of two-field husbandry, which leaves half the land sit fallow, in some southern and eastern provinces by the fourteenth century. The two-field system was dominant in eastern Sweden by the sixteenth century (Myrdal and Söderberg 1991, 530). By the early nineteenth century three-field agriculture was found in the more densely settled south (parts of central Sweden—Väster- and Östergötland—and in the southernmost province of Skåne, which became Swedish in 1658 [Smith 1967, 237; Myrdal and Söderberg 1991, 530; Magnusson 1996, 56]). Thus, regions of late medieval Sweden offer an example of the communal open field system in a very early stage of development (see chap. 1).

Nevertheless, despite differing in intensity, the Swedish system was

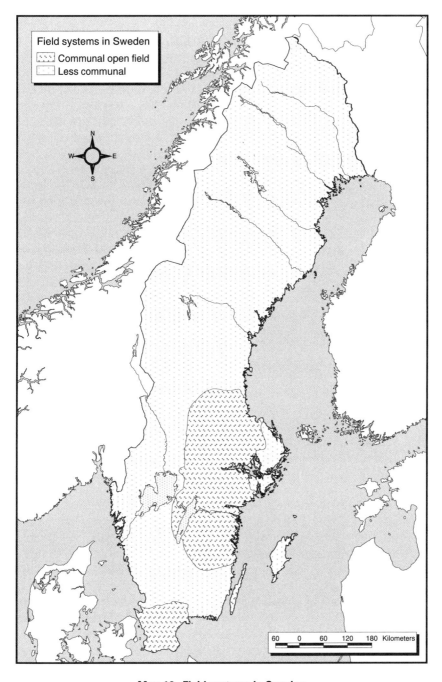

**Map 16. Field systems in Sweden**

recognizably similar to the Continental communal open field system. Each strip of land (*bandparcell,* or *teg*) in the fields (*vångar*) was allocated in a regular fashion according to *solskifte,* or sun division, a practice that appears to have also existed in open field England and Denmark (see chap. 2; Goransson 1961; Söderberg 1996, 27). In *solskifte* strips in the field are arranged clockwise, according to the passage of the sun across the sky from east to west (for practical purposes, south being combined with east). Farmers occupied strips in the same sequence in every field, following the sequence of houses along the village street. Individual strips were not necessarily equal in size, although they tended to be long and narrow. As a result, a single holding was made up of many strips of land. Instances occurred of villagers holding more than one hundred strips in the same village. Bundles of adjacent strips, or *tegar,* made a *fall* (alternatively, *teglag, parcellag*), equivalent to the English furlong and the French *quartier* (Dahl 1961, 57). The average farm in Sweden at this time consisted of a *mantal* (a unit devised for taxation purposes that parallels the German *Hufe* and the English *hide* [see chap. 1]). A *mantal* of land may have consisted of 9 or so hectares (about 22 acres) (Mead 1981, 37), although it was by no means a consistent land measure (Rydeberg 1985, 188). In addition to the fields proper were common woodlands and pasture (*utmark*) and meadowland (*odaläng*) (Olai 1983, 239).

Authorities everywhere used the *solskifte* division as an aid in assessing taxes. The limits of the *solskifte* often coincided with those of the judicial provinces (Göransson 1961). By the thirteenth century *solskifte* appears in the provincial law codes of all provinces in eastern Sweden: the Östgöta-Law, the Upplands-Law, the Västmanna-Law, the Dala-Law, and the Södermanna-Law. This indicates that the communal open field region of medieval Sweden consisted of most of the provinces of the east: Östergötland and northeast Småland, Öland, Uppland with Gästrikland, the plains of Västergötland (Winberg 1977, 335); the southeast corner of Dalarna (or Dalecarlia [see *Times Concise Atlas of World History,* 77]), Västmanland, Närke and Södermanland (Göransson 1961, 80; Mead 1981, 37). The communal open field system also characterized the Danish province of Skåne (see map 16). Thus, in Sweden there was a close correspondence between the best agricultural land (of the plains) and the communal open field system.

In all communal regions the system of land division by *solskifte* was supported by church, nobility, and state as a readily identifiable key to land ownership and therefore to tax assessment. As in the Continent, regions of communal agriculture in Sweden tended to be the most manorialized part of Sweden. Here is where the majority of land owned by the nobility or the church (called *frälse* land) was concentrated (Sawyer and

Sawyer 1993, 46, 109, 130; Kirby 1990, 40). Land was known as *kyrkjord* if it were owned by the church and the clergy and *frälsejord* if it were owned by the nobility. The largest manorial estates (*säterier*) tended to be located near centers of administration in the south and around Stockholm (Sawyer and Sawyer 1993, 130).[1] Manorial estates were smaller in hilly Småland and rare in the forested areas of Uppland (Mead 1981, 60–61). Some estates had a manorial demesne, especially in eastern Sweden (the counties of Uppland, Södermanland, and Östergötland and the plains of Västergötland), although its share of total noble land was negligible (Jutikkala 1975; for Västergötland, see Winberg 1977, 337). All noble and church land was tax-exempt. For the nobility and gentry the tax exemption was in exchange for military service.

A large percentage of peasants (by Swedish standards) in these regions were tenants of noble landowners and not freeholders or tax peasants (*skattebönder*).[2] For example, figures from Östergötland (for the middle of the sixteenth century) show that only a seventh of the peasantry were freeholders (Østerud 1978, 78). Tenants on noble land paid dues and rents directly to their manorial lord. In Sweden rent was composed of a wide range of money rents and rents in kind. In addition, peasants typically also owed their lords labor services, such as field work and cartage. This was particularly the case if there was a demesne farm. This *corvée* labor persisted in some of these regions to the eighteenth century (e.g., in Västmanland, see Gaunt 1977, 186). Distant tenants tended to pay rents in kind and rarely were responsible for labor services (Sawyer and Sawyer 1993, 140). Some also had to turn to their overlords for justice, as some nobles had right of trial and punishment over their tenants (Dahlgren 1973, 109). Rent-paying tenants rarely were obliged, however, to pay taxes to the Crown also.

Not all farmers in communal regions were tenants, however. Some were tax-paying peasants who were (at least in principle) freeholders, or *skattebönder*. Freehold peasants on tax land, or *skattejord,* owed taxes to the Crown as ruler of the realm, unlike tenants on noble and church lands who paid rents to their respective landlords. Freeholders were the most privileged peasant class. They owned the largest farms and in general enjoyed a higher social standing than other peasants (Dahlgren 1973, 106). They were the only category of peasants with the right to sell their land. As long as they paid their dues to the Crown, they had permanent possession of their landholdings (although if they did not pay them, they could be removed from their land [see Rydeberg 1985, 185]). Many communal regions even contained a majority of freeholders, fully involved in communal open field farming. For example, although southeastern Dalarna was communal open field land, Dalarna was held almost entirely by freeholders (Österberg 1991, 156, 158). Gaunt (1977, 190) gives another example of a communal open field region occupied entirely by tax-paying peasants in the parish of Västerfärnebo in central Sweden in the seventeenth century.[3] The existence in Sweden of large villages and communal farming systems *without* manorial overlordship is an important clue to the origin of field systems (as discussed in chap. 1).

Compared to open field regions on the Continent, manorial control in the communal regions of Sweden was relatively light, as it was throughout Sweden. Manors were typically small and labor services comparatively slight. Most nobles did not engage in direct farming of their demesnes (Heckscher 1954, 29). There are no precise figures, but at the end of the Middle Ages over half of the land of the Swedish realm was freehold, or *skattejord,* only 5.6 percent was Crown land, while about 40 percent was owned by the nobility and the church (Heckscher 1954, 30–31; Metcalf 1995, 525).[4]

In communal regions by the eighteenth century the traditional inheritance system featured primogeniture, in which the oldest son usually took over the farm and bought out his coinheritors at a reasonable price (Østerud 1978, 109). This does not meant that it was always the predominant family structure in these regions, and in some occasions farms were divided (Gaunt 1978, 74). Yet, at this time, peasants under the domain of local noblemen (usually communal areas) were not allowed to split up their holdings. Although this evidence is for the eighteenth century, we may presume these were traditional practices in these regions, particularly since they conflicted with the state laws of the time, which specified divided inheritance with sons awarded double the share of daughters (Löfgren 1974, 34). How far back these practices date, however, is obscure.

### Less-Communal Open Fields and Enclosures

Regions of less-communal open fields and enclosures were located in western Sweden (the provinces of Västergötland—excluding the plain area, Dalsland, and Värmland) and in the forested areas of Småland (south) and the far north outside of the river valleys (see map 16). In these regions, individual farms ("lonely farms") and hamlets predominated (Heckscher 1954, 28; Teitsson 1981, 184). The majority of peasant farmers were *skattebönder,* or tenants of the Crown, the most privileged peasant classes (e.g., in Värmland in the west; see Österberg 1991, 156, 158). Tenants on Crown-land or *kronojord* owed dues to the Crown but to the Crown as landowner rather than as ruler of the realm. Although not as privileged as freeholders or *skattebönder,* they were considered to have more security of tenure than *frälse*-peasants, since a nobleman was more likely than the

Crown to want to evict a tenant. The freedom of the peasantry was in part a result of the frontier nature of many of these regions. Many enclosures and private fields were products of new clearing in the forest, as their names attest (Sawyer and Sawyer 1993, 9). As in Germany, "clearing made free" in Sweden also. There were very few residential manors owned by noblemen (Sandnes 1981, 85). One-course systems with no rotations were most common in these regions (Söderberg 1996, 27), although two-, three-, and even four-course rotations could also be found (e.g., in Värmland; see Magnusson 1996, 56). Communal regulation and coordination of rotations was largely absent in these regions.

In the north, also, single farms and hamlets were the primary settlement form. In cold and remote Upper Norrland, however, settlement had been concentrated strongly on the coast and some miles up the larger rivers. The greater part of the settlement was in the form of larger villages, although this appears to have been a rather unique situation (Sandnes 1981, 88; see also 185). Most of the land in the north was Crown land or freehold. By the sixteenth century Norrland in Sweden was held almost entirely by freeholders (Sawyer and Sawyer 1993, 141; Østerud 1978, 78; Sandnes 1981, 88). Throughout the north there was little noble land, and there were no manors, or *säterier* (Jutikkala 1975).

In these less-communal regions, at least in the eighteenth century, partible inheritance was common (Löfgren 1974, 36). For example, in the province Dalarna (Dalecarlia)—much of which was a less-communal region—partible inheritance was the rule (Löfgren 1974, 36; Christiansen 1978, 55). Once again, it is uncertain how old this custom was in these regions, yet the similarity to the pattern we have seen previously in late medieval England (and to a lesser extent in other places) is suggestive.

## Agrarian Change in Late Medieval and Early Modern Sweden

In late medieval Sweden there are few records of agrarian matters (Heckscher 1954, 17; Magnusson 1996, 53). With state centralization and increased state control in the early modern period, records improved greatly in quality. Yet there is much we may never know about rural life and society in Sweden in both periods. There is some evidence of regional differences along lines hypothesized in chapter 2. The region of most interest for our purposes is western Sweden, to the south of Göteborg, which, although hilly in many places, was home to a more congenial ecology than the north and was characterized by less-communal field systems. Thus, we would expect more development and change there than in the more communal parts of the south. There is some evidence of a progressive rural sector in the west by the sixteenth century and in other less-communal regions in the seventeenth and eighteenth centuries. On the whole, however, as with most European countries, agriculture throughout Sweden did not begin to change until the eighteenth century, with an agricultural revolution in the nineteenth century. The model of chapter 3 suggests that a comparatively sparse population and poor ecology promoted this outcome, along with comparatively uncertain property rights and oppressive state policies from the sixteenth century on. In what follows I trace the economic history of Sweden over the period from the fourteenth through the seventeenth centuries. As much as possible, I also describe regional differences in agrarian change throughout the same period.

### Agriculture in Late Medieval Sweden

In late medieval Sweden, due to the sparse population and correspondingly limited trade, much Swedish agriculture was subsistence oriented and specialization in rural products was unusual (Mead 1981, 58). There was a more arable focus (producing cereals) in the fertile plain lands of the communal east and south and a more pastoral focus (producing butter) in the hillier, less-communal west, a distinction that endured through the next centuries (Gissel 1981a, 149). Yields from crop and stock varied from place to place but appear to have been rather poor everywhere (Mead 1981, 60).

As in Continental Europe, the best land of Sweden (communal and less-communal regions alike) was devoted largely to grain growing, yet, unlike Continental Europe, little wheat was grown. Grain crops included barley, rye, and oats, with barley predominating in the Middle Ages (Heckscher 1954, 28; Gissel 1981a, 145; yield ratios discussed below are typically those for barley and rye). In the communal regions of the south peas, beans, flax, hemp, and vegetables were also grown outside of the open fields. In addition to the arable fields, villages possessed commons and hay meadows, both of which provided animal fodder. Meadows probably were subject to private rights but not so the forest, which, presumably with few exceptions, was held entirely in common (Heckscher 1954, 29). Oxen were used for plowing, as draft animals and as a source of meat. The horse was little used, except for personal transportation and by the military. Evidence from rents from the fourteenth and fifteenth centuries suggests a monetized economy. These regions—Östergötland, and Svealand (around Stockholm)—were the major grain-producing regions of Sweden (Gissel 1981a, 153), although only a small proportion of the total was for local sale or export. Danish Skåne was another important grain-producing area.

In the less-communal west cultivation of grain also predominated, although seed/yield ratios were typically lower than in the east. Slash-and-burn cultivation appears to have been less common than in the east and rotation systems more varied. As in the north, fishing and hunting played an important part as a secondary means of livelihood, particularly in more peripheral districts. There was also a lively pastoral economy. In Västergötland and parts of Halland (Denmark) there was much production for the market, and there were a large number of small trading centers at the estuary of the Gota River. Evidence from rents in western Sweden also suggest a money economy. This area produced considerable butter and other agricultural products (Sandnes 1981, 107; Gissel 1981a, 153) for internal consumption and for export. As export figures suggest, butter was the most important export of late medieval Sweden, although butter ceased to be exported by the end of the fifteenth century (Heckscher 1954, 48).

### Fourteenth-Century Crisis

In the later Middle Ages Scandinavian countries shared in the agrarian crisis that afflicted most of northwestern Europe at the same time (Magnusson 1996, 38–39). In addition to demographic decline caused by the plague, the climate may have cooled somewhat, and precipitation may have increased, although evidence suggests that effects of climate change were neither drastic nor long lasting (Teitsson 1981, 176). Of more import was the political turmoil in Sweden at this time. In 1389 Sweden was taken over by the queen of Denmark and Norway, Margrete. In 1397 the queen's nephew Eric of Pomerania was crowned king of Sweden, Norway, and Denmark. This inaugurated the Kalmar Union, which continued intermittently throughout the fifteenth century, finally to fall apart in the 1520s (Heckscher 1954, 286).

Demographic decline coupled with a general fall in agricultural prices led to the desertion of settlements in Sweden, as in other parts of Europe. Cultivated land and farmsteads were abandoned, mostly over the period from the latter part of the fourteenth century to the mid-fifteenth century (Mead 1981, 62; Sandnes 1981, 86). There is evidence that, as in other parts of Europe, rents began to fall at this time in all regions of Sweden in response to the shortage of tenants. Desertion of settlements followed a regional pattern. Research shows generally *less* desertion in regions of large villages (often communal areas) and *more* desertion of farms in regions of individual farms, a finding that appears opposite to what we have seen in England and Germany at the same time (Sandnes 1981, 78; see also chaps. 4 and 7). In Sweden, however, the highest rate of desertion of farms was found in a communal area: the Northern Vedbo Hundred in the northernmost part of Småland. Here the desertion of farms has been calculated to have been about 36 percent. In other communal areas percentages were lower (11 percent in Närke, 10–12 percent in Södermanland, 10 percent in Skåne). These are generally lower than the percentage that has been calculated for one less-communal region, Western Värmland, where the percentage of farms deserted has been calculated to be about 20 percent.

Swedish regional differences may not reverse the English pattern entirely, however, as there may have been much more desertion of farms in the communal regions than these figures suggest. This is because in regions of large villages, if the entire village was not deserted, the source material and methodology used make it difficult to establish the desertion of individual farms within the village (Sandnes 1981, 106). This was less true if there were smaller villages and a large proportion of individual farms, as in the Northern Vedbo Hundred. Moreover, desertion is clearest in less-communal areas where settlement tended to be in individual farms, such as Western Värmland. This bias may be responsible for the pattern we see.

Desertion promoted a change in the distribution of land ownership at this time, as many deserted holdings found their way into the hands of the nobility or the church. Newly acquired holdings often were used for pasture farming, because, as in parts of France, England, and Germany at the same time, low prices of cereals discouraged arable husbandry (Sawyer and Sawyer 1993, 162; Österberg 1981, 209). Here we see a regional difference. To incorporate deserted acreage into estates and convert it to pasture was most common in the communal regions of southern and central Sweden, where there were already large estates and demesne farms. In less-communal regions, on the other hand, land was much less likely to be incorporated into large estates and was more likely to be resettled (Österberg 1981, 209). In such areas desertion of farms did not become permanent. Thus, events in the communal regions of Sweden and Denmark were more likely to follow the eastern European pattern, where the landowning nobility increased their control over the land in the period following the crisis of the fourteenth century, rather than a western European pattern, where the opposite was often true.

Throughout Sweden the amount of land held by the nobility and the church began to expand, a process that was to continue until the Reformation (Sawyer and Sawyer 1993, 135). During the fifteenth century the

Crown attempted to impose restrictions on expansion of *frälse* land, although this only may have prompted the nobility to attempt to consolidate their landholdings (Kirby 1990, 40). Despite the increase in noble land, however, there was no increase in demesne farming at this time. Estates typically were leased out to many tenants to farm. Bollerup's manor in Danish Skåne, consisting of 130 tenanted holdings distributed over four parishes, is an example of the latter (Mead 1981, 60).

### Sixteenth Century

The sixteenth century was a time of economic boom in Sweden, as in most parts of Europe (Myrdal and Söderberg 1991, 523; Metcalf 1995, 545). By this time the Union of Kalmar had dissolved and Sweden was largely independent of Denmark-Norway. The population began to grow quickly. As in France and Germany, population growth slowed in the latter half of the sixteenth century, particularly in the communal regions of eastern Sweden (Myrdal and Söderberg 1991, 527; Pounds 1990, 256). Towns in Sweden remained small (Pounds 1990, 224).

Population growth in the early sixteenth century promoted settlement of new lands and the creation of new farms. Gustavus Vasa indirectly encouraged the settlement of Crown lands in the north by exempting colonists from several years of taxation (Mead 1981, 63; Österberg 1991, 159). At this time settlement expanded considerably in the north and also in the more peripheral regions of the south and west (Mead 1981, 75; Myrdal and Söderberg 1991, 523; Magnusson 1996, 38–39). From 1530 to 1630 the number of building units almost doubled in Sweden (Magnusson 1996, 40). Such new settlement helped maintain the numbers of freehold or tax peasants in Sweden. For example, about half of the new settlements in Värmland and Närke (in central Sweden) were freehold or tax farms (Österberg 1991, 158).

Politically, Sweden was becoming united under the Vasa Dynasty and was developing as a political power. The central state was becoming more powerful, a process that was aided by the Reformation and Crown expropriation of church lands under Gustavus Vasa (r. 1523–60). Reflecting the development of greater central control, fortified strongholds multiplied in Scandinavia at this time and were used as centers of administration and tax collection. Externally, the Swedes gained greater control over the Baltic trade, due to the diminished power of the Hanseatic League (Mead 1981, 58). The rising importance of the Baltic in European trade and the decline of the Hanse's monopoly brought economic boom to Scandinavian kingdoms (Metcalf 1995, 545). During the boom both urban and rural dwellers appear to have thrived. The mining industry expanded. In the agricultural sector in the latter part of the century Denmark and Sweden again shifted from grain to livestock production, since animal fats were in high demand and Scandinavians were better able to compete successfully in this sphere than in grains (Myrdal and Söderberg 1991, 526). At this time rye overtook barley as the most common grain in eastern Sweden, although barley remained the dominant crop in northern Sweden (Heckscher 1954, 259; Myrdal and Söderberg 1991, 526). Yields also rose, from an average of perhaps 3 in the 1400s and early 1500s to yields of from 3 to 7 by the mid-sixteenth century (Magnusson 1996, 54–55).

Myrdal and Söderberg (1991) find evidence of regional differences in agricultural change at this time. Better implements (heavier plow shares for deeper tilling, lighter plow, use of iron harrow) and improved cultivation techniques (multiple plowings) began to be used in the early sixteenth century in the grain-producing, communal regions of eastern Sweden. These improved techniques were responsible for an increase in production at this time in eastern Sweden. As a result, seed/yield ratios improved and could reach 7 to 1. There was, however, no corresponding shortening of fallow periods, no use of leguminous crops, and no increase in fertilization of the fields. This led to overuse of the soil and eventually to falling production. In a study of grain production using tithe registers for 1539–1600 Myrdal and Söderberg (1991, 526) found falling production over the century in the traditional cereal-growing plains of Sweden, although they declined from a high level, and per capita harvests were typically larger than elsewhere. Less-communal western Sweden (Västergötland, Dalsland, and Värmland) and Småland were more dynamic, although they started from a lower level (see also Magnusson 1996, 38–39). Seed/yield ratios were typically lower in this region. In this region cattle raising and dairy farming were also important activities and were the primary basis for the prosperous rural economy in these regions in the later sixteenth century.

Other research shows the health of the rural economy in less-communal western Sweden in the sixteenth century. Österberg has found evidence in Värmland (in western Sweden c. 1540–1600) of a substantial change from cultivation of barley and mixed grain to cultivation of oats in the sixteenth century. Her research shows a comparatively complex peasant society in this region, in which several farms had capital goods and especially livestock (mostly cattle). Numbers of livestock were high and suggest trade in animal products. In addition, there was wide variation in the wealth of the peasantry, belying the egalitarianism typically assumed of the Swedish peasantry at the time. The peasantry also possessed a number of horses, which were important to the work of clearing new land, proceeding apace in this area (Österberg 1991, 133, 143). The predominance of livestock, existence of horses, and indications of market orientation suggest a differentiated and prosperous peasant economy in this western region of Sweden at this time.

On the whole, however, the economic growth of the sixteenth century petered out and did not keep pace with population growth. Increasing demands by an expansionist state contributed to the stagnation of the agrarian economy in all regions of Sweden by the seventeenth century (Myrdal and Söderberg 1991, 523; Magnusson 1996, 40). All over Sweden manorial, Crown, and ecclesiastical dues increased in complexity (Österberg 1991, 139), and in general the tax burden in Sweden began to rise very quickly from the 1560s. The number of extra taxes was often two per year (Österberg 1991, 139). In addition, the northern Seven Years' War (1563–70) with Denmark-Norway led to the plundering and burning of many farms along the frontier. Increased taxation and warfare caused a notable, although temporary, settlement regression in Sweden in many regions after this date. The term deserted (*öde*) was introduced in tax records to mean that a farm had not paid its taxes (Jutikkala 1981, 128).

The increased tax burden created by the state and the accompanying erosion of peasant status provoked peasant unrest. There were several peasant uprisings during the reign of Gustavus Vasa, of which the most serious was the Dacke Feud in Småland in 1542–43. In the spring of 1543 the king launched an offensive into Småland and defeated the rebels in battle (Kirby 1990, 34–35; Österberg 1991, 147). Surprisingly, the increase in taxation from the 1560s on did not provoke such unrest (excluding the club war—*klubbekriget*—in Finland in the 1590s). Instead, many peasants turned to the Crown begging for tax reductions and exemptions (Österberg 1991, 129). In regions affected by the war with Denmark-Norway, the Crown was responsive and began to issue general deeds of exemption for burnt and pillaged homesteads. This may have lessened dissatisfaction with new taxation.

### Seventeenth Century

The Swedish population continued to grow during the seventeenth century, although more slowly. Under Gustavus Adolphus (r. 1611–32) the Swedish population totaled about 900,000. One hundred years later, in 1720, it was about 1.44 million. Internal colonization again took place, particularly in forested lands of the north (Heckscher 1954, 117). The seventeenth century was most characterized by the expansionist policies of the Swedish Crown, increasing taxation, and further stagnation of the rural economy.

Initially, the principal aim of Sweden's expansionist policy was the acquisition of territory in the eastern Baltic area (Kirby 1990, 123).[5] Open conflict in northern Europe began in the sixteenth century with the entrance of Russian and Tatar troops into Livonia in January 1558 and continued intermittently until the Peace of Westphalia in 1648. The Russians and Tatars were defeated, leaving Sweden and Poland as the two primary protagonists in Livonia after the 1580s. A turning point was reached in 1621, when Livonia was captured as Riga fell to the Swedish army. By this means Sweden succeeded in establishing control over most of Livonia and over the mouth of the River Neva. This was the beginning of Swedish control in northern Germany and its age of empire, which endured for the remainder of the century (Kirby 1990, 107). Next Sweden was drawn into the Thirty Years' War in Germany (1630). Gustavus Adolphus extended Swedish control through northern Germany, an advance checked by his death on the battlefield of Lützen (1632). In the Peace of Westphalia (1648) Sweden secured its control of parts of northern Germany, including parts of Pomerania, the city of Wismar, and Bremen-Verden (Heckscher 1954, 286). It acquired territory closer to home also. After war with Denmark-Norway (1643–45), Sweden permanently acquired several provinces on the southern tip of the Scandinavian peninsula (Heckscher 1954, 128; Sawyer and Sawyer 1993, 79). The provinces were Gotland, Halland, Skåne, and Blekinge (from Denmark) and Jämtland, Härjedalen, and Bohuslän (from Norway).

Territorial expansion and warfare required vast sums, which Sweden did not have (Åström 1973, 58). Much of the money for the war effort came from outside of Sweden proper. The most important source of revenue came from Swedish control of the Baltic ports, through which came all grain exports from eastern Europe to the west. An arrangement worked out between Sweden and Poland allowed Gustavus Adolphus to levy tolls on ships trading in the Baltic. To collect these tolls, Swedish officials were placed at the ports of Thorn, Lübeck, Königsberg, and Danzig (Downing 1992, 196; Mead 1981, 67). The tolls were collected from 1628 to 1635 and were highly lucrative (Åström 1973, 92). Although not as large as the revenue from these Prussian tolls, French subsidies were also a major source of revenue for the Swedish war effort. France was not the only state that financed Sweden, as money also came from Holland, England, Spain, and some German states, although French subsidies were the largest and most enduring of the foreign subsidies. They were paid in 1632–33, 1637–48, 1657–66, and 1672–78 (Åström 1973, 94). They became the primary source of Swedish war finance once the Prussian tolls were lost. The Peace of Westphalia also supplied Sweden with revenue to pay for its war costs, as it awarded Sweden a large amount of cash with which to pay off its armies.

Yet this money did not suffice for war expenses, and the Crown also attempted to increase its revenues from Sweden itself. It created monopolies on the salt and grain trades. Controls on all trade throughout the period became stricter and more widespread, particularly on the iron and copper trades, which formed an important part of state revenues. Already, under the Hanseatic system, a limited number of ports had introduced monopoly controls. In 1617 Stockholm became a staple town for the trading centers of the Bothnian Sea. Eventually, Stockholm proclaimed a monopoly of the tar trade for the whole of its Baltic territories (Heckscher 1954, 100–101), much to the annoyance of the English, who were their main customers for the tar. Internal taxation also was revised and expanded. During the Thirty Years' War the provincial bailiff system was systematized, and new royal officials were introduced into the countryside (Downing 1992, 200). Tax records were improved. The old established land registers ( *jordeböcker*), which expressed taxation in terms of the *hemman,* or *mantal,* and which were maintained at the provincial level, gradually were replaced by more complete taxation maps (Mead 1981, 102). Greater taxation was not borne readily by the peasantry. Resistance to activities of land surveyors, who estimated yields on different qualities of land in order to determine the tax rate, is illustrated by a royal instruction of 1688 that declared that "no one shall hinder the land surveyor" in the execution of his duties.

In addition, as a quick way of raising money and troops, in the early seventeenth century the Crown sold off, or gave, a large proportion of its landholdings to the nobility (and, to a lesser extent, the peasantry) (Rydeberg 1985, 184). In part this was a deliberate policy, especially by Gustavus Adolphus and Axel Oxenstierna, who was chancellor of the realm from 1611 to 1654. Both men were convinced that natural (in-kind) economy should be replaced by a money economy, especially in the field of public finances (Heckscher 1954), and they saw alienating Crown lands as a means to this end. Yet, by and large, the natural economy remained. Payments of rent continued to be in kind. The only difference was that they were made to a new (noble) recipient and not the Crown. When alienation was in the nature of a pure grant of land, the Crown received no payment for it at all. The result was both declining Crown revenues and the loss of much of the Crown land. Revenues of Crown lands and other customary revenues decreased between 1633 and 1677 (Åström 1973, 82). Almost all the estates Gustavus Vasa had acquired from the church in the sixteenth century thus were transferred to the aristocracy in the early seventeenth century and many more besides (Heckscher 1954, 117–18; Rydeberg 1985, 184). The peasantry particularly suffered a degradation of their status, as formerly Crown and tax peasants became peasants on noble land. By 1652 only about 28 percent of total landholdings remained in the possession of the peasantry and the Crown.

## The *Reduktion*

In the long run the drawbacks of alienation were clear, and the policy began to be reversed. This occurred under Charles X to a very moderate degree and under Charles XI (after 1660) in a far more drastic fashion. Above all, the peasantry agitated for a reversal of the process of alienation, or *reduktion,* as it came to be called. In 1650 the unhappy consequences of the alienation of Crown lands were presented in the *Riksdag* by the peasant estate. The peasant estate urged the queen to resume all alienated freehold and Crown land. Queen Christina used the agitation to help ensure the succession of her cousin, Karl Gustav, who promised to bring about the resumption of Crown lands. The pressure for a complete *reduktion* came to a head in the *Riksdag* of 1680, when the three non-noble estates (those of the peasants, townsmen, and miners) presented a motion calling for the resumption of alienated lands (Kirby 1990, 252, 254). At this point the policy of alienation was fully reversed, and a large-scale restoration of alienated lands was carried out (Heckscher 1954, 119; Rydeberg 1985, 184). By 1687 much of the *reduktion* had been completed. It solved the Crown's fiscal problems. In 1693 the king was able to announce that he did not require the estates to grant any extraordinary aids. The finances of the kingdom were declared to be in a healthy state (Kirby 1990, 252–57).

The reversion had momentous consequences for the peasants. In the long run the number of freehold peasants was increased as a result of the *reduktion,* while the nobility's share of the land shrank. The aristocracy, which in 1655 had controlled 72 percent of the farmland, possessed less than 33 percent by the end of the century (Østerud 1978, 83; Rydeberg 1985, 185). During the same period the numbers of freeholders, or tax peasants, doubled (Downing 1992, 202; see also Heckscher 1954, 126). Freeholders and tenants on Crown land, who through alienation of their taxes and dues to a lord had lost some of their former independence, now regained their former status. It is evident that their general position was thereby improved. This was particularly true of freeholders, who now had about one-third of the land at their partial disposition in 1700 (Østerud 1978, 84; Rydeberg 1985, 185).

As Heckscher notes, however, "one must not imagine that the landlords were submitted to terrible suffering and deprivation" by the *reduktion* (1954, 121). Although the size of noblemen's estates was reduced from the middle to the end of the seventeenth century, the nobility still possessed more land than before the alienation to them of royal lands a hundred years earlier. Moreover, now their holdings were more concentrated in one area, as the *reduktion* had greatest effect on scattered farms and pieces of land (which had once belonged to the Crown), which now found their way to the peasantry (Østerud 1978, 88, 83). The main inconvenience of the confiscation was confusion in property relations. Titles to land were disputed sometimes for decades, with endless litigations necessary to decide whether a certain piece of land belonged to the noble or to the Crown. Often ownership simply was reshuffled. While many great landlords lost their holdings, many large estates accrued to reversion administrators and the king's favorites (Heckscher 1954, 123).

Few manorial demesnes reverted to the Crown, as the Crown had very limited interest in acquisition of them. Such demesnes had to be operated on a larger scale, and by that time the Crown managed practically no large-scale agriculture. Thus, manorial demesnes remained in the hands of the nobility. For example, in Uppland and Södermanland (eastern Sweden) most estates with demesnes remained in the possession of the nobility and gentry (Hecksher 1954, 120–21; Østerud 1978, 83). The *reduktion* did not interrupt a trend toward large-scale demesne farming in Sweden, which had begun earlier in the century in a process parallel to the transition from *Grundherrschaft*[6] to *Gutscherrschaft*[7] in Prussia and Poland at the same time (see chap. 7; Heckscher 1954, 128; Østerud 1978, 86, 88). In particular, there had been a rapid expansion in the size of manor farms (*säterier*) in southeastern Sweden in the years immediately following the Peace of Westphalia (1648), with the return of a large number of officers from the war (Jutikkala 1975, 161). This change was encouraged by the fact that manorial home farms paid fewer taxes than scattered noble land, and they supplied duties from the peasantry.

In terms of public finance the *reduktion* entailed a return to a natural economy, which persisted longer in Sweden than in any other comparable country. The renaissance of a natural economy was most clearly reflected in the organization of the armed forces. Resumed land became the basis of the *indelningsverk* (which dates to 1682), a military system based on the exchange of land for military service. Each officer was granted either a large landholding or a percentage of the revenue from one (Downing 1992, 204; Mead 1981, 104). A property that supported a cavalryman and his horse in lieu of taxation was called a *rusthåll*, its owners *rusthållare.* Such properties were owned usually by "persons of quality" or wealthier farmers. Eventually, this system supported a force of five thousand officers in Sweden. In addition, a fixed number of regular soldiers was required from each province. They were supported by groups of wealthier peasants in exchange for freedom from conscription. The soldiers were provided with a cottage and a smallholding, and they were supposed to engage in farming when not needed for military duties. This method of financing the army meant that the army tended to be composed of peasants rather than warriors. Even civil servants were funded in this way, as they were assigned specific shares in the Crown's revenue from peasants. Thus, all civilian and military officials of the Crown became bound to the soil from which they received their livelihood (Heckscher 1954, 124–28).

Although the *reduktion* had promoted demesne farming and increased the amount of freehold in Sweden, it did little to encourage agricultural development. Throughout the seventeenth century increasing taxation had a negative effect on agrarian change and improvements. For example, increasing taxation from the end of the sixteenth century discouraged the clearing of new farms (Jutikkala 1981, 141). Österberg (1991, 143) also notes a slackening in new settlement in western Värmland after about 1565, when taxation began to increase rapidly. As Jutikkala notes, new taxes were assessed mostly on the basis of the number of farms, so it made no sense for farmers to clear new farms for the sake of a few tax-free years (1981, 141).

Nor did the development of demesne farming improve agricultural productivity in the communal regions of the east, although there were some changes. In eastern parts of this region—parts of Västmanland and Västergötland, most of Östergötland, the important provinces around Lake Mälaren, and the coastal strip in the south of Norrland—a two-field system, in which half of the land was left fallow every years, was now customary (Magnusson 1996, 56). The three-field system, which divided land between fall crops, spring crops, and fallow, occurred in some districts in the south of Sweden (Skåne, which had been Swedish since 1658, and Småland), along the shores of Lake Vättern, and on the islands of Öland and Gotland (Heckscher 1954, 152). Cereal growing remained the main concern of these farms, and yields remained poor compared to other European countries such as England, the Netherlands, and France at the same time. In (communal) central Sweden, the primary grain-growing region, average yields in the seventeenth century were 3 to 5 times the seed sown (Mead 1981, 80; Myrdal and Söderberg 1991, 529; Magnusson 1996, 52). This compares to an average of 6 to 1 and higher in England and the Netherlands around 1700 (Pounds 1990, 279). Assuming lower average yields in the less-communal regions of around 2 to 4 (Magnusson 1996, 52), this suggests that Swedish yields in general averaged about 4 to 1— lower than average in France but higher than average in Germany (Myrdal and Söderberg 1991, 529). Low yields did not mean that agricultural output did not increase. As population grew, so did output. In the best lands of the south provinces such as Östergötland consistently had a grain surplus (Gaunt 1996, 410), and other southern provinces continued to pay rents in grain (Gissel 1981a, 149). Most of the increase, however, came from the cultivation of new land rather than from gains in productivity. Even with the extension of cultivation through internal colonization, increases in food production were insufficient given population growth (Heckscher 1954, 115–16). Sweden was not self-sufficient in grain and typically supplemented its own production with grain imported from Livonia and other Baltic lands (Åström 1973, 70; Mead 1981, 80). In 1685, for example, after the failure of the harvest in central Sweden, the Baltic provinces supplied Stockholm with 153,145 hectoliters of grain (Kirby 1990, 241).

The rural economy in many less-communal regions retained a pastoral focus, and yield ratios for cereals were typically lower than in the cereal plains of the east (Myrdal and Söderberg 1991, 529). For example, in western Sweden most rents were paid in butter or money, not grain (Gissel 1981a, 149). In Västergötland the trend toward the use of horses rather than oxen continued, and over the century oxen came to be replaced by horses (Magnusson 1996, 59). In the colonial areas in the north seed/yield ratios were also low, probably less than 3 to 1 (Åström 1973, 62).

There is evidence, however, that conditions in the less-communal areas were better than those in communal areas. Gaunt (1977) examined one less-communal (Skinnskatteberg) and four communal parishes (Västerfärnebo, Kolbäck, Lovö, and Björksta), all in central Sweden, from the seventeenth to the eighteenth centuries. One of these communal parishes Västerfärnebo, was a village of free farmers and not tenants. He found that all the communal areas produced more grain for the market (the less-communal Skinnskatteberg always had a deficit of grain), but he found that on several indicators the less-communal region had the highest levels of economic well-being. Families were largest and had the most complicated structures in the less-communal region. In Skinnskatteberg the household size averaged about 7 people. In Västerfärnebo it averaged about 5.9, and in the manor-dominated parishes it averaged about 4. There were also more children born per family in less-communal Skinnskatteberg (7.3 for men, 5.7 for women) than any of the other parishes (the number is higher for men because of the remarriage of men with still-fertile women). Looking at figures for the number of surviving children, both Skinnskatteberg and Västerfärnebo were similar in having just over 2.5 surviving children per woman (Gaunt 1977, 203), numbers of surviving children were much lower in the manorialized parishes. Furthermore, Gaunt gives evidence of innovative, labor-intensive agricultural techniques in less-communal Skinnskatteberg, noting: "In no other area have I found such a variety of growing methods in use simultaneously." He also notes that problems such as the abandonment of land because of infertility and farm turnover were much more common in the manor-dominated parishes. In the communal, non-manor-dominated parish of Västerfärnebo economic difficulties were suppressed by the extra work possibilities available from the cartage business, but agriculture itself produced little surplus and gave an average crop yield of only 4 to 6 to 1 if fertilized every three or 4 years (Gaunt 1977, 187, 193, 190). None of the innovative agricultural techniques found in Skinnskatteberg were used.

### Eighteenth Century

The early eighteenth century saw a momentary lull in population growth in Sweden, as the pestilence crossed the Baltic to Sweden in 1710, carrying off as many as 40,000 people in Stockholm (Kirby 1990, 352). After this episode, however, the population began to grow again. From 1749 on official publications of vital statistics begin to appear—by far the oldest regular compilation of its kind (Heckscher 1954, 133). These figures show that the population grew steadily throughout the eighteenth century, from 1.4 million in 1700 to 2.3 million in 1800 (Winberg 1978, 170; Kirby 1990, 355). In the long-settled areas of the south smallholdings began to multiply. There was an important difference in new settlements of the eighteenth century. While the seventeenth century had been a period in which forest regions had been plowed up and used for agriculture, in the eighteenth century the new land brought under cultivation was largely in old, settled regions (Heckscher 1954, 154). In communal Sweden, where noble estates were most numerous, the number of new leasehold farms (*torp*) increased significantly (Kirby 1990, 355). In the same regions the number of cotters and landless people also increased rapidly, especially at the end of the century (Heckscher 1954, 154, 171; Winberg 1978, 171). This was in part due to a resistance by noblemen in these regions to the division of peasant lands (Gaunt 1977, 192), although from the middle of the eighteenth century resistance to subdivision of the parental farm lessened (Østerud 1978, 109). Overall the population remained overwhelmingly rural. In Sweden and Finland less than a tenth of the population lived in towns (Winberg 1978, 170). In 1760 about 78.6 percent of the population were rural dwellers, most of whom were supported by agriculture. This share remained almost constant for more than a hundred years; as late as 1870, it was 72.4 percent (Heckscher 1954, 133–47). Civil servants, the officers of the armed services (now well established in Sweden/Finland in their rural residences and landholdings), and clergy were the local elite of the rural community (Mead 1991, 131).

As before, economic growth in the eighteenth century was notable in less-communal western Sweden, where the value of *mantal* was tripled between 1730–34 and 1770–74 in terms of the value of the rent and tithes paid to the Crown, while it was weaker in the communal regions of the east where there were many large estates (Jonsson, Köll, and Pettersson 1990, 125–26). In the regions of peasant agriculture in the west improvements came from expansion of the area under cultivation coupled with the intensification of traditional methods. Agriculture in the communal areas continued to employ a regular two- and, more rarely, a three-field system of agriculture, with one field in a fallow rotation. The common denominator for all these methods was a permanent separation between fields and meadows. Fields were reserved for cereals, and fodder crops typically were not grown (Østerud 1978, 162). As a result, crop yields per acre did not improve and remained about 5 to 1 (Gaunt 1977, 190). In this region most additional food supplies came not from increases in yields per acre but from expansion of the area under cultivation (Heckscher 1954, 153).

All over Sweden there was an expansion of oats cultivation and the introduction of the potato, which increased in use in the second half of the eighteenth century (see Gadd 1983, 339, 341, 344). Potatoes did not catch on initially, but then people found they could be used for distilling vodka. This caused their popularity to increase, and the general effect was to facilitate the introduction of the crop for other purposes as well. Since the mash from the distilling process was used for cattle feeding, the introduction of the potato also indirectly advanced livestock farming and hence (presumably) improved agriculture. Potatoes also were used in human diets, and all these things together meant that the introduction of potatoes improved nutrition and thus contributed to a fall in the death rate in the nineteenth century (Winberg 1977, 331).

### Domestic Industry

During the eighteenth century domestic industry for the production of textiles increased considerably. This industry was concentrated in less-communal parts of western and northern Sweden (a pattern we have seen in England, and France). In these regions, in the west, (Västergötland), in the north (in Dalarna and Ångermanland), also in the south (in parts of Småland), the rural population may have devoted more time to crafts than to agriculture. Linen and wool cloth were the main products, but some households also produced wood, iron, and leather goods. Furniture and carriages were other important products. These products were sold all over the country by traveling peddlers, traditionally from the western province of Västergötland. Furthermore, the market area of domestic industry was not limited to Sweden, as exports seem to have been considerable (Heckscher 1954, 189–90).

Rural domestic industry was actively discouraged by the Crown, which preferred that such activities be confined to urban areas where they could be monitored more closely. Nevertheless, despite royal opposition, industries continued to thrive in these regions. In the nineteenth century the influence of the old household industry was especially strong in the so-called Seven Hundreds—seven of the hundreds of Älvsborg County in western Sweden—where the modern cotton industry came to be concentrated. This industry relied on traditional skills, from the old household industry, of the population in the area (Heckscher 1954, 232).

In some regions of Sweden (e.g., Bergslagen in Dalecarlia) mining and associated activities, like charcoal burning, had been important economic activities since the late Middle Ages (Myrdal and Söderberg 1991, 534; Isacson 1979, 177). These regions provided iron and copper for both a domestic and international market, and for a time Sweden even dominated the European market for these metals. Furthermore, income from iron and copper exports made up a large proportion of total state revenues. In these regions agriculture played a secondary role in the rural economy, and market relations were necessarily well developed for the sale of metal products and the exchange of metal products for grain. In the seventeenth century tar burning became an important market activity for many peasant households, particularly in Småland and western Finland.

### The Enclosures

In 1746 Jacob Faggot published an influential paper on problems associated with Sweden's communal open field system. He proclaimed open fields "the nurse of the country's poverty" and suggested that old communal practices be discarded and that land consolidation and enclosure proceed apace. The first move toward a realization of Faggot's ideas was taken very soon after his first proposal, with the Field Consolidation Act of 1749 (*storskiftet*). This relied on consensus for repartition and thus did not have much effect. In 1757 a new act, and subsequently the Surveying Act of 1783, enabled the individual villager to demand consolidation of his holdings (Heckscher 1954, 155–56; Dahl 1961).

These policies aimed at abolition of the *bytvång* (village compulsion) and the strip system and at partition of the commons and wastelands among individual villagers. Peasant resistance to redistribution and consolidation was sometimes intense (Bäck 1984, 309). Typically, it was greatest when some villagers were to be deprived of their houses and buildings in the village and settled on isolated homesteads. This not only made it necessary to erect new buildings, but, more important, it often left the relocated farmer uprooted and broke up the solidarity of the village. Where there were consolidated estates and hence a single owner of many land-holdings, it was easier to consolidate land—for example, in Skåne. As a result, parts of this province were soon far ahead in field reforms, and by 1822 a great deal of all the land in Skåne had been redistributed (Heckscher 1954, 157). Consolidation was more difficult in areas of the country where land was primarily in peasant possession and there were many freeholders, as in Dalarna (Dahl 1961, 67; Østerud 1978, 146). On the other hand, sometimes there was no resistence to consolidation on the part of peasant landowners, who not infrequently initiated a request for consolidation (e.g., in Ekebyborna [see Olai 1983, 238]), and evidence suggests that in general the peasantry as a class were divided on the issue (Bäck 1984, 308)

Unlike in the English midlands, enclosure in Sweden led to neither flight from the land nor a decrease in the number of smallholdings.[8] On the contrary, peasant farming tended to be stimulated by the tendency to parcel larger farms into smaller consolidated lots with independent owners. Thus, while enclosure stimulated the move to large farms in midland England, it had the reverse effect in Sweden (Heckscher 1954, 161; Olai 1983, 241). There it led to the proliferation of small family farms. The consolidation and enclosure movement was successful, however, in breaking down the communal system, and by 1870 enclosure of former communal land largely had been accomplished. These farms also had clearer legal title to their land than at any time in the past (Olai 1983).

### The Agricultural Revolution

By the second half of the eighteenth century an agricultural expansion began in Sweden. High grain prices during the Napoleonic Wars promoted the change (Winberg 1978, 171). Arable areas were expanded, production was increased, and Sweden was exporting grain by 1830. Peasant farms throughout Sweden led the way in these changes, particularly in the west and northeast (Gadd and Jonsson 1990, 28; for Dalecarlia, see Isacson 1979, 186). On the peasant holdings traditional implements were improved; new crops and new methods of crop rotation and animal husbandry were introduced. The introduction of iron plows and threshers accelerated with the boom period of the 1850s (Gadd 1983, 341). The manor farms of the south also participated in these changes and were ahead in the introduction of new, factory-produced tools and implements such as grain drills and horse rakes. The peasantry were reluctant to take up these comparatively expensive tools, and it was not until the 1870s that they were taken up on peasant holdings (Østerud 1978, 162–64; Jonsson, Köll and Pettersson 1990, 128).

As a result of such changes, throughout the agricultural lands of southern Sweden the fallow was reduced (Gadd 1983, 344). The growing of wheat expanded, while the growing of rye contracted (Heckscher 1954, 259). New soil increasingly began to be cultivated, and the reclamation of land expanded particularly from the 1820s (Winberg 1977, 332). Between 1866 and 1870 output of cereal crops more than doubled. Famine crises declined in number (Heckscher 1954, 258–60). Grain exports, mostly from the south and west, increased (Winberg 1978, 170). In southern and western Sweden the possibility of exporting grain in turn led to increases in the value of land (Østerud 1978, 179).

In many ways, however, this agricultural revolution was too little, too late. The appearance of American grain on European markets in the late 1870s imparted a heavy blow to farmers. In Sweden farmers called for protection against cheap grain imports (Mead 1981, 236). Tariffs were raised. Nevertheless, the tendency to switch from cereal production to more profitable animal farming was too strong to be checked by the relatively moderate tariffs (Heckscher 1954, 257; Østerud 1979, 177). Eventually, Sweden became an exporter of meat and dairy produce and a net importer of grain (Østerud 1979, 177).

Furthermore, despite changes and improvements, an already substantial landless and impoverished class continued to grow (Winberg 1977, 331; Isacson 1979, 179). Winberg notes that in the period between 1750 and 1850, while the number of peasants in Sweden rose by 10 percent, the number of the landless more than quadrupled (1977, 331). Many of these people were able to support themselves as wage earners, as the changes in agriculture created a new demand for day laborers, and, after the middle of the nineteenth century, there was a further demand for workers in industry. Nevertheless, the economic expansion did not always suffice to cater to all. For example, Isacson found in a study of the parish of By in Southern Dalecarlia in the early nineteenth century that, despite dramatic increases in grain production, there emerged a group of agriculturalists whose members had little chance of economic or social mobility or owning their own land (1979, 185). This class was most susceptible to economic fluctuations. Thus, although famine crises were fewer than before, in the 1860s peasants still on occasion consumed bread made with bark and mosses of various kinds (Moberg 1973, 47). Mass emigration to North America became a major safety valve during the last three to four decades of the nineteenth century. Nearly a million people emigrated from Sweden between 1850 and 1910, most going to North America (Østerud 1978, 187).

In addition, the Swedish population remained overwhelmingly rural.

As late as 1870, 72.4 percent of the population were supported by agriculture (Heckscher 1954, 133–47; Østerud 1978, 75). The census of 1910 was the first to show an agricultural population of less than one-half of the total population (48.8 percent). Not until 1936 did industry employ a larger share of the population than agriculture (Heckscher 1954, 214).

In sum, agricultural productivity in the best farming lands of Sweden began to rise significantly only after the enclosure movement had begun to eradicate the old communal farming systems in these regions, which had been an obstacle to technical change and innovation. There are signs of a growing rural economy in the less-communal regions of Sweden (notably western Sweden) from the sixteenth to the nineteenth centuries; however, in general, development everywhere in Sweden was hindered by oppressive taxation policies from the end of the sixteenth century. Other factors specific to the national context—uncertain property rights and misguided Crown policies in economic matters—also played a part in stifling agrarian change throughout Sweden.

## Factors Specific to the Protonational Context

### State Institutions

In England and the Netherlands the maintenance of some democracy at the national level had positive consequences for rural development. We may expect the same to have occurred in Sweden. The maintenance of democracy did limit taxation in Sweden, at least before the early seventeenth century. From the seventeenth century, however, Crown taxation became a burden on the rural economy. In addition, unlike the English and Dutch cases, an important deficiency in Sweden was a high level of uncertainty concerning property rights in the different types of land (Olai 1983, 240; Winberg 1985, 237), which increased transaction costs, and discouraged production and trade.

Like England, Sweden saw both early national unification and state centralization. This was promoted by several factors. First, in such a sparsely populated land there was greater political interest in unification than in many countries. Second, the estates and fiefs of the landed nobility were scattered over many different provinces, such that it was rare for any noble to dominate any particular region of the country. No noble had the territorial base to establish an independent principality. Furthermore, communications in Sweden were aided by a long coastline and the existence of extensive winter roads (for sleds). As it was impossible to block all these communication routes, this promoted linkages between all parts of Sweden.

With national unification came a national economy and a single coinage. Regional differences in coinage disappeared in the Middle Ages, and local tolls and other economic barriers between provinces were rarer than in any other country, including England (Heckscher 1954, 37). There was also centralized law. While the provincial law codes date to the thirteenth century, comprehensive codes for the whole kingdom were produced in the 1350s under Magnus Eriksson (Sawyer and Sawyer 1993, 17; Gustafsson 1994, 32). The Land Law of 1350 itself was a written constitution outlining fundamental principles governing relations among the Crown, nobility, clerics, burghers, and peasants.

Like many places in Europe, the late medieval period saw the development of democracy in Sweden. The Land Law became the foundation of Swedish democracy. Significantly, it specified that decisions about extra taxation were to be made by the bishop, lawman, six aristocrats, and six others from each province (Sawyer and Sawyer 1993, 98). During the fifteenth century representatives of provincial assemblies were summoned to special meetings of the Swedish royal council to approve and publicize decisions, rather than to help make them. Meetings of this kind were the basis for the development of the Swedish *Riksdag,* a central assembly equivalent to the English Parliament. The meeting at Arboga in 1435 traditionally is considered the first Swedish parliament—a little later than the first national English Parliaments and the French Estates-General (Downing 1992, 188; see Heckscher 1954, 285). The *Riksdag,* with separate estates of nobles, other landowners, townsmen, and miners, first appeared in a clearly recognizable form at the so-called Reformation *Riksdag* held in 1527 at Västerås (Sawyer and Sawyer 1993, 98).

The separate estates were not equally important in the *Riksdag,* however. The Estate of the Nobility was the most privileged estate, and it retained its predominance and influence in the *Riksdag* until the eighteenth century (Østerud 1978, 69). Before the Reformation the clergy were also privileged. Both the nobility and the clergy were treated separately from the mass of the rural population both in terms of law and taxes (Metcalf 1995, 526). In addition, the nobility and the clergy were the only estates who had a political voice in the royal council, which had a great deal of power during the late medieval period. Councillors claimed the right to approve new members proposed by kings. During minorities and vacancies they had great latitude as representatives of the kingdom, controlling royal castles and fiefs and choosing the next king (Sawyer and Sawyer 1993, 98). Although the nobility and clergy were the most influential estates in the *Riksdag,* the common people also had some influence in Swedish democracy. At the provincial level each province initially had a representative assembly (*landsthing*), made up of magnates and men from the hundreds, although the *landsthing* disappeared early in most provinces except Norrland. At the local level was the hundred moot, which was an informal assembly in which the free, or tax, peasants openly debated and decided local matters (Scott 1977, 64; Sawyer and Sawyer 1993, 84). By the fifteenth century the moot had become a popularly elected permanent organization, both a court of law and an administrative body in charge of elections to the peasant estate of the *Riksdag,* public works, local taxes, and charities (Downing 1992).

Local participation in Swedish democracy endured through the early modern period. As the house of Vasa consolidated its control, they, like the early Tudors, rallied commoners and peasants to their side in disputes with the magnates. As in England, though the power of the king vis-à-vis the aristocracy increased, it was at the expense of perpetuating the influence of the lower orders in the political process. One consequence of this step was the maintenance of the power of the *Riksdag* and the continuing influence of peasant estate within it. Throughout the financial strains of the seventeenth century, and during the reign of an absolute monarch like Charles XI, the *Riksdag* retained the right to give consent to any new taxation (Åström 1973, 98) and to the levying of troops (Dahlgren 1973, 180). Within the *Riksdag* the peasant estate was not uninfluential, particularly on matters that did not elicit concerted opposition from the more powerful noble estate (Bäck 1984; Gustafsson 1994). For example, the peasant estate were important proponents of the *reduktion* of the seventeenth century, as noted earlier. The continued control of the *Riksdag* over taxation also helped keep taxation comparatively low, at least until the early seventeenth century (Österberg 1991, 162), although by the 1620s it was reaching oppressive levels, and by the beginning of the eighteenth century the greater part of the surplus on a freeholder's farm was taken as a tax by the Crown (Winberg 1985, 230). As noted, this had negative effects on the rural economy. By the eighteenth century the tax on freehold stopped increasing, which allowed for subsequent improvements in the rural economy in the eighteenth and nineteenth centuries (Gadd and Jonsson 1990, 23).

Along with the development of democracy in Sweden came the development of a national legal system. By the fifteenth century the hundred court was the most important lower court, although the Fjärding Thing (one fourth of a hundred) was responsible for petty matters. In the hundred court a chief was assisted by two judges and "the twelve," a kind of jury whose members decided matters of fact and declared guilt or innocense. The twelve, called the *nämnd,* became a permanent part of the court and thus somewhat different from the Anglo-Saxon jury (Scott 1977, 64). The judicial revolution in Sweden came in the seventeenth century. From 1614 state courts of appeal (*hovrätter*) were created in a few places and took control of the lower courts, and a part of the Council of the Realm came to function as a supreme court. A new Supreme Court was created in 1789.

Despite the maintenance of democracy and the development of a national legal system, however, property rights in land remained uncertain in Sweden until the eighteenth and nineteenth centuries. This was true of all kinds of land: *kyrkjord, frälsejord* (noble land) and *skattejord* (freehold or tax land). Land owned by the church and the aristocracy was subject to confiscation by the Crown, as the church lands were during the Reformation and some noble land during the *Reduktion* of the late seventeenth century. Even rights to freehold or tax land were comparatively uncertain. The state occasionally claimed to have *dominum directum* to the farms of *skattebönder,* or tax peasants, a kind of superior ownership. The *skattebönder* did not obtain full legal ownership of their land until 1789 (Jonsson, Köll, and Pettersson 1990, 132). Further uncertainty was created by the *bördsrätt,* an institution that was included in the provincial laws of the thirteenth century and which persisted into the nineteenth century. According to the *bördsrätt,* if a person wished to sell land he or she had inherited, his or her relatives had first refusal on the land (Winberg 1985, 232). The seller was obliged to advertise the sale of the land at the local court. Any relative who wished to buy the land had about two years to do so, at a price determined by six people, three appointed by the seller and three appointed by the relative wishing to buy. The *bördsrätt* was supposed to have a two-year limit; after this time relatives' claims to the land lapsed. Yet, if a relative could claim that there existed a common ancestor who had not distributed the estate among all relatives at some point in the past, even more than one hundred years previously, then the relative could lay claim to part of the farm. Since kinship in Sweden was reckoned through both sexes—that is, it was cognatic—this meant a very large group of people potentially could have a claim to a farm. These practices maintained uncertainty in property rights and in effect limited individual rights to land. Disputes about who had the right to redeem property were common (e.g., in eighteenth-century Örebro [see Rydeberg 1985, 187]). These problems persisted until the law of 1720 limited the group of relatives with a claim to land, while a law of 1805 limited claims on land whose purchase had been confirmed before the local court (Winberg 1985, 240). Moreover, property rights in land were rarely recorded in writing, as with English copyhold, and this promoted uncertainty and disputes about ownership rights. Land disputes were often decided by parties bringing with them large numbers of "oath-helpers" who vouched for their rights before the local court (Winberg 1985, 240). One positive effect of the *storskifte* (consolidation) legislation in Sweden was that it enabled many property holders to obtain for the first time a legal document describing their property rights in writing (Olai 1983, 238).

Nor did maintenance of democracy in Sweden mean enlightened Crown policies with regard to economic matters. Most of the medieval and early modern monarchs and local lords tried to limit trade, commerce, shipping, and handicraft to the towns, although many took no radical measures against rural pursuit of these activities (Heckscher 1954, 72; Österberg 1991, 140). Like most medieval and early modern monarchs, they also habitually granted monopolies over particular trades and industries to various groups and towns, which inhibited economic growth. In addition, some early Swedish kings had a predilection for a natural economy. Gustavus Vasa is the best example here. For spending purposes he preferred goods to money, and payments were effected in kind rather than money. This policy was not entirely detrimental to trade, but it made it more difficult. Indeed, Gustavus's other policies did much to increase trade in Sweden. Gustavus himself was a ceaseless trader, and in other respects he worked to improve communications through Sweden and otherwise facilitate trade (Heckscher 1954, 65, 66). The predilection for natural economy persisted in Sweden through the seventeenth century, as noted earlier.

## Coinage

Crown policy seems to have been misguided particularly with regards to the coinage. Among other things this may explain why natural economy persisted so long in Sweden. The right of coinage was the prerogative of the Royal Mint, such that individuals possessed no right to have plate struck into coin. Regular coinages began to be issued in Sweden in the twelfth century. The mark was the basic unit as well as the highest. Originally, the mark was a unit of weight, as was the pound (*libra*), which was the base of the old French *livre* as well as the still current pound sterling (Heckscher 1954, 59, 57). This money was issued only sporadically. Foreign currencies circulated freely, due in part to the frequent debasement of the Swedish currency (Sawyer and Sawyer 1993, 8). By 1520 no less than sixteen to eighteen marks in coin were required to make one mark in silver, which implies a decline to one-eighth or one-ninth of the relation prevailing in the thirteenth century (Heckscher 1954, 58).

In response to debasement Gustavus Vasa struck a coin of stable value called the daler, which had almost exactly the same silver content as many foreign *thaler* coins in common use at the time. The Swedish daler never was used as much as its foreign counterpart. Nevertheless, the daler remained unaffected by fluctuations in the value of other Swedish coins, and its silver content remained constant. It became the *riksdaler,* which retained its original value for centuries, even though the rest of the currency often suffered debasement. Thus, the Swedish population had at least one sound currency on which they could rely in the midst of general monetary confusion and continual debasement (Heckscher 1954, 76–77).

The greatest monetary folly in Sweden was the introduction in 1625 of a second, inferior copper standard. This was to affect the Swedish monetary system adversely for 150 years to come. It was initially introduced as a clumsy way of raising the foreign price of copper. Since Sweden had a monopoly on copper, the idea was that, if part of the copper supplies were used for Swedish coinage, the export price could be raised. The policy was not very successful, in part because so little currency was used in Sweden that proportionately little copper was used (Heckscher 1954, 88, 89). Yet the copper standard survived until currency reform in 1776, although it was made largely irrelevant in 1745, when inconvertible paper money was introduced.

The copper standard was a serious inconvenience. The price of copper was barely more than one-hundredth that of silver, so that a copper coin had to weigh about a hundred times as much as a silver coin of equal value. This led to coinage of ridiculous size and weight. The ten-daler piece weighed about 43 pounds (19.7 km) , and the two-daler piece, which was the standard coin, measured about 9.5 inches (240 mm) diagonally. The total weight required for ordinary payments could be staggering, and the transportation of any sizable sum required wagons or sleds. This proved particularly obstructive to the treasury in collection of tax revenues, as transporting revenue from the provinces to Stockholm posed grave problems (Heckscher 1954, 88–89; Kirby 1990, 238). At the same time, the copper coins drove out the use of the more convenient silver coins, as it usually was cheaper to pay in copper than in silver.

The copper standard had only one redeeming value: the inconvenience of such monstrous copper coins encouraged the introduction of paper money. Sweden had the first paper money in Europe. In 1656 a Livonian of Dutch extraction founded one of Sweden's first banks. Five years later it occurred to him to issue bank notes. The issue of paper money was equivalent to receipt of interest free deposits, which made them highly popular with managers of the bank. The managers issued an excessive volume of bank notes, however, and a run on the bank caused the bank to close. It created a general fear of paper money that persisted for almost a century, although after its failure the bank was taken over in 1668 by the *Riksens Ständers Bank,* today known as the *Riksbank,* which is the oldest existing bank in Europe (Heckscher 1954, 92). The reopened bank was not permitted to issue notes, and its operations remained limited. By the end of the century the Crown had become its largest customer (Kirby 1990, 239).

Needless to say, such monetary difficulties, including a literally massive currency, inhibited the growth of a money economy and the development of trade in Sweden and thus also inhibited the development of agriculture. Coupled with growing royal taxation and uncertainty in property rights, these factors worked to inhibit substantial agrarian change in Sweden through the early modern period. It was not until these factors were changed, beginning in the eighteenth century, that agricultural development began in Sweden.

## Conclusion

In Sweden ecological conditions were most favorable for agriculture in the southern part of the Swedish peninsula, particularly the central region. Yet only in the west was there a predominance of less-communal agricultural systems. Here there is evidence of a prosperous peasant (pastoral) economy from the sixteenth century and rural industry. There is also evidence that peasant agriculture in western Sweden (along with that in the northeast) led the way in the agricultural revolution in the eighteenth and nineteenth centuries (Gadd and Jonsson 1990). Gaunt's evidence (1977) for the seventeenth and eighteenth centuries also suggests that economic conditions in the rich lands of the south were poorer in the communal parts than in the less-communal parts of that region. This evidence supports the hypothesis that agrarian change would be most rapid in less-communal regions, all else being equal.

All over Sweden, however, agricultural progress was slowed by a sparse population, uncertainty of land rights, and misguided Crown policies regarding trade and coinage. After the sixteenth century royal taxation also increased dramatically and deterred peasant production for the market. As a result, the innovative methods already common in parts of England and the Netherlands—complex rotations, extensive use of fertilizers, growing of fodder crops—were seldom employed in any part of Sweden before the eighteenth century. In the eighteenth century the enclosures (*skiften*) began to break down communal farming systems, and this, along with improvements in peasant property rights and stable levels of taxation, promoted subsequent agricultural improvement and change.

As noted previously, Sweden makes a good test case for examining the effect of local institutions separate from class relations, as communal institutions existed despite comparatively light manorial control in many regions of Sweden. In fact, even without high levels of manorialization, there is evidence that communal systems of agriculture limited agricultural improvement and agrarian change in the most fertile part of Sweden. This Swedish evidence suggests that, despite the correlation between communal agricultural systems and feudal social structures throughout Europe, it was the former, and not the latter, that was ultimately responsible for the economic stagnation characteristic of communal regions.

CHAPTER 9

# Conclusion: Rural Institutions and Agrarian Change in the Preindustrial West

> The consequence is that economics must pay close attention
> to local institutions, because they matter for behavior.
> —Robert Solow, "Notes on Coping"

### The Role of Rural Institutions in Agrarian Change

The purpose of this book has been to note the systematic patterning of rural institutions and the field systems they produced across Europe and to point to their role in creating regional patterns of agrarian change in preindustrial England, the Netherlands, France, the German lands, and Sweden. Following Bloch (1966a), we may classify field systems into three types according to the extent of communal agricultural practices: communal open field systems, less-communal open field systems, and enclosed, noncommunal systems. Despite some local variation, the three types of field systems were found in each of the five countries examined here. To simplify the analysis I have grouped the less-communal field systems with enclosed, noncommunal field systems as one "less-communal" category. Given this classification, we can say that, in general, agrarian change was least likely in regions of communal agriculture and most likely in regions of less-communal agriculture. This does not mean that all less-communal regions were home to dynamic agricultural economies or that all communal regions were entirely backward. This was far from the case, as other factors also shaped the regional pattern of change. Ecology, demography, local class relations, access to markets, state policies and institutions, and warfare also determined outcomes in the different regions. This meant that by the end of the time period covered here the communal regions of midland England, for example, were more productive than many less-communal regions on the Continent. The point to be made here is that these other factors worked in conjunction with local conditions and to explain regional outcomes fully we must refer to both sets of factors.

Thus, in England a favorable conjuncture of factors in regions of the east and southwest—less-communal agricultural systems, a benign ecology, comparatively weak overlordship, access to markets, low levels of state oppression, and state-protected property rights in land—promoted a prosperous and thriving rural economy by the late medieval period. These regions were the first to experience the rise of large farms and contractual labor relations, enclosure, and the introduction of the agricultural improvements that, when diffused throughout southern England during the early modern period, would make the English agricultural revolution possible. Further to the north and west a more inhospitable and mountainous ecology coupled with little access to markets inhibited agrarian change throughout the period examined here. In the midland and central regions, where ecological conditions were highly favorable for agriculture and there was easy access to the major markets, communal agricultural systems and strong overlordship slowed the process of change. Changes to improve productivity such as enclosure were difficult and created a great deal of social upheaval in these regions. They were eventually compelled with state aid in the form of the enclosure acts and other means of coercion. It was only then that these regions began to participate fully in the rise of agricultural productivity now called the English agricultural revolution. Even so, as late as the nineteenth century, average wheat yields were higher in the less-communal regions than in the regions where communal agriculture had been dominant.

As in eastern and southwestern England, in most of the Netherlands both local and state conditions promoted agrarian development and change. Less-communal field systems, weak overlordship, easy access to markets, comparatively unoppressive state regimes, and legal support for property rights led to the development of a flourishing rural sector at a very early date. Only in the border regions of communal agriculture in the southeast, where the seigneurial system persisted into the modern period, was little change noticeable. Despite the political upheavals of the later sixteenth century and the subsequent economic decline of the southern Netherlands, rural prosperity endured in the north and paved the way for the golden age of the Dutch Republic in the seventeenth century. In the south a troubled period during the seventeenth century was followed by a rural economic revival in the eighteenth century, which helped propel the first European industrial revolution.

Conditions were less favorable for change in France, the German lands, and Sweden. In France much of the best agricultural land in the north and northeast was characterized by communal farming systems. Manorial overlordship was initially strong in these regions, although its strength dwindled over the early modern period. In the north there were only small pockets of less-communal agriculture (in Flanders and part of Normandy), and this is where most agricultural change and improvement occurred. In the south ecological conditions sometimes did not favor agriculture, and some of the more isolated mountainous regions had little access to markets. Less-communal farming systems coupled with market access in some parts of the south (in and around Guyenne and Provence) promoted change and rural development. Yet in all the more progressive regions of France, in both north and south, encroaching oppression by a growing and corrupt state bureaucracy, coupled with a lack of protection for property rights, promoted the emergence of a backward, subsistence-oriented rural economy by the eighteenth century. In the nineteenth century it was the south, not the northeast, that was the poorest area of France.

In the southwest of the German lands rural conditions were very similar to those of northeastern France. Here there were communal farming systems, fertile soils, and access (by river) to most of the major markets of western Europe. As in France, local overlordship was initially quite strong in these regions and weakened over the early modern period. Unlike in France, however, there was no real national state (the framework provided by the Holy Roman Empire was loose), and over time the power of princes and other territorial rulers tended to increase. An associated trend was the increase in legal support for peasant rights provided by a variety of princely and other regional court systems, and in most parts of the west hereditary rights to land remained relatively secure. In these regions of communal rights, however, such legal protection often served to increase, not decrease, the transaction costs associated with communal rights, as they were subject to continual negotiation. Constant warfare was also a problem. As a result, little large-scale agrarian improvement occurred, although private gardens and vineyards could be highly productive.

Further to the north and east of Germany conditions initially were favorable for rural development. There were less-communal farming systems, access to markets via water, a privileged peasant class, and benign territorial overlordship. These promoted a highly productive and innovative rural sector in the late medieval period, especially in the northwestern region close to the urban markets of the Low Countries. In the eastern area, however, refeudalization, extensive warfare, and the growth of Prussian absolutism after the fifteenth century arrested these developments. It was only in northwestern Germany, where peasant freedoms persisted, that a dynamic rural economy lasted to modern times.

As in northern France and southern Germany, the best agricultural lands of southern Sweden were characterized by communal farming systems, and there is likewise evidence that communal farming systems inhibited agrarian change. Unlike other places, however, in general overlordship was weak throughout Sweden. Further to the north and west there were less-communal farming systems, but ecological conditions were often less favorable for agriculture. In fact, in much of the north subarctic conditions placed constraints on arable agriculture. In the west conditions were less severe, and there is evidence of peasant prosperity, growing agricultural productivity, and rural industry in the seventeenth century and after. In Sweden, however, state-level conditions worked against change in any region. First, despite the emergence of a national legal system, due to the absence of exclusive rights to land in many regions and the customary institution of the *bördsrätt,* property rights in land remained open to negotiation throughout Sweden. Second, as in France, the rise of Swedish absolutism in the early modern period, coupled with heavy taxation and the implementation of policies that restricted trade and penalized producers, inhibited development in rural Sweden. It is significant that when these conditions changed—taxation ceased to rise, property rights became individualized, and the currency was reformed—agricultural productivity began to rise in eighteenth-century Sweden.

From these cases it is clear that less-communal rural institutions were an essential element in creating agrarian change (as expected from hypothesis 1 in chap. 3). All the most innovative agricultural regions in Europe—in England, the Netherlands, Flanders, and northwestern Germany—were less-communal areas. Change in communal regions came only after great pressure from outside. In many of these regions of Europe communal farming systems persisted into the twentieth century, finally to disappear in the aftermath of World War II.

It is also clear that local class relations influenced change but not in the way Brenner (1985, 1989) and others (e.g., O'Brien 1996) have argued. That is, agrarian change was most likely where territorial lords were comparatively *weak* and where peasants had strong property rights in land (supporting hypothesis 2 in chap. 3). In England, the Netherlands, France, Germany, and Sweden regional analysis suggests that the perpetuation of feudal relations and manorial control hindered change, while the presence of a large free peasantry promoted change. Furthermore, rather than promoting a subsistence orientation (as Brenner's model suggests), strong peasant property rights in the less-communal regions of England, the Netherlands, and northwest Germany promoted commercialization of agriculture and agrarian change. It was only in communal regions, such as midland England, northern France, and southwest Germany, that support for peasant property rights helped maintain peasant economies that were primarily subsistence oriented. Yet the case of Sweden shows that a strong version of the reverse argument cannot be made either. That is, it was not manorial control alone that inhibited agricultural change in communal regions of Europe. In southern Sweden, where overlordship was historically weak compared to Continental Europe and "peasant villages" were common, change was still slow on the best agricultural lands, in part because they were handicapped by communal agricultural systems.

In addition, we can also see that, while ecology influenced the course of change, it was not decisive. This is demonstrated by the case of the Netherlands and parts of southern England and eastern Germany. These regions can only be described as ecologically marginal, yet in them less-communal rural institutions promoted early agrarian change and development. Nor was location on some of the best agricultural land of Europe enough to promote sustained agricultural development in communal regions of northern France and southwest Germany. Thus, support for hypothesis 3 (in chap. 3) is equivocal.

Population also appears important in promoting change, supporting hypothesis 4, although this is confounded by the fact that increasing rural prosperity also led to greater population density. Once again, however, by itself a dense population was not enough to promote development, as we see from parts of northern France, southwestern Germany, and midland England. These were regions of comparatively dense population since medieval times, yet agricultural development and change in these regions was not as early or extensive as in other less-communal regions.

In the cases examined here necessary causes of agrarian change, besides less-communal systems of agriculture and weak manorial over-lordship, appear to have been market access (supporting hypothesis 4) and legal protection for property rights (supporting hypothesis 5). Of all these additional factors market access emerges as the most important. All the positive cases of agrarian change were in regions where access to markets for agricultural commodities (typically by water) was relatively easy. Remote areas far from markets—parts of central and southern France, northern and western England, and northern Sweden—all saw little development and change throughout the period examined here. The analysis here also makes clear, however, that market access alone was not enough to promote extensive rural development and agrarian change. Parts of northern France, central England, and southwestern Germany are examples in which this was the case.

The last factors were also necessary, but not sufficient, to promote agrarian change. Protection of exclusive rights in land provided by a central state or some other governing body as a third party was a crucial element, one that was present in both positive cases—England and the Netherlands. Lack of protection for property rights in France (associated with generally high levels of corruption) and in early modern Prussia was a factor inhibiting economic change. Alone, however, third-party support for property rights was not enough to guarantee development, as we saw in communal parts of England, Germany, and Sweden. In these regions support for property rights often had the effect of increasing transaction costs, as communal rights became the subject of extensive litigation.

Low levels of taxation and the absence of warfare were not necessary factors for agricultural development (contradicting hypotheses 6 and 6a). Heavy taxation limited the scope of agrarian change, as we have seen in many regions of early modern France, eastern Germany, and Sweden. Yet heavy taxation alone did not prevent development. Parts of the northern Netherlands endured extremely high levels of taxation during the Revolt and the following Eighty Years' War (1568–1648), for example, with little long-term damage to the rural economy. Nor did comparatively low levels of taxation always promote development, as we saw in communal regions of England and in southwestern Germany in the early modern period. Indirect taxation through state control of trade and prices also damaged economies, as we have seen in France and Sweden. But, since this was present to some extent in all the cases examined here in all historical periods, it cannot be concluded that it always prevented economic development. Last, warfare, in that it both destroyed rural economies and promoted the rise of autocracy, was detrimental to rural development, as the cases of the German lands and the southern Netherlands illustrate. On the other hand, the resilience of the rural economy to the disasters of wars is also apparent in places like the southern Netherlands and northwestern Germany. These places showed a remarkable ability to bounce back from the devastation inflicted by warfare and invading troops.

In sum, most of the hypotheses presented in chapter 3 are supported by the historical evidence, exceptions being hypotheses concerning the role of ecology, taxation by the state, and warfare. The analysis also shows, however, that none of the factors promoting change (i.e., less-communal local institutions, weak overlordship, market access, and state support for property rights) alone is sufficient to promote agricultural development and agrarian change. Instead, a combination of all four factors is necessary.

One other notable finding emerges from the cases examined here. Less-communal local institutions not only promoted agrarian change and development; they may also have promoted rural industry too. Throughout Europe there was some correlation between less-communal field systems, agrarian change, and the appearance of local rural industry, although the correlation was far from perfect. Thus, the regions that we have noted as regions of comparatively rapid agrarian change and development: eastern and southwestern England, much of the Netherlands, Normandy, parts of southern France, northwestern Germany, eastern Germany, and western Sweden were all notable for rural industry at an early date. The Netherlands is the most outstanding case in this regard. I have not explored the causal mechanism behind this correlation to any extent. It may have occurred because of the high population densities in many less-communal regions (which created a surfeit of labor and thus promoted the emergence of by-employments such as rural industry); it may also have been a result of the lack of manorial and community control over economic activities typical of less-communal regions.[1] Last, rural prosperity created by agrarian change no doubt created a demand for the products of rural industry and thus stimulated growth of industry.

### Implications for Theories of Agrarian Change

These findings have several implications for current theories of agrarian change in preindustrial Europe. Neo-Marxists such as Brenner (1985, 1989, 48) suggest that commercialized, capitalist agriculture was most likely to emerge in areas where commercially oriented landlords were powerful enough to dispossess a subsistence-oriented peasantry but not so powerful that they could enserf them (see also Moore 1966; Anderson 1974; O'Brien 1996). Yet, as noted, the regional analysis I present suggests the opposite was true. Agrarian development almost always occurred in regions of few communal rights, where feudal lords were *least* powerful relative to the peasantry and where there was little peasant dispossession (see also Overton 1996, 205). A decline in peasant rights almost always was accompanied by a decline in agricultural productivity; there was no curvilinear relationship (as implied by Brenner's thesis). The steady decline in agricultural production in eastern Germany during the period of refeudalization during the sixteenth and seventeenth centuries is testimony to this (see chap. 7). So, too, is the decline of parts of southern and western France after they were fully incorporated into the French kingdom of the north after the sixteenth century (see chap. 6).

Nor are these findings consistent with modernization theories of the rise of the west. In common with traditional Marxist theories, modernization theories view development as fundamentally a result of the development of technology (Rostow 1960; see also Young 1994), which, however, may be retarded by traditionalist cultures. According to this approach, improvement and innovation in agriculture would be associated with "progressive cultures," while a lack of improvement and innovation would be associated with the maintenance of traditional cultures and a "subsistence mentality." Here I find that, although cultural differences existed between regions and may have been (in part) a cause of regional differences in economic development, these regional differences in cultures were themselves a logical product of the economic organization in which they were embedded. Thus, it is regional differences in economic organization, rather than differences in culture per se, that is the more fundamental explanation of regional differences in development.

Modernization theory would predict further that less innovative areas soon would change in response to contact with more developed areas and that convergence would occur as similar technologies and modes of economic organization emerged everywhere. Yet this is not what we see in preindustrial Europe. Regional differences persisted, despite similar basic agricultural technologies in all regions. Nor did economic development in more progressive regions automatically lead to imitation by less progressive regions and thus the decline of regional differences, as modernization theory predicts. Regional differences in rural structures and development throughout Europe were surprisingly enduring. In many places it took the catastrophes of World Wars I and II to eradicate them finally. Even so, their effects on farm sizes and regional landscapes still can be seen to this day. Travelers in northern France, southern England, and many other places can still note the changes that Young, Hardy, and others remarked on hundreds of years before.

Last, the findings pose problems for a world system approach to development (Wallerstein 1974). Although they do not contradict such an approach, they draw attention to internal causes of economic change within what were to become nation-states rather than external causes (such as relations between states and the nature of the global economy). Relations between states and colonial relations had little impact on regional differences within the countries discussed here. The analysis of the effects of local institutions and other factors presented here can complement a world system analysis, however, by showing how the network of relations between states in the European world system was first created. That is, it shows how eastern Germany (as with other parts of eastern Europe) came to be assigned a peripheral role in the European world economic system, despite a prosperous agricultural economy in the later Middle Ages. It also shows how the south of France in particular came to be assigned to the semi-periphery, and it can account for the discrepancies in development within the core of western Europe—that is, between northern France, England, and the Netherlands.

The findings support predictions drawn from the new institutional economics and make most sense within that theoretical framework. Local institutions, local class relations, market access, and legal support for property rights were important in determining regional economic outcomes because they shaped choices and costs for individuals and, consequently, those individuals' behavior, as discussed in chapter 3. Where these factors meant that the costs of production and change were low relative to benefits, development was more likely. Where they were high relative to benefits, development was least likely. I have followed Coase (1960), in paying special attention to social costs (transaction costs; i.e., costs of defining and enforcing property rights, of measuring the valuable attributes of what is being exchanged, and monitoring the exchange process), and North and Thomas (1973), in applying Coase's insight to historical development. More particularly, I have highlighted the role of local institutions in shaping field systems and transaction (and other) costs. In communal field systems communal rights raised transaction costs because they were difficult to protect and were open to negotiation. Other costs (such as costs of innovation) were also raised in the communal system because individual economic freedom was restricted. This slowed the process of change in communal regions. Less-communal rights lowered transaction costs because they were comparatively easy to protect. Other costs were also lower because individuals had more economic freedom to do what they wanted with their land and resources.

This application to agrarian change in preindustrial Europe is novel, insofar as other applications of the new institutional economics to development have focused on social costs created by state, not local, institutions (Barzel 1989; de Soto 1989; Campbell and Lindberg 1990; Bates 1990; North 1990a; Root 1994). The cases and histories I have presented here make it clear that a focus on state institutions is inadequate. For example, new institutionalists have stressed the importance of state support for property rights. Yet, as we have seen, this was a necessary but not sufficient condition for regional development. In regions where communal rights predominated, state support for property rights actually served to increase some of the transaction costs associated with communal rights. Thus, state policies and actions influenced local dynamics, yet alone they cannot explain different regional outcomes.

The goal in this book has been to add to, and strengthen, the contributions of the new institutional economics to the study of economic change. I hope that what is presented here marks something of a new beginning (or a revival) in the study of the development of western Europe—that is, in addition to institutional arrangements at the state level, local institutional arrangements will attract the attention they deserve. Such a change in emphasis has begun already in the study of political change (Mettam 1988; Henschall 1992; Putnam 1993; Major 1994); it is overdue in the study of economic change.

## Rural Origins of the Modern World

The implications of this study extend beyond support for the use of the new institutional economics in understanding economic change in history. Previous studies of the rise of the West using a variety of theoretical frameworks have tended to see agrarian change as being imposed by urban and other landowning "capitalists" and the peasantry as largely an impediment to change. Marxists, beginning with Marx himself, have often considered the peasantry as a conservative, reactionary "sack of potatoes" and a force against change (Marx 1906, 808–9). Other analyses in this tradition have suggested that the peasantry were pushed aside in the process of modernization by enclosers and others (Poianyi 1944, 35; Scott 1976; Braudel 1982, 254) or were used by others (Brenner 1987, 1989).

Analyses based on the neoclassical tradition have also tended to stress the role of the large landowners in agricultural innovation, change, and increasing agricultural production (e.g., in Sweden [see Heckscher 1954]). Particularly in the English case, it is the rise of large farms run by enterprising landlords that is usually considered the motive force behind the English agricultural revolution (see Allen 1988a; Bates 1988). Analysts such as Le Roy Ladurie (1987, 340) and de Planhol and Claval (1994, 157) have stressed the importance of large-scale agriculture in improving agricultural productivity in France. Similarly, the role of the large Junker estates in eastern Germany in grain production has often been stressed (e.g., Carsten 1954; Wallerstein 1974; Brenner 1987).

This analysis does not seek to deny that large farms and entrepreneurial landowners were important in the agricultural revolution in Europe. It suggests, however, that, at least in a few regions of Europe, peasants were active agents of modernization, rather than merely its victims. By improving their methods, increasing their efforts, and producing for the market, they helped make the modern world possible. English historians have been aware of the role of common people in economic development (Power 1963 [1922]; Croot and Parker 1987, 83; Cooper 1978), as have Dutch (de Vries and van der Woude 1997, 197) and, more recently, Swedish (Jonsson, Köll, and Pettersson 1990) and, to a lesser extent, German economic historians (Hagen 1985, 1989). Yet the anglocentric notion that the English were always different, to the extent of MacFarlane's (1978) claim that there never was a "peasantry" in England, has also been common (at least among English speakers). Instead, this analysis suggests that, at least in communal regions, there was a peasantry in England, just as there were regions of enterprising small farmers on the Continent. In all cases what mattered was not so much the language or ethnic origin of the people or whether or not they have been labeled "peasants" but, rather, the incentive structure they faced. This incentive structure was provided by the nature of social institutions, both local and national, coupled with other factors, in the region where they lived. In a few regions where this incentive structure promoted development, agrarian capitalism emerged spontaneously and was not a foreign imposition. For this reason we can say that the modern world, rather than being antirural, on the contrary has strong rural roots.

# Notes

## Chapter 1

1. There are some exceptions. For example, Goldstone (1988) examined the effects of regional factors in shaping agrarian outcomes. Other sociologists have been very aware of the regional differences in agrarian structures but have primarily concerned themselves with explaining other outcomes, often in later time periods (on revolts, see Markoff 1985; and on voting patterns, see Brustein 1988).

2. Partly as a way around this problem, Bloch advocated the use of nontraditional techniques in the study of rural life, such as the examination of the contemporary landscape itself, either by aerial photography or otherwise; or the study of maps, linguistic evidence, and so on. Meitzen's study (1895) itself was based on a novel source of evidence: maps and ancient Roman land surveys. By and large, however, such nontraditional techniques have been used sparsely.

3. The study of regional differences in agrarian organization recently has become confined to historical geography and archaeology (e.g., Smith 1967; Clout 1977; Crumley and Marquardt 1987), which have tended to focus on field patterns and settlement forms to the neglect of social and economic phenomena. Thus, the study of field systems has been confined to a specialist literature, in which it has been easily ignored. The growing unpopularity of ethnic explanations of regional differences may have contributed to a general decline in the emphasis placed on the regional differences themselves, hence also a decline in the effort to delineate their full character and significance (cf. Rösener 1992, 65).

4. de Vries (1984, 155) uses a measure of urban potential that measures the accessibility of a city to the inhabitants of all other cities.

5. Widespread acceptance of ecological explanations also has meant that the few subsequent comparative scholars and others who have treated regional differences often have done so in a flawed or incomplete way (see Hopcroft 1995).

6. England and the Netherlands, however, did not experience this seventeenth-century downturn to the same extent as other European countries.

## Chapter 2

1. A four-field (or more than four-field) system was possible within the confines of the communal system, yet there is little evidence of it in the late medieval period.

2. Many have suggested that communal regulation only existed because of the nature of the two- or three-field system. The Swedish evidence suggests, however, that communal control of agriculture predates common rotations and fallowing. In parts of Sweden there were no common rotations or any regular fallowing; nevertheless, there was strong village control of cropping and fallowing (Heckscher 1954).

3. As in America of de Tocqueville's time.

4. Other plough types used in these regions include swing and foot plows. These plows were distinguished from the *araire*, or stick plow, by the presence of a moldboard (for turning the furrow) and coulter (for cutting the sod). They were similar to the wheeled plow, except they lacked wheels.

5. Hallam (1981) suggests that these regions in eastern England were simply in a higher stage of development than communal open field regions. In eastern England population was dense, ecology generally favorable, and there was access to urban markets, all of which influenced agricultural practice and served to break down communal agriculture. Yet this hypothesis concerning the evolution from communal agriculture to less-communal agriculture is problematic because there is no evidence that these areas in eastern England were ever characterized by a system of communal agriculture such as that found in the midlands of England.

6. For more complete reviews, see Dahlman 1980; and Dodgshon 1980.

7. This may be less true in the communal regions of northern France, which in Roman times were characterized by large *villae* and open fields. These types persisted through the period of Germanic invasions into the Carolingian period, although scattered habitation did become more common at this time (de Planhol and Claval 1994, 52, 71).

8. In recognition of these problems, Homans (1988c, 155) has argued the reverse. That is, he suggests that it was easier for warlords to consolidate their control in regions where the population already was clustered together in villages and governed by a central, communal body, thus resulting in the correlation between degree of manorialization and the communal open field system.

9. Other authors suggest the land-use system adopted was simply a rationalized version of the communal open field system of the West (Mayhew 1973); others claim they reflect the nature of the Slavic field systems already in place in the East (Thorpe 1961; Aubin 1966).

## Chapter 3

1. Note that information costs are also considered transaction costs.

2. Bloch (1966a, 38) also notes that this was a problem that only occurred in champion (communal open field) regions.

3. As reflected in the English saying that "enclosure made a good farmer better but a bad farmer worse."

4. Some attention also has been given to the role of informal normative institutions (North 1990a, 23; Knight 1992; Putnam 1993).

**Chapter 4**

1. Although Overton (1996, 26) notes that all such maps are only approximations.

2. Few areas of late medieval or early modern England were predominantly pastoral regions, as virtually all regions had some mixture of "corn and horn" as befits a subsistence-oriented rural economy (Kussmaul 1990, 3).

3. Mate (1991, 132) notes: "In 1438–9 and again in 1481–2 the London market was bolstered with wheat and other grains from the south-east. Similarly in 1474–5, when Castile was suffering from a severe shortage of grain, Spanish merchants exported over 4,000 quarters of grain from Kentish ports."

4. Agricultural productivity in some parts of East Anglia reached levels in the late medieval period not attained again until the early eighteenth century, at the height of the agricultural revolution (Campbell 1991, 179).

5. Tenants could be free peasants or otherwise. Tenant farms should not be confused with the home farms of manorial lords—the demesnes. These tended to shrink in size after 1350.

6. After the late medieval period the tendency for the very largest farms to be found in the east and southwest disappeared. In the midlands and central regions the enclosure movement of the fifteenth and subsequent centuries threw many small peasant proprietors off their land and destroyed communal open field systems, making way for the rise of large, consolidated farms in the eighteenth century (Wordie 1983; Allen 1988a, 121; Grigg 1989). By 1850 very large farms (of over 100 acres) predominated in these regions (see map 5). By this date all of England had become a nation of relatively large farms, and average farm sizes across England exceeded those of farms on the Continent (which they still do to this day).

7. Horses have an advantage over oxen in both speed and strength. For example, they can work 1.5 times faster than oxen (Overton 1996, 125).

8. Brenner's (1989) argument that enclosing landlords destroyed village solidarity is most appropriate in these regions.

9. About half of this enclosure took place after 1800 (Wordie 1983). By this later date the nature of enclosure had changed somewhat and was more likely than previously to be for arable purposes, although enclosure for pasture farming was still common in the midlands (Beckett 1982). Furthermore, enclosure affected mostly the commons and wastes of the parish or manor, rather than the open fields proper.

10. Many counties in the north, west, east, and southwest had less than 4 percent of their area enclosed by act of parliament. They were Northumberland, Durham, Cumberland, Westmoreland, and Lancashire in the north; Cheshire, Staffordshire, Shropshire, Herefordshire, and Monmouthshire on the Welsh border; Somerset, Devon, and Cornwall in the southwest; Essex, Sussex, and Kent in the southeast. Of these the counties of Lancashire, Devon, Cornwall, and Kent had none of their open field area enclosed by act of parliament (Clay 1984, 73).

11. Large farms often have been given credit for England's agricultural productivity, especially in the seventeenth and eighteenth centuries, at which time average

farm size in England was substantially greater than on the Continent. Comparative studies have shown, however, that large farms are not necessarily associated with a productive agriculture (see Bates 1988, 507–9, for a review). The regional evidence presented here may help resolve the issue, as it suggests that it was the specific conjuncture of large farms with smaller, more innovative free farms that promoted a productive agriculture in both eastern and southwestern England.

12. The last documented famine in England was 1622–23, when people starved to death in Cumberland, Westmoreland, and perhaps also some Durham parishes (Overton 1996, 141).

13. Through the seventeenth and eighteenth centuries the cloth industry of East Anglia and the west country also continued to flourish, although by the nineteenth century it was in decline (Pounds 1990, 290).

14. The aversion to debasement meant, however, that bullion was attracted overseas to foreign mints, where, because of the inflated price of the coinage, bullion sellers could receive a better price. To avoid losing all bullion, the English Crown tried to prevent the export of all specie (Munro 1972), although this was not entirely effective. Shortage of specie remained a problem for the Crown.

15. In a biography of Thomas William Coke (a nineteenth-century descendant who was both politician and agriculturalist), the author notes that Edward's father acquired land at Mileham (Norfolk) in 1554 and that "there is no doubt that Robert was resident at Mileham four years earlier, either as a tenant or upon land acquired in some other manner; for there in February, his illustrious son, Edward, was born" (Stirling 1912, 2).

16. By the eighteenth century per capita taxes in England were heavier than taxes in France (Mathias and O'Brien 1976; Levi 1988, 120; Henshall 1992, 113; Hoffman and Norberg 1994, 301).

17. In addition, as I have argued in more detail elsewhere (Hopcroft, 1999), enforced reliance on indirect taxes may have given extra power to parliaments responsible for granting taxes the king needed.

## Chapter 5

1. Based on Huppertz (1939, 126).

2. The Low Countries, in fact, had been a trading center for centuries. Already in the early Middle Ages the region of the Meuse, Rhine, and Scheldt had served as a base for the Frisians in their trading operations between western Europe and Scandinavia (Van der Wee 1993, 7). In Carolingian times Frisian cloth was sold over all of Europe, although there is some debate about whether it actually was produced in Frisia (van Houtte 1977, 17). At this time the towns of Dorestad and Quentovic (in Frisia) were the major trading centers. Small trading settlements also emerged at Tournai, Ghent, Bruges, Antwerp, Dinant, Namur, Huy, Liège, and Maastricht. Frisian coins were circulated extensively all over Europe as far as Iceland and Russia by the ninth century. Around 1100 they were the universal trading currency (van Houtte 1977, 51). The Frisian trade declined, however, in the tenth and eleventh centuries. The economy of the Mediterranean region revived, and

Frisian traders were ill equipped to take advantage of this revival. Viking, Magyar, and Saracen attacks contributed to the decline of Frisian trade. In the northern Netherlands, Utrecht and some of the towns of Ijssel (Kampen, Zwolle, and Deventer) became heirs to the Frisian legacy.

3. Or about 3.7–9.3 acres to 0.4–3.7 acres.

4. Secular principalities included the counties of Flanders and Hainaut, the duchies of Brabant and Limburg, the county of Namur, the county of Loon, the counties of Holland and Zeeland, and the county (after 1339, duchy) of Guelders. The ecclesiastical principalities were Liège and Utrecht.

5. This tripartite organization of estates obtained in Brabant, Flemish Flanders, Zeeland, Utrecht, Artois, Hainaut, Namur, and Luxembourg (de Schepper 1994, 516).

6. The king's council itself was replaced by three new independent councils: the Council of State, the Privy Council, and the Council of Finance. The Privy Council retained its function as the highest court of appeal for judgments of the "Council of Justice" and the provincial courts. The Privy Council also had important responsibilities in the nomination of councillors, fiscal officers, and procurators-general to provincial councils. In addition, it could authorize a wide variety of deviations from the common law. Last, it could extrajudicially influence proceedings and judgments in any trial before any other court (de Schepper 1994, 508).

7. In its financial practices and institutions, however, Amsterdam, the financial center of the northern Netherlands, borrowed more from northern Italy, Bruges, and southern France than from Antwerp. Amsterdam intentionally avoided the system formerly in use in Antwerp (use of letters obligatory [promissory notes] as the customary mode of payment). Instead, all payments were made through the Bank of Amsterdam using bills of exchange (Van der Wee 1993, 146).

8. It appears that the business lunch is a very old tradition.

## Chapter 6

1. These border regions of France, currently part of France, have varied historically in their national affiliation. All of Flanders and Artois had been part of the Burgundian-Hapsburg Netherlands in the fourteenth century, although French influence remained strong. Artois and part of Flanders were annexed from Burgundy in 1477 then ceded to the Spanish in 1498, only to be retaken by France in 1659 (see *Times Concise Atlas of World History,* 72, 80).

2. Tithe receipts refer to receipts of money paid to the church (traditionally 10 percent of income, although this varied in practice). They are the best indicators of trends in agricultural production in France but are poor measures of absolute outputs.

3. I owe this point to John Markoff (personal communication).

4. An important exception are the hilltop villages of the Mediterranean region (de Planhol and Claval 1994, 147), which were probably a response to the insecurity promoted by Arab invasions.

5. Forster (1970) contrasts the different practices in England and France

regarding tenant farmers in the eighteenth century as follows: "English landlords did not raise rents as rapidly and as frequently as did French landlords in the eighteenth century. It was simply not the custom to raise rent on a 'sitting tenant,' and even annual leases were renewed if not automatically, at least so regularly that tenant families stayed on for lifetimes, even generations—or thought they would. This was not true in France, where the turnover of tenants on most estates was legend. The dispatch with which French landlords notified their old tenants to pay the increase, including the infamous *pot de vin,* or see their lease auctioned is in striking contrast to English practice."

6. Various reasons have been advanced about why the south and west turned to sharecropping and not leasing at this time. Duby suggests that it was the depressed economic conditions of the south and west as compared to the north (Duby 1968, 356–57). Similarly, Wallerstein regards sharecropping as simply a concomitant of a semi-peripheral (read "poor") area: sharecropping was "a sort of second best, chosen by the landed classes of southern France and northern Italy as a partial response to the creation of a capitalist world economy, in the form of semicapitalist enterprises, appropriate to semi-peripheral areas" (1974, 107).

7. Excluding the wars of the French Revolution, which were in part on French soil, and the peasant counterrevolution and its suppression.

8. As distinguished from the *pays d'états.* In the latter the regional *états* (representative assemblies) continued to be responsible for the levying and collecting of taxes (see map in Major 1994, 2). In 1601 the *pays d'états* included Brittany, Guyenne, Languedoc, Burgundy, Dauphiné, and Provence.

9. For example, Markoff (1996, 252) notes that in the eighteenth century regional judiciaries did little about lords who concocted newly profitable "traditions," such as the right to rent out village land to commercial stock raisers.

10. In 1989 the average farm in England was 65.1 hectares (about 160 acres), while it was only 27 hectares (about 67 acres) in France ("Europe's Latest Farming Muddle" 1991, 16).

## Chapter 7

1. This may be misleading, however, because it does not reflect taxes on the proceeds of viticulture, which was very common in these regions of southern Germany (see discussion later in this chapter).

2. This was a development of the later Middle Ages. In ancient German law judgments were given by the *Schöffen,* and the judge was simply their mouthpiece and executive officer. In the course of time the judge probably came much more to act on his own under control of the jurisdictional lord (Du Boulay 1983).

3. The most common titles for mayor in the north and the east of Germany were *Schulze* or *Bauermeister;* in the south of the country the title was *Schultheiss, Ammann,* or *Vogt* ( Rösener 1992, 165).

4. This map is a simplified version of Huppertz 1939, 126.

5. The *Esch* has already been described for the eastern Netherlands. The *Esch*

was a closed system of long strips of arable land that were often enclosed. The strips were fertilized regularly with sod cut from the heath in the village commons, which was enriched in turn with manure from animals that grazed there. The sod then raised the level of the strips of land, so the *Esch* was elevated.

6. The term *refeudalization* is a misnomer. There was no "feudalism" in the area originally, so it could not have been reintroduced, as the term implies. Second, it implies an economic backwardness and disenfranchisement of the peasantry in this region that now appears overstated in light of recent evidence (e.g., Hagen 1985; 1989 [I thank T. Robisheaux for pointing this out to me]).

7. A *Hufe* was a variable measure of land, supposedly sufficient to maintain a peasant family (probably about 20–30 acres).

8. Attempts to provide a supreme imperial court, competent to hear appeals from all subjects even in the absence of the emperor, were a development of the fifteenth century and were not very successful (Du Boulay 1983, 86).

9. This was in part because princes thought a Romanist judge would serve them better politically. It was also because litigants preferred advocates who had been to a university, whether in Italy or Germany. Popular judges were happy to call in more educated arbitrators who could comprehend technical writing and produce a written opinion behind the scenes (Du Boulay 1983, 89).

## Chapter 8

1. These areas remained the most manorialized regions of Sweden as late as the eighteenth century (Gustafsson 1994, 37).

2. There were no real serfs or slaves, however. Slaves were being freed before the twelfth century (Sawyer and Sawyer 1993, 132), and the institution itself had disappeared by the fourteenth century (Downing 1992, 187). *Skattebönder* are comparable to English freeholders. The *skattebönder* owned their farms but owed dues to the Crown (Rydeberg 1985, 184).

3. These were not unknown in other places. Overton (1996, 157) notes that in 1606 the manor at Wigston Magna, just south of Leicester in England, was bought by the tenants. The community at Wigston Magna subsequently became a "peasant village" in which common rights remained, but there was no large landowner, and the field system was organized by the village, not the manor.

4. These figures exclude Finland and the provinces of Gotland, Härjedalen, Jämtland, Blekinge, Halland, Skåne, and Bohuslän, which only became Swedish in 1658 (Heckscher 1954, 128).

5. The motivations for this policy are debated. Weibull (1933) thought that the goal of Gustavus Vasa and his successors was to secure Sweden from Danish encirclement by breaking through the ring, giving Sweden unhindered economic and political links with the rest of Europe. Attman (1985) thought that it was a means to gain control of the Russian trade, at least after 1562. Kirby suggests that other motivations, such as the security of the realm and the prestige of ambitious monarchs, may have been as important (1990, 124).

6. This involves relatively restricted rights and control for the landlord; duties from tenants are collected mainly in rents.

7. This involves large-scale farming by compulsory labor services from peasants who were hereditarily bound to the manorial estate.

8. An exception seems to be the fate of the former *frälsebönder* (tenants of the nobility). During the period of enclosure and reform they were either evicted and replaced by landless laborers, or their farms were sold to freeholders (Winberg 1978, 171).

## Chapter 9

1. Others have noted the correlation between rural industry and the absence of landed estates (cf. Kriedte, Medick, and Schlumbohm 1977, 47–56, 266–71, 197–201).

# Bibliography

Abel, Wilhelm. 1955. *Die Wüstungen des Ausgehenden Mittelalters.* Stuttgart: Gustave Fischer Verlag.

————. 1978a. *Geschichte der deutschen Landwirtschaft vom frühen Mittelalter bis zum 19. Jahrhundert.* Stuttgart: Eugen Ulmer.

————. 1978b. *Agricultural Fluctuations in Europe from the Thirteenth to the Twentieth Centuries.* New York: St. Martin's Press.

Allen, Robert C. 1988a. "The Growth of Labor Productivity in Early Modern English Agriculture." *Explorations in Economic History* 25:117–46.

————. 1988b. "Inferring Yields from Probate Inventories." *Journal of Economic History* 48:117–25.

————. 1992. *Enclosure and the Yeoman: The Agricultural Development of the South Midlands, 1450–1850.* Oxford: Oxford University Press.

Allen, Robert C., and Cormac O'Gráda. 1988. "On the Road again with Arthur Young: English, Irish and French Agriculture during the Industrial Revolution." *Journal of Economic History* 48:93–116.

Allison, K. J. 1957. "The Sheep-corn Husbandry of Norfolk in the Sixteenth and Seventeenth Centuries." *Agricultural History Review* 5(1): 12–30.

Anderson, Perry. 1974. *Lineages of the Absolutist State.* London: New Left Books.

Ardant, Gabriel. 1971. *Histoire de l'impôt.* Paris: Fayard.

Åström, Sven-Erik. 1973. "The Swedish Economy and Sweden's Role as a Great Power." *Sweden's Age of Greatness 1632–1718,* 58–101. New York: St Martin's Press.

Attman, A. 1985. *Swedish Aspirations and the Russian Market during the Seventeenth Century.* Acta Regiae Societatis Scientiarum et Litterarum Gothoburgensis. Humaniora 24. Göteborg: Kungl. Vetenskaps-och Vitterhets-Samhallet.

Aubin, Hermann. 1966. "The Lands East of the Elbe and German Colonization Eastwards." In *The Cambridge Economic History of Europe,* vol. 1, ed. M. M. Postan, 449–87. Cambridge: Cambridge University Press.

Bäck, Kalle. 1984. English summary. In *Bondeopposition och bondeinflytande under frihetstiden. Centralmakten och östgötabördernas reaktioner i näringspolitiska frågor,* 304–12. Stockholm: Historiska institutionen.

Bailey, Mark. 1989. *A Marginal Economy?* Cambridge: Cambridge University Press.

Bardet, J. P., P. Chaunu, J. M. Gouesse, P. Gouhier, A. and J. M. Vallez. 1987.

"Laborieux par nécessité: L'économie normande du XVIᵉ au XVIIIᵉ siècle."
In *Histoire de la Normandie,* ed. M. de Boüard, 287–318. Paris: Privat.

Barraclough, G. 1962. *The Origins of Modern Germany.* Oxford: Basil Blackwell.

Barzel, Yoram. 1989. *Economic Analysis of Property Rights.* Cambridge: Cambridge University Press.

Bates, Robert H. 1988. "Lessons from History, or the Perfidy of English Exceptionalism and the Significance of Historical France." *World Politics* 40(4): 498–516.

———. 1990. "Macropolitical Economy in the Field of Development." In *Perspectives on Positive Political Economy,* ed. James E. Alt and Kenneth A. Shepsle, 31–56. Cambridge: Cambridge University Press.

Bates, Robert H., and Da-Hsiang Donald Lien. 1985. "A Note on Taxation, Development, and Representative Government." *Politics and Society* 14(1): 53–70.

Beckett, J. V. 1982. "The Decline of the Small Landowner in Eighteenth- and Nineteenth-Century England: Some Regional Considerations." *Agricultural History Review* 30, pt. 2: 97–111.

———. 1989. *A History of Laxton—England's Last Open-Field Village.* Oxford: Basil Blackwell.

———. 1990. *The Agricultural Revolution.* Oxford: Basil Blackwell.

Bennett, M. K. 1935. "British Wheat Yields for Seven Centuries." *Economic History* (February): 12–29.

Beresford, M. W. 1979. *Medieval England: An Aerial Survey.* New York: Cambridge University Press.

Biddick, Kathleen. 1985. "Medieval English Peasants and Market Involvement." *Journal of Economic History* 45:823–31.

Bieleman, Jan. 1990. "Rural Change in the Dutch Province of Drenthe, 1600–1910." In *Recent Doctoral Research in Economic History,* ed. Erik Aerts and Herman Van der Wee, 43–50. Leuven: Leuven University Press.

Bishop, T. A. M. 1935. "Assarting and the Growth of the Open Fields." *Economic History Review* 6:26–40.

Blickle, Peter. 1981. *The Revolution of 1525: The German Peasants' War from a New Perspective.* Trans. Thomas A. Brady Jr. and H. C. Erik Midelfort. Baltimore: Johns Hopkins University Press.

———. 1992. *Communal Reformation: The Quest for Salvation in Sixteenth Century Germany.* Trans. Thomas Dunlap. Atlantic Highlands, NJ: Humanities Press.

Bloch, Marc. 1966a. *French Rural History.* Berkeley: University of California Press.

———. 1966b. *Land and Work in the Middle Ages Collected Essays.* New York: Harper Torchbooks.

———. 1966c. "The Rise of Dependent Cultivation and Seignorial Institutions." In *The Cambridge Economic History of Europe,* ed. M. M. Postan, 235–89. 2d ed. Cambridge: Cambridge University Press.

———. 1971 [1913]. *The Ile-de-France.* Ithaca, NY: Cornell University Press.

Blockmans, W. P. 1994. "Voracious States and Obstructing Cities: An Aspect of State Formation in Preindustrial Europe." *Cities and the Rise of States in Europe, AD 1000–1800,* 218–50. Boulder, CO: Westview Press.

———. 1996. "The Growth of Nations and States in Europe before 1800." *European Review* 4:241–51.

Blum, Jerome. 1961. *Lord and Peasant in Russia from the Ninth to the Nineteenth Century.* Princeton: Princeton University Press.

Bois, Guy. 1984. *The Crisis of Feudalism.* Cambridge: Cambridge University Press.

Bonnaud, Pierre. 1977. "Peopling and the Origins of Settlement." In *Themes in the Historical Geography of France,* ed. H. D. Clout, 21–72. London: Academic Press.

Boserup, Ester. 1965. *The Conditions of Agricultural Growth.* Chicago: Aldine.

Bourde, A. J. 1958. "L'agriculture à l'anglaise en Normandie au XVIIIe siècle." *Annales de Normandie,* 215–33.

Brady, Thomas A., Jr. 1996. "Economic and Social Institutions." In *Germany: A New Social and Economic History,* vol. 1, *1450–1630,* ed. Bob Scribner, 259–83. New York: Arnold.

Brady, Thomas A., Jr., Heiko A. Oberman, and James D. Tracy. 1994. "Introduction: Renaissance and Reformation, Late Middle Ages and Early Modern Era." In *Handbook of European History, 1400–1600,* ed. Thomas A. Brady Jr., Heiko A. Oberman, and James D. Tracy, 1:xiii–xxiv. Leiden: Brill.

Braudel, Fernand. 1982. *The Wheels of Commerce.* New York: Harper and Row.

———. 1984. *The Perspective of the World.* New York: Harper and Row.

———. 1990. *The Identity of France.* New York: Harper and Row.

Brenner, Robert. 1987. "Agrarian Class Structure and Economic Development in Pre-Industrial Europe." In *The Brenner Debate: Agrarian Class Structure and Economic Development in Pre-Industrial Europe,* ed. T. H. Aston and C. H. E. Philpin, 10–63. Cambridge: Cambridge University Press.

———. 1989. "Economic Backwardness in Eastern Europe in Light of Developments in the West." In *The Origins of Backwardness in Eastern Europe,* ed. Daniel Chirot, 15–52. Berkeley: University of California Press.

Britnell, R. H. 1991. "Eastern England." In *The Agrarian History of England and Wales,* vol. 3: *1348–1500,* ed. Edward Miller, 53–66, 194–209, 611–23. Cambridge: Cambridge University Press.

Brunet, Pierre. 1955. "Problèmes relatifs aux structures agraires de la Basse-Normandie." *Annales de Normandie* 5:115–34.

Brustein, William. 1988. *The Social Origins of Political Regionalism, 1849–1981.* Berkeley: University of California Press.

Cameron, Rondo. 1993. *A Concise Economic History of the World.* 2d ed. New York: Oxford University Press.

Campbell, B. M. S. 1980. "Population Change and the Genesis of Commonfields on a Norfolk Manor." *Economic History Review* 33:174–92.

———. 1981. "Commonfield Origins: The Regional Dimension." In *The Origins of Open-Field Agriculture,* ed. Trevor Rowley, 112–29. Totowa, NJ: Barnes and Noble.

———. 1983. "Arable Productivity in Medieval England: Some Evidence from Norfolk." *Journal of Economic History* 43:379–404.

———. 1984. "Population Pressure, Inheritance and the Land Market in a Fourteenth Century Peasant Community." In *Land, Kinship and Life-cycle,* ed. R. M. Smith, 87–134. Cambridge: Cambridge University Press.

———. 1988. "The Diffusion of Vetches in Medieval England." *Economic History Review,* 2d ser., 41(2): 193–208.

———. 1991. "English Seignorial Agriculture." In *Land, Labour and Livestock,* ed. B. M. S. Campbell and Mark Overton, 148–80. Manchester: Manchester University Press.

Campbell, B. M. S., and Ricardo Godoy. 1986. "Commonfield Agriculture: The Andes and Medieval England Compared." Proceedings of the Conference on Common Property Resources Management, 323–58. Washington, DC: National Academy Press.

Campbell, B. M. S., and John P. Power. 1989. "Mapping the Agricultural Geography of Medieval England." *Journal of Historical Geography* 15(1): 24–39.

Campbell, John L., and Leon N. Lindberg. 1990. "Property Rights and the Organization of Economic Activity by the State." *American Sociological Review* 55(5): 634–47.

Cameron, Rondo. 1982. "Technology, Institutions and Long-Term Economic Change." In *Economics in the Long View: Essays in Honour of W. W. Rostow,* ed. Charles P. Kindleberger and Guido di Tella, 1:27–43. New York: New York University Press.

———. 1993. *A Concise Economic History of the World: From Paleolithic Times to the Present.* New York: Oxford University Press.

Carsten, F. L. 1954. *The Origins of Prussia.* London: Oxford University Press.

———. 1959. *Princes and Parliaments in Germany: From the Fifteenth to the Eighteenth Century.* Oxford: Clarendon Press.

Chambers, J. D., and G. E. Mingay. 1966. *The Agricultural Revolution, 1750–1880.* London: B. T. Batsford.

Chayanov, A. V. 1986. *The Theory of Peasant Economy.* Madison: University of Wisconsin Press.

Chevalier, Bernard. 1994. "France from Charles VII to Henry IV." In *Handbook of European History, 1400–1600,* ed. Thomas A. Brady Jr., Heiko A. Oberman, and James D. Tracy, 1:369–401. Leiden: Brill.

Chirot, Daniel. 1985. "The Rise of the West." *American Sociological Review* 50(2): 181–94.

———. 1989. "Causes and Consequences of Backwardness." In *The Origins of Backwardness in Eastern Europe,* ed. Daniel Chirot, 1–14. Berkeley: University of California Press.

Christiansen, Palle Ove. 1978. "The Household in the Local Setting: A Study of Peasant Stratification." In *Chance and Change, Social and Economic Studies in Historical Demography in the Baltic Area,* ed. Sune Åkerman, Hans Chr. Johansen, and David Gaunt, 50–60. Odense: Odense University Press.

Clague, Christopher. 1997. "The New Institutional Economics and Economic

Development." In *Institutions and Economic Development*, 13–36. Baltimore and London: Johns Hopkins University Press.

Clark, Gregory. 1988. "The Cost of Capital and Medieval Agricultural Technique." *Explorations in Economic History* 25:265–94.

———. 1991. "Yields per Acre in English Agriculture, 1250–1860: Evidence from Labour Inputs." *Economic History Review* 44(3): 445–60.

Clark, Samuel. 1995. *State and Status: The Rise of the State and Aristocratic Power in Western Europe*. Montreal: McGill-Queen's University Press.

Clay, C. G. A. 1984. *Economic Expansion and Social Change: England, 1500–1700*, vol. 1, *People, Land and Towns*. Cambridge: Cambridge University Press.

Clout, Hugh D. 1977. *Themes in the Historical Geography of France*. London: Academic Press.

Coase, Ronald H. 1960. "The Problem of Social Cost." *Journal of Law and Economics* 3:1–44.

Coleman, D. C. 1977. *The Economy of England, 1450–1750*. Oxford: Oxford University Press.

———. 1983. "Proto-Industrialization: A Concept Too Many." *Economic History Review* 36(11): 435–49.

Cooper, J. P. 1978. "In Search of Agrarian Capitalism." *Past and Present* 80:20–65.

Crafts, N. F. R. 1985. *English Economic Growth during the Industrial Revolution*. Oxford: Oxford University Press.

Croot, Patricia, and David Parker. 1987. "Agrarian Class Structure and the Development of Capitalism: France and England Compared." In *The Brenner Debate: Agrarian Class Structure and Economic Development in Pre-industrial Europe*, ed. T. H. Aston and C. H. E. Philpin, 79–90. Cambridge: Cambridge University Press.

Crumley, Carole L., and William H. Marquardt. 1987. *Regional Dynamics: Burgundian Landscapes in Historical Perspective*. New York: Academic Press.

Dahl, Sven. 1961. "Strip Fields and Enclosure in Sweden." *Scandinavian Economic History Review* 9(1): 56–67.

Dahlgren, Stellan. 1973. "Charles X and the Constitution." In *Sweden's Age of Greatness, 1632–1718*, ed. Michael Roberts, 174–203. New York: St Martin's Press.

Darby, H. C. 1969. *An Historical Geography of England before A.D. 1800*. Cambridge: Cambridge University Press.

———. 1973. *A New Historical Geography of England*. Cambridge: Cambridge University Press.

Davis, John H. R. 1973. *Land and Family in Pisticci*. New York: Humanities Press.

de Boüard, M. 1988. "La Normandie ducale: économies et civilisations." In *Histoire de la Normandie*, ed. M. de Boüard, 159–94. Paris: Privat.

de Planhol, X. 1957. "Essai sur la genèse du paysage rural de champs ouverts." *Annales de l'Est*, no. 21:414–23.

———. 1988. *Géographie historique de la France*. Fayard.

de Planhol, Xavier, with Paul Claval. 1994. *An Historical Geography of France.* Trans. Janet Lloyd. Cambridge: Cambridge University Press.

de Schepper, Hugo. 1994. "The Burgundian Habsburg Netherlands." In *Handbook of European History, 1400–1600,* ed. Thomas A. Brady Jr., Heiko A. Oberman, and James D. Tracy, 1:499–534. Leiden: Brill.

de Soto, Hernando. 1993. "The Missing Ingredient: What Poor Countries Need to Make Their Markets Work." *Economist* 328(7828): 8–12.

de Vries, Jan. 1974. *The Dutch Rural Economy in the Golden Age, 1500–1700.* New Haven and London: Yale University Press.

de Vries, Jan, and Ad van der Woude. 1997. *The First Modern Economy.* Cambridge: Cambridge University Press.

Delisle, Léopold. 1903. *Études sur la condition de la classe agricole et l'état de l'agriculture en Normandie au Moyen Âge.* Paris: n.p.

Dewald, Jonathan. 1987. *Pont-St-Pierre, 1398–1789: Lordship, Community and Capitalism in Early Modern France.* Berkeley: University of California Press.

Despois, M. 1957. Discussion of "Essai sur la genese du paysage rural de champs ouverts." *Annales de L'Est,* no. 21:423–24.

Dewindt, Edwin Brezette. 1972. *Land and People in Holywell-cum-Needingworth.* Toronto: Pontifical Institute of Medieval Studies.

Deyon, P. N.d. *Contribution à l'étude des revenus fonciers en Picardie. Les fermages de l'Hôtel-Dieu d'Amiens et leurs variations de 1515 à 1789.* Lille: R. Giard.

———. 1988a. "La Picardie, frontière du royaume (XVIe–XVIIe s.)." In *Histoire de la Picardie,* ed. Robert Fossier, 243–60. Paris: Privat.

———. 1988b. "Les progrès économiques et les sociétés provinciales (XVIe–XVIIIe s.)." In *Histoire de la Picardie,* ed. Robert Fossier, 261–90. Paris: Privat.

———. 1988c. "Forces et faiblesses de l'ancien régime." In *Histoire de la Picardie,* ed. Robert Fossier, 313–28. Paris: Privat.

Dickens, A. G. 1987. "The Early Expansion of Protestantism in England, 1520–1558." *Archiv für Reformationsgeschichte* (*Archive for Reformation History*) 78:187–221.

Dion, R. 1934. *Essai sur la formation du paysage rural français.* Tours: Arrault et cie.

Dodgshon, Robert A. 1980. *The Origin of British Field Systems: An Interpretation.* London: Academic Press.

Dodwell, Barbara. 1939. "The Free Peasantry of East Anglia." *Norfolk Archaeology* 27:145–57.

———. 1967. "Holdings and Inheritance in Medieval East Anglia." *Economic History Review,* 2d ser., 20:53–66.

Douglas, David C. 1927. *The Social Structure of Medieval East Anglia.* Oxford Studies in Social and Legal History vol. 9. Oxford: Clarendon Press.

Dovring, Folke. 1965. "The Transformation of European Agriculture." In *The Cambridge Economic History of Europe,* vol. 1, *The Industrial Revolutions and After: Incomes, Population and Technological Change,* ed. H. J. Habakkuk and M. M. Postan, 604–72. Cambridge: Cambridge University Press.

Downing, Brian. 1992. *The Military Revolution and Political Change.* Princeton: Princeton University Press.

Du Boulay, F. R. H. 1965. "Who Were Farming the English Demesnes at the End of the Middle Ages?" *Economic History Review,* 2d ser., 17(3): 443–55.

———. 1983. *Germany in the Later Middle Ages.* New York: St. Martin's Press.

Duby, Georges. 1968. *Rural Economy and Country Life in the Medieval West.* Columbia: University of South Carolina Press.

Dupont-Ferrier, Gustave. 1976. *Études sur les institutions financières de la France à la fin du moyen age.* I. *Les élections et leur personnel.* II. *Les finances extraordinaires et leur mécanisme.* Genève: Slatkine-Megariotis Reprints.

Dyer, C. C. 1991. "The West Midlands." In *The Agrarian History of England and Wales,* vol. 3, *1348–1500,* ed. Edward Miller. Cambridge: Cambridge University Press.

Eggertsson, Thráinn. 1990. *Economic Behavior and Institutions.* Cambridge: Cambridge University Press.

Elias, Norbert. 1990. *Über den Prozeß der Zivilisation: soziogenetische und psychogenetische Untersuchungen. Bd. 1. Wandlungen des Verhaltens in den weltlichen oberschichten.* Suhrkamp: Frankfurt am Main.

Emigh, Rebecca Jean. 1997. "The Spread of Sharecropping in Tuscany: The Political Economy of Transaction Costs." *American Sociological Review* 62:423–42.

Ertman, Thomas. 1997. *Birth of the Leviathan: Building States and Regimes in Medieval and Early Modern Europe.* Cambridge: Cambridge University Press.

"Europe's Latest Farming Muddle." 1991. *Economist,* February 23, 6–17.

Fenoaltea, Stefano. 1988. "Transaction Costs, Whig History and the Common Fields." *Politics and Society* 16(2–3): 171–240.

Finberg, H. P. R. 1951. *Tavistock Abbey: A Study in the Social and Economic History of Devon.* Cambridge: Cambridge University Press.

Forster, Robert. 1970. "Obstacles to Agricultural Growth in Eighteenth Century France." *American Historical Review* 75(6): 1600–1615.

Fossier, R. 1988. "La société Picard au moyen âge." In *Histoire de la Picardie,* ed. Robert Fossier, 135–76. Paris: Privat.

Fourquin, Guy. 1990. *Histoire économique de l'Occident medieval.* Paris: Armand Colin.

Fox, H. S. A. 1991. "Devon and Cornwall." In *The Agrarian History of England and Wales,* vol. *1348–1500,* ed. Edward Miller. Cambridge: Cambridge University Press.

Fryde, E. B. 1991. "Royal Fiscal Systems and State Formation in France from the 13th to the 16th Century, with Some English Comparisons." *Journal of Historical Sociology* 4(3): 236–87.

Fryde, E. B., and Natalie Fryde. 1991. "Peasant Rebellion and Peasant Discontents." In *The Agrarian History of England and Wales,* vol. 3, *1348–1500,* ed. Edward Miller. Cambridge: Cambridge University Press.

Fulbrook, Mary. 1990. *A Concise History of Germany.* Cambridge: Cambridge University Press.

Fussell, G. E. 1983. *Agricultural History in Great Britain and Western Europe before 1914.* London: Pindar Press.

Gadd, Carl-Johan. 1983. "English Summary." In *Järn Och Potatis. Jordbruk, teknik och social omvandling i Skaraborgs län 1750–1860,* 339–47. Göteborg: The Institute.

Gadd, Carl-Johan, and Ulf Jonsson. 1990. "Agrarian History as a Sub-Field of Swedish Economic History." *Scandinavian Economic History Review* 38(2): 18–30.

Ganshof, François Louis, and Adriaan Verhulst. 1966. "Medieval Agrarian Society in Its Prime: France, the Low Countries, and Western Germany." In *The Cambridge Economic History of Europe,* vol. 1, *The Agrarian Life of the Middle Ages,* 291–339. Cambridge: Cambridge University Press.

Gaunt, David. 1977. "Pre-Industrial Economy and Population Structure." *Scandinavian Journal of History* 2:183–210.

———. 1978. "Household Typology: Problems, Methods, Results." In *Chance and Change, Social and Economic Studies in Historical Demography in the Baltic Area,* ed. Sune Åkerman, Hans Chr. Johansen, and David Gaunt, 69–83. Odense: Odense University Press.

———. 1996. Review of *Peasantry to Capitalism: Western Östergötland in the Nineteenth Century,* by Göran Hoppe and John Langton. *Economic History Review* 49(2): 409–10.

Gilbert, Martin. 1968. *British History Atlas.* London: Weidenfeld and Nicolson.

Gissel, Svend. 1981a. "Rents and Other Economic Indicators." In *Desertion and Land Colonization in the Nordic Countries c. 1300–1600,* ed. Svend Gissel, Eino Jutikkala, Eva Österberg, Jørn Sandnes, and Björn Teitsson, 143–71. Stockholm: Almqvist and Wiksell International.

———. 1981b. "Trade and Supply: The Commercial Background to the Development of Settlements." In *Desertion and Land Colonization in the Nordic Countries c. 1300–1600,* ed. Svend Gissel, Eino Jutikkala, Eva Österberg, Jørn Sandnes, and Björn Teitsson, 188–204. Stockholm: Almqvist and Wiksell International.

Gissel, Svend, Eino Jutikkala, Eva Österberg, Jørn Sandnes, and Björn Teitsson, eds. 1981. *Desertion and Land Colonization in the Nordic Countries c. 1300–1600.* Stockholm: Almqvist and Wiksell International.

Godoy, Ricardo. 1991. "The Evolution of Common-Field Agriculture in the Andes: A Hypothesis." *Comparative Studies in Society and History* 33(2): 395–414.

Goldstone, Jack. 1988. "Regional Ecology and Agrarian Change in England and France, 1500–1700." *Politics and Society* 16(2–3): 265–86.

———. 1991. *Revolution and Rebellion in the Early Modern World.* Berkeley: University of California Press.

Göransson, Sölbr. 1961. "Regular Open Field Pattern in England and Scandinavian *Solskifte." Geografiska Annaler* 43B:80–101.

Goubert, Pierre. 1960. *Beauvais et le Beauvaisis de 1600 à 1730.* Paris: S.E.V.P.E.N.

———. 1973. *The Ancien Régime.* London: Weidenfeld and Nicolson.

———. 1986. *The French Peasantry in the Seventeenth Century.* Cambridge: Cambridge University Press.

Gray, H. L. 1915. *English Field Systems.* Cambridge, MA: Cambridge University Press.

Greif, Avner. 1994. "Cultural Beliefs and the Organization of Society: A Historical and Theoretical Reflection on Collectivist and Individualist Societies." *Journal of Political Economy* 102(51): 912–50.

Grigg, David. 1989. *English Agriculture: An Historical Perspective.* Basil Blackwell.

Gustafsson, Harald. 1994. *Political Interaction in the Old Regime: Central Power and Local Society in the Eighteenth-Century Nordic States.* Trans. Alan Crozier. Lund: Studentlitteratur.

Hagen, William W. 1985. "How Mighty the Junkers? Peasant Rents and Seigneurial Profits in Sixteenth-Century Brandenburg." *Past and Present* 108:80–116.

———. 1989. "Seventeenth-Century Crisis in Brandenburg: The Thirty Years' War, the Destabilization of Serfdom, and the Rise of Absolutism." *American Historical Review* 94:302–35.

Hallam, H. E. 1981. *Rural England, 1066–1348.* Sussex: Harvester Press.

Hardy, Thomas. 1960 [1891]. *Tess of the D'Urbervilles.* New York: Dodd, Mead.

Harley, C. K. 1992. "The Industrial Revolution: A Macroeconomic Assessment." In *The Industrial Revolution: An Economic Assessment,* ed. Joel Mokyr. Boulder, CO: Westview Press.

Heckscher, Eli F. 1954. *An Economic History of Sweden.* Trans. Göran Ohlin. Cambridge: Harvard University Press.

Henshall, Nicholas. 1992. *The Myth of Absolutism.* London and New York: Longman.

Hoffman, Philip T. 1988. "Institutions and Agriculture in Old Regime France." *Politics and Society* 16:241–64.

———. 1991. "Agricultural Productivity Growth in France: Regional Variation." Paper presented at the All-U.C. Group in Economic History, University of California, Davis, November 8–10.

———. 1996. *Growth in a Traditional Society: The French Countryside, 1450–1815.* Princeton: Princeton University Press.

Hoffman, Philip, and Kathryn Norberg. 1994. "Conclusion." *Fiscal Crises, Liberty, and Representative Government, 1450–1789,* 299–313. Stanford: Stanford University Press.

Holborn, Hajo. 1959. *A History of Modern Germany: The Reformation.* New York: Knopf.

Homans, G. C. 1941. *English Villagers of the Thirteenth Century.* Cambridge, MA: Cambridge University Press.

———. 1987a. "The Explanation of English Regional Differences." In *Certainties and Doubts: Collected Papers, 1962–1985.* New Brunswick: Transaction Books.

————. 1987b. "The Anglo-Saxon Invasions Reconsidered." In *Certainties and Doubts: Collected Papers, 1962–1985*. New Brunswick: Transaction Books.

————. 1988a [1962]. "The Frisians in East Anglia." In *Sentiments and Activities: Essays in Social Science*, 158–81. New Brunswick: Transaction Books.

————. 1988b [1962]. "The Puritans and the Clothing Industry in England." In *Sentiments and Activities: Essays in Social Science*, 182–91. New Brunswick: Transaction Books.

————. 1988c. [1962]. "The Rural Sociology of Medieval England." In *Sentiments and Activities: Essays in Social Science*, 145–57. New Brunswick: Transaction Books.

Hopcroft, Rosemary L. 1994a. "The Social Origins of Agrarian Change in Late Medieval England." *American Journal of Sociology* 99(6): 1559–95.

————. 1994b. "The Origins of Regular Open Field Systems in Pre-Industrial Europe." *Journal of European Economic History* 23(3): 563–80.

————. 1995. Comment: "Conceptualizing Regional Differences in Eighteenth Century England." *American Sociological Review* 60(5): 791–96.

————. 1997. "Rural Organization and Receptivity to Protestantism in Sixteenth-Century Europe." *Journal for the Scientific Study of Religion* 36(2): 158–81.

————. 1999. "Maintaining the Balance of Power: Taxation and Democracy in England and France, 1340–1688." *Sociological Perspectives* 42(1): 69–95.

Hoyle, R. W. 1990. "Tenure and the Land Market in Early Modern England: Or a Late Contribution to the Brenner Debate." *Economic History Review*, 2d ser., 43(1): 1–20.

Huppertz, Barthel. 1939. *Räume und Schichten Bäuerlichen Kulturformen in Deutschland*. Bonn: Ludwig Röhrscheid Verlag.

Hyams, P. R. 1980. *King, Lords and Peasants in Medieval England*. Oxford: Oxford University Press.

Isacson, Maths. 1979. "English Summary." In *Ekonomisk tillväxt och social differentiering 1680–1860. Bondeklassen i By socken, Kopparbergs län*, 176–87. Stockholm: Almqvist and Wiksell International.

Jacquart, Jean. 1975. "Immobilisme et Catastrophes." In *Histoire de la France rurale*, ed. Georges Duby and Armand Wallon, 2:159–344. Paris: Seuil.

Johnson, Arthur H. 1909. *The Disappearance of the Small Landowner*. Oxford: Clarendon Press.

Jones, E. L. 1965. "Agriculture and Economic Growth in England, 1660–1750: Agricultural Change." *Journal of Economic History* 25:1–18.

————. 1968. "Agricultural Origins of Industry." *Past and Present* 40:58–71.

————. 1987. *The European Miracle*, 2d ed. Cambridge: Cambridge University Press.

————. 1988. *Growth Recurring*. Oxford: Clarendon Press.

Jonsson, Ulf, Anu Mai Köll, and Ronny Pettersson. 1990. "The Dynamics of Change in Swedish Agriculture (1700–1850)." In *Structures and Dynamics of Agricultural Exploitations*, ed. Erik Aerts, Maurice Aymard, Juhan Kahk, Gilles Postel-Vinay, and Richard Sutch, 124–37. Leuven: Leuven University Press.

Juillard, E, A. Meynier, X. de Planhol, and G. Sautter. 1957. *Structures agraires et paysages ruraux: un quart de siècle de recherches françaises.* Annales de l'ést, no. 17.

Jutikkala, Eino. 1975. "Large Scale Farming in Scandinavia in the Seventeenth Century." *Scandinavian Economic History Review* 20(2): 159–66.

———. 1981. "The Way Up." In *Desertion and Land Colonization in the Nordic Countries c. 1300–1600,* ed. Svend Gissel, Eino Jutikkala, Eva Österberg, Jørn Sandnes, and Björn Teitsson, 115–42. Stockholm: Almqvist and Wiksell International.

Kerridge, Eric. 1968. *The Agricultural Revolution.* New York: A. M. Kelley.

———. 1969. *Agrarian Problems in the Sixteenth Century and After.* New York: Barnes and Noble.

———. 1992. *The Common Fields of England.* Manchester: Manchester University Press.

King, Edmund. 1973. *Peterborough Abbey, 1086–1310.* Cambridge: Cambridge University Press.

———. 1991. "The East Midlands." In *The Agrarian History of England and Wales,* vol. 3: *1348–1500,* ed. Edward Miller. Cambridge: Cambridge University Press.

Kirby, David. 1990. *Northern Europe in the Early Modern Period: The Baltic World, 1492–1772.* London and New York: Longman.

Knight, Jack. 1992. *Institutions and Social Conflict.* Cambridge: Cambridge University Press.

Kriedte, Peter, H. Medick, and J. Schlumbohm. 1977. *Industrialisierung vor der Industrialisierung Gewerbliche Warenproduktion auf dem Land in der Formations-periode des Kapitalismus.* Gottingen: Vandenhoeck und Ruprecht.

Lamond, E., ed. 1929 [1581]. *A Compendious or Briefe Examination: A Discourse of the Common Weal of this Realm of England.* Ed. from the mss. by the late Elizabeth Lamond. Cambridge: Cambridge University Press.

Landes, David S. 1986. "What Do Bosses Really Do?" *Journal of Economic History* 46(3): 585–623.

Langdon, John. 1986. *Horses, Oxen and Technological Innovation.* Cambridge: Cambridge University Press.

Langland, William. 1981 [1378]. *The Vision of Piers Plowman.* London: British Broadcasting Commission.

Le Roy Ladurie, Emmanuel. 1987. *The French Peasantry, 1450–1660.* Berkeley: University of California Press.

Le Roy Ladurie, Emmanuel, and Joseph Goy. 1982. *Tithe and Agrarian History from the Fourteenth to the Nineteenth Centuries.* Cambridge: Cambridge University Press.

Leonard, E. M. 1962. "The Inclosure of Common Fields in the Seventeenth Century." In *Essays in Economic History,* vol. 2, ed. E. M. Carus-Wilson. London: Edward Arnold.

Levi, Margaret. 1988. *Of Rule and Revenue.* Berkeley: University of California Press.

Lewis, Archibald R. 1984. "Patterns of Economic Development in Southern France, 1050–1271 A.D." *Medieval Society in Southern France and Catalonia,* 57–83. London: Variorum Reprints.

Löfgren, Orvar. 1974. "Family and Household among Scandinavian Peasants: An Exploratory Essay." *Ethnologia Scandinavica,* 17–52.

Macfarlane, Alan. 1978. *The Origins of English Individualism.* Oxford: Blackwell.

Magnusson, Lars. 1996. *Sveriges Ekonomiska Historia.* Stockholm: Rabén Prisma.

Major, J. Russell. 1994. *From Renaissance Monarchy to Absolute Monarchy.* Baltimore: Johns Hopkins University Press.

Mann, Michael. 1986. *The Sources of Social Power.* Cambridge: Cambridge University Press.

———. 1988. *States, War and Capitalism.* Oxford: Blackwell.

Markoff, John. 1985. "The Social Geography of Rural Revolt at the Beginning of the French Revolution." *American Sociological Review* 50:761–81.

Martin, John E. 1983. *Feudalism to Capitalism: Peasant and Landlord in English Agrarian Development.* London: Macmillan.

Marx, Karl. 1906. *Capital.* New York: Modern Library.

Mate, Mavis. 1986. "The Estates of Canterbury Cathedral Priory before the Black Death, 1315–1348." *Studies in Medieval and Renaissance History* 8:1–26.

———. 1991. "Kent and Sussex." In *The Agrarian History of England and Wales,* vol. 3, *1348–1500,* ed. Edward Miller. Cambridge: Cambridge University Press.

Mathias, Peter, and Patrick O'Brien. 1976. "Taxation in Britain and France, 1715–1810: A Comparison of the Social and Economic Incidence of Taxes Collected for the Central Government." *Journal of European Economic History* 5:601–50.

Mayhew, Alan. 1973. *Rural Settlement and Farming in Germany.* London: Batsford.

McCloskey, Donald. 1975. "The Persistence of English Common Fields." In *European Peasants and Their Markets,* ed. W. N. Parker and E. L. Jones, 73–119. Princeton: Princeton University Press.

McCloskey, Donald N. 1976. "English Open Fields as Behavior towards Risk." In *Research in Economic History,* vol. 1. Greenwich, CT: JAI.

Mead, W. R. 1981. *An Historical Geography of Scandinavia.* New York: Academic Press.

Meitzen, August. 1895. *Siedelung und agrarwesen der Westgermanen und Ostgermanen, der Kelten, Romer, Finnen und Slawen. [The Settlement and Agrarian Structure of the Western and Eastern Germanic Tribes, Celts, Romans, Finns and Slaves].* 3 vols. Berlin: W. Hertz.

Melton, James Van Horn. 1988. *Absolutism and the Eighteenth-Century Origins of Compulsory Schooling in Prussia and Austria.* Cambridge: Cambridge University Press.

Merton, Robert K., and Alice S. Rossi. 1957. "Contributions to the Theory of Reference Group Behavior." In *Social Theory and Social Structure,* by Robert K. Merton, 225–80. Rev. and enlarged ed. Glencoe, IL: Free Press.

Metcalf, Michael F. 1995. "Scandinavia, 1397–1560." In *Handbook of European History, 1400–1600,* ed. Thomas A. Brady Jr., Heiko A. Oberman, and James D. Tracy, 2:523–50. Leiden: Brill.

Mettam, Roger. 1988. *Power and Faction in Louis XIV's France.* New York: Basil Blackwell.

Meynier, A. 1959. *Les paysages agraire.* Paris: Librairie Armand Colin.

Miller, Edward. 1991. "The Southern Counties." In *The Agrarian History of England and Wales,* vol. 3: *1348–1500,* ed. Edward Miller, 42–52, 182–93, 596–610. Cambridge: Cambridge University Press.

Moberg, Vilhelm. 1973. *A History of the Swedish People.* 2 vols. Trans. Paul Britten Austin. New York: Dorset Press.

Moeller, Bernd. 1977. *Deutschland im Zeitalter der Reformation.* Göttingen: Vandenhoeck and Ruprecht.

Moore, Barrington. 1966. *Social Origins of Dictatorship and Democracy.* Boston: Beacon Press.

Moreton, C. E. 1992. *The Townshends and Their World: Gentry, Law and Land in Norfolk c. 1450–1551.* Oxford and New York: Clarendon Press.

Morineau, Michel. 1970. *Les faux-semblants d'un démarrage économique: agriculture et démographie en France au XVIIIe siècle.* Paris: Armand Colin.

Munro, John H. A. *Wool, Cloth, and Gold: The Struggle for Bullion in Anglo-Burgundian Trade, 1340–1478.* Toronto: University of Toronto Press.

———. 1994. "Patterns of Trade, Money and Credit." In *Handbook of European History, 1400–1600,* ed. Thomas A. Brady Jr., Heiko A. Oberman, and James D. Tracy, 1:147–95. Leiden: Brill.

Myrdal, Janken, and Johan Söderberg. "English Summary." In *Kontinuitetens dynamik. Agrar ekonomi i 1500-talets Sverige,* 523–35. Stockholm: Almqvist and Wiksell International.

Nee, Victor. 1996. "The Emergence of Market Society: Changing Mechanisms of Stratification in China." *American Journal of Sociology* 101(4): 908–49.

Neveux, Hugues. 1975. "Declin et repris: la fluctuation biseculaire 1330–1560." In *Histoire de la France rurale,* ed. Georges Duby and Armand Wallon, 2:9–158. Paris: Seuil.

———. 1980. *Vie et declin d'une structure économique Les grains du Cambrésis fin du XIVe siècle -debut du XVIIe siècle.* Paris: Ecole des hautes études en sciences sociales.

North, D. C. 1981. *Structure and Change in Economic History.* New York: Norton.

———. 1982. "The Theoretical Tools of the Economic Historian." In *Economics in the Long View: Essays in Honour of W. W. Rostow,* ed. Charles P. Kindleberger and Guido di Tella. New York: New York University Press.

———. 1990a. *Institutions, Institutional Change and Economic Performance.* Cambridge: Cambridge University Press.

———. 1990b. "Institutions and a Transaction-Cost Theory of Exchange." In *Perspectives on Positive Political Economy,* ed. James E. Alt and Kenneth A. Shepsle, 182–94. Cambridge: Cambridge University Press.

———. 1994. "Economic Performance through Time." *American Economic Review* 84(3): 359–68.

North, D. C., and R. P. Thomas. 1973. *The Rise of the Western World.* Cambridge: Cambridge University Press.

O'Brien, Patrick Karl. 1996. "Path Dependency, or Why Britain Became an Industrialized and Urbanized Economy Long before France." *Economic History Review* 49(2): 213–49.

O'Brien, P. K., and D. Heath. 1982. "The Efficiency of British and French Agriculture, 1815–1914." In *Prestations paysannes, dîmes, rente fonçiere et mouvement de la production agricole a l'époque préindustrielle,* ed. Joseph Goy and Emmanuel Le Roy Ladurie, 733–47. Paris: Ecole des hautes études en sciences sociales.

Olai, Birgitta. 1983. "English Summary." In *Storskiftet i Ekebyborna. Svensk jordbruksutveckling avspeglad i en östgötasocken,* 234–43. Stockholm: Almqvist and Wiksell International.

Olson, Mancur. 1997. "The New Institutional Economics: The Collective Choice Approach to Economic Development." *Institutions and Economic Development,* 37–66. Baltimore and London: Johns Hopkins University Press.

Österberg, Eva. 1981. "Social Aspects." In *Desertion and Land Colonization in the Nordic Countries c. 1300–1600,* ed. Svend Gissel, Eino Jutikkala, Eva Österberg, Jørn Sandnes, and Björn Teitsson, 205–29. Stockholm: Almqvist and Wiksell International.

———. 1991. *Mentalities and Other Realities: Essays in Medieval and Early Modern Scandinavian History.* Lund: Lund University Press.

Østerud, Øyvind. 1978. "Agrarian Structure of the Old Peasant Society." In *Agrarian Structure and Peasant Politics in Scandinavia: A Comparative Study of Rural Response to Economic Change,* 69–110. Oslo: Universitetsforlaget.

Overton, Mark. 1990. "Re-estimating Crop Yields from Probate Inventories." *Journal of Economic History* 50:931–35.

———. 1991. "The Determinants of Crop Yields in Early Modern England." In *Land, Labour and Livestock: Historical Studies in European Agricultural Productivity,* ed. B. M. S. Campbell and Mark Overton, 284–322. Manchester: Manchester University Press.

———. 1996. *Agricultural Revolution in England. The Transformation of the Agrarian Economy, 1500–1850.* Cambridge: Cambridge University Press.

Overton, Mark, and Bruce M. S. Campbell. 1991. "Productivity Change in European Agricultural Development." In *Land, Labour and Livestock: Historical Studies in European Agricultural Productivity,* ed. B. M. S. Campbell and Mark Overton. Manchester: Manchester University Press.

Parain, Charles. 1941. "The Evolution of Agricultural Technique." In *The Cambridge Economic History,* vol. 1, ed. J. H. Clapham and Eileen Power. Cambridge: Cambridge University Press.

Pautard, Jean. 1965. *Les disparités régionales dans la croissance de l'agriculture française.* Paris: Gauthier-Villars Editeur.

Pignede, Bernard. 1966. *Les Gurungs: une population himalayenne du Nepal.* Paris: Mouton and Co.

Pirenne, Henri. 1937. *Economic and Social History of Medieval Europe.* San Diego: Harcourt Brace Jovanovich.

Plaisse, Andre. 1961. *La Baronnie du Neubourg: essai d'histoire agraire, économique et sociale.* Paris: Presses Universitaires de France.

Poland, Burdette C. 1957. *French Protestantism and the French Revolution: A Study in Church and State, Thought and Religion, 1685–1815.* Princeton: Princeton University Press.

Polanyi, Karl. 1944. *The Great Transformation: The Political and Economic Origins of Our Time.* Boston: Beacon Press.

Postan, M. M. 1952. "The Trade of Medieval Europe: The North." In *The Cambridge Economic History,* ed. M. M. Postan and E. E. Rich, 2:119–256. Cambridge: Cambridge University Press.

———. 1973. *Essays on Medieval Agriculture and General Problems of the Medieval Economy.* Cambridge: Cambridge University Press.

Pounds, N. J. G. 1990. *An Historical Geography of Europe.* Cambridge: Cambridge University Press.

Power, Eileen. 1963 [1922]. *Medieval People.* New York: Barnes and Noble.

Press, Volker. 1994. "The Habsburg Lands: The Holy Roman Empire, 1400–1555." In *Handbook of European History, 1400–1600,* ed. Thomas A. Brady Jr., Heiko A. Oberman, and James D. Tracy, 1:437–66. Leiden: Brill.

Price, Roger. 1983. *The Modernization of Rural France: Communications Networks and Agricultural Market Structures in Nineteenth-Century France.* New York: St. Martin's Press.

Prince, Hugh. 1977. "Regional Contrasts in Agrarian Structure." In *Themes in the Historical Geography of France,* ed. Hugh Clout, 129–84. New York: Academic Press.

Putnam, Robert D. 1993. *Making Democracy Work: Civic Traditions in Modern Italy.* Princeton: Princeton University Press.

Raftis, J. Ambrose. 1964. *Tenure and Mobility.* Toronto: Pontifical Institute of Medieval Studies.

Ragin, Charles C. 1987. *The Comparative Method: Moving beyond Qualitative and Quantitative Strategies.* Berkeley: University of California Press.

*Rand McNally Atlas of World History.* 1984. Chicago: Rand McNally.

Ransom, Roger, Richard Sutch, and Gary Walton. 1982. *Explorations in the New Economic History: Essays in Honor of Douglass C. North.* New York: Academic Press.

Riches, Naomi. 1967. *The Agricultural Revolution in Norfolk.* London: Frank Cass.

Robinson, Geroid Tanquary. 1932. *Rural Russia under the Old Regime.* New York: Longmans, Green.

Robisheaux, Thomas. 1989. *Rural Society and the Search for Order in Early Modern Germany.* Cambridge: Cambridge University Press.

———. 1994. "The World of the Village." In *Handbook of European History,*

*1400–1600,* ed. Thomas A. Brady Jr., Heiko A. Oberman, and James D. Tracy, 1:79–112. Leiden: Brill.

Root, Hilton L. 1987. *Peasant and King in Burgundy: Agrarian Foundations of French Absolutism.* Berkeley: University of California Press.

———. 1994. *The Fountain of Privilege: Political Foundations of Markets in Old Regime France and England.* Berkeley: University of California Press.

Rösener, Werner. 1992. *Peasants in the Middle Ages.* Trans. Alexander Stützer. Urbana and Chicago: University of Illinois Press.

Rostow, W. W. 1960. *The Stages of Economic Growth: A Non-communist Manifesto.* New York: Cambridge University Press.

Roth, Guenther, and Claus Wittich. 1978. *Economy and Society.* 2 vols. Berkeley: University of California Press.

Rowley, Trevor. 1986. *The High Middle Ages.* London: Routledge and Kegan Paul.

Russell, J. C. 1948. *British Medieval Population.* Albuquerque: University of New Mexico Press.

Rydeberg, Göran. 1985. "English Summary." *Skatteköpen i Örebro län 1701–1809,* 184–91. Uppsala: Almqvist and Wiksell International.

Sabean, David Warren. 1984. *Power in the Blood: Popular Culture and Village Discourse in Early Modern Germany.* Cambridge: Cambridge University Press.

———. 1990. *Property, Production and Family in Neckarhausen, 1700–1870.* Cambridge: Cambridge University Press.

Samsonowicz, Henryk, and Antoni Maczak. 1985. "Feudalism and Capitalism: A Balance of Changes in East-Central Europe." In *East-Central Europe in Transition: From the Fourteenth to the Seventeenth Century,* ed. Antoni Maczak, Henryk Samsonowicz, and Peter Burke, 6–23. Cambridge: Cambridge University Press.

Sandnes, Jørn. 1981. "Settlement Developments in the Late Middle Ages (approx. 1300–1540)." In *Desertion and Land Colonization in the Nordic Countries c. 1300–1600,* ed. Svend Gissel, Eino Jutikkala, Eva Österberg, Jørn Sandnes, and Björn Teitsson, 78–114. Stockholm: Almqvist and Wiksell International.

Sawyer, Birgit, and Peter Sawyer. 1993. *Medieval Scandinavia.* Minneapolis: University of Minnesota Press.

Sayer, Derek. 1992. "A Notable Administration: English State Formation and the Rise of Capitalism." *American Journal of Sociology* 97(5): 1382–1415.

Schilling, Heinz. 1991. *Civic Calvinism in Northwestern Germany and the Netherlands (16th to 19th Centuries).* Kirksville, MO: Sixteenth Century Journal Publishers.

Schofield, R. S. 1965. "The Geographical Distribution of Wealth in England, 1334–1649." *Economic History Review,* 2d ser., 18(3): 483–510.

Scott, Franklin D. 1977. *Sweden: The Nation's History.* Minneapolis: University of Minnesota Press.

Scott, James C. 1976. *The Moral Economy of the Peasant.* New Haven: Yale University Press.

Scott, Tom. 1996. "Economic Landscapes." In *Germany: A New Social and Economic History,* vol. 1, *1450–1630,* ed. Bob Scribner, 1–31. New York: Arnold.

Scribner, Bob. 1996. "Communities and the Nature of Power." In *Germany: A New Social and Economic History,* vol. 1, *1450–1630,* ed. Bob Scribner, 291–325. New York: Arnold.

Seebohm, F. 1890. *The English Village Community.* London: Longmans, Green and Co.

Sexauer, Benjamin. 1976. "English and French Agriculture in the Late Eighteenth Century." *Agricultural History* 50(3): 491–505.

Sion, Jules. 1909. *Les paysans de la Normandie orientale.* Paris: Armand Colin.

Sivéry, Gérard. 1977–79. *Structures agraires et vie rurale dans le Hainaut à la fin du Moyen Âge.* Villeneuve-d'Ascq: Publications de l'Université de Lille III.

Skocpol, Theda. 1979. *States and Social Revolutions.* New York: Cambridge University Press.

Slicher van Bath, B. H. 1963a. *Yield Ratios, 810–1820.* Wageningen: A. A. G. Bijdragen (10).

————. 1963b. *The Agrarian History of Western Europe, AD 500–1850.* New York: St. Martin's Press.

Small, Albion. 1994 [1895]. "The Era of Sociology." Reprinted in the *American Journal of Sociology* 100(1): ix–xxiii.

Smith, C. T. 1967. *An Historical Geography of Western Europe before 1800.* New York: Praeger.

Söderberg, Johan. 1996. *Sveriges Ekonomiska Och Sociala Historia.* Malmö: Liber-Hermods.

Solow, Robert. 1992. "Notes on Coping." In *Eminent Economists,* ed. Michael Szenberg, 270–74. Cambridge: Cambridge University Press.

Somers, Margaret R. 1993. "Law, Community and Political Culture in the Transition to Democracy." *American Sociological Review* 58(5): 587–620.

Spufford, Peter. 1965. "Assemblies of Estates, Taxation and Control of Coinage in Medieval Europe." In *Congrès internationale des sciences historiques, études présentées à la Commission l'histoire des assemblées d'états.* Louvain: Nauwelaerts.

Stacey, Robert C. 1986. "Agricultural Investment and the Management of the Royal Demesne Manors, 1236–1240." *Journal of Economic History* 46:919–34.

Stone, E. 1956. "The Estates of Norwich Cathedral Priory, 1100–1300." Ph.D. diss., Oxford University.

Stone, L. 1960. "Discussion of Trevor-Roper's General Crisis." *Past and Present* 18:31–33.

Sussman, Nathan. 1993. "Debasements, Royal Revenues, and Inflation in France during the Hundred Years' War, 1415–1422." *Journal of Economic History* 53(1): 44–70.

Tawney, R. H. 1912. *The Agrarian Problem in the Sixteenth Century.* London and New York: Longmans, Green and Co.

Te Brake, William H. 1985. *Medieval Frontier: Culture and Ecology in Rijnland.* College Station: Texas A&M University Press.

Teitsson, Björn. 1981. "Geographical Variables." In *Desertion and Land Colonization in the Nordic Countries c. 1300–1600,* ed. Svend Gissel, Eino Jutikkala, Eva Österberg, Jørn Sandnes, and Björn Teitsson, 172–87. Stockholm: Almqvist and Wiksell International.

t'Hart, Marjolein C. 1993. *The Making of a Bourgeois State. War, Politics and Finance during the Dutch Revolt.* Manchester and New York: Manchester University Press.

Thirsk, J. 1964. "The Common Fields." *Past and Present* 29:3–25.

———. 1967. "The Farming Regions of England." In *The Agrarian History of England and Wales,* vol. 14, *1500–1640,* ed. Joan Thirsk. Cambridge: Cambridge University Press.

———. 1984. *The Rural Economy of England.* London: Hambledon Press.

Thoen, Erik. 1993. "The Count, the Countryside and the Economic Development of the Towns in Flanders from the Eleventh to the Thirteenth Century, Some Provisional Remarks and Hypotheses." *Studia Historica Œconomica,* ed. Erik Aerts, Brigitte Henau, Paul Janssens, and Raymond van Uytven, 259–78. Leuven: Leuven University Press.

———. 1990. "Economie rurale et demographie en Flandre pendant le bas moyen age et le debut des temps modernes." In *Recent Doctoral Research in Economic History,* ed. Erik Aerts and Herman Van der Wee, 31–39. Leuven: Leuven University Press.

Thornton, Christopher. 1991. "The Determinants of Land Productivity on the Bishop of Winchester's Demesne of Rimpton, 1208–1403." In *Land, Labour and Livestock,* ed. Bruce M. S. Campbell and Mark Overton. Manchester: Manchester University Press.

Tilly, Charles. 1989. "Cities and States in Europe, 1000–1800." *Theory and Society* 18:563–84.

———. 1992. *Coercion, Capital, and European States, AD 990–1992.* Cambridge: Blackwell Publishers.

———. 1994. "Entanglements of European Cities and States." In *Cities and the Rise of States in Europe, AD 1000 to 1800,* 1–27. Boulder, CO: Westview Press.

*Times Concise Atlas of World History.* 1992. London: HarperCollins.

Titow, J. Z. 1965. "Medieval England and the Open Field System." *Past and Present* 22:86–192.

Toffin, Gerard. 1984. *Société et religion chez les Newar du Nepal.* Paris: Editions du centre national de la recherche scientifique.

Topolski, Jerzy. 1985. "A Model of East-Central European Continental Commerce in the Sixteenth and the First Half of the Seventeenth Century." In *East-Central Europe in Transition: From the Fourteenth to the Seventeenth Century,* ed. Antoni Maczak, Henryk Samsonowicz, and Peter Burke, 128–39. Cambridge: Cambridge University Press.

Tullock, Gordon. 1987. *Autocracy.* Dordrecht: Kluwer Academic Publishers.

Turner, Michael. 1982. "Agricultural Productivity in England in the Eighteenth

Century: Evidence from Crop Yields." *Economic History Review,* 2d ser., 35:489–505.

Tusser, Thomas. 1965 [1573]. *Fiue hundreth points of good husbandry Vnited to As many of good huswiferie.* Early English Books Series, STC 24375. Ann Arbor, MI: University Microfilms.

Usher, Abbot Payson. 1913. *The History of the Grain Trade in France, 1400–1710.* Cambridge: Harvard University Press.

Van der Wee, Herman. 1993. *The Low Countries in the Early Modern World.* Trans. Lizabeth Fackelman. Brookfield, VT: Variorum.

Van der Wee, Herman, with E. Van Cauwenberghe. 1993. "Agrarian History and Public Finances in Flanders, 14th to 17th Century." In *The Low Countries in the Early Modern World,* by Herman Van der Wee, 69–83. Trans. Lizabeth Fackelman. Brookfield, VT: Variorum.

Van Deursen, A. T. 1991. *Plain Lives in a Golden Age: Popular Culture, Religion and Society in Seventeenth-Century Holland.* Trans. Maarten Ultee. Cambridge: Cambridge University Press.

van Houtte, J. A. 1977. *An Economic History of the Low Countries, 800–1800.* New York: St Martin's Press.

Vinogradoff, P. 1892. *Villainage in England.* Oxford: Clarendon Press.

von Thadden, Rudolf. 1987. *Prussia: The History of a Lost State.* Trans. Angi Rutter. Cambridge: Cambridge University Press.

Wallerstein, Immanuel. 1974. *The Modern World System.* New York: Academic Press.

Weibull, C. 1933. "Gustaf II Adolf." *Scania* 6:1–22.

Williamson, Oliver E. 1975. *Markets and Hierarchies: Analysis and Anti-Trust Implications.* New York: Free Press.

———. 1985. *The Economic Institutions of Capitalism: Firms, Markets, Relational Contracting.* New York: Free Press.

Williamson, Tom. 1988. "Explaining Regional Landscapes: Woodland and Champion in Southern and Eastern England." *Landscape History* 10:5–13.

Wilmot, Sarah. 1996. "The Scientific Gaze: Agricultural Improvers and the Topography of South-West England." In *Topographical Writers in South-West England,* ed. Mark Brayshay, 105–35. Exeter: University of Exeter Press.

Winberg, Christer. 1977. "English Summary." In *Folkökning och proletarisering. Kring den sociala strukturomvandlingen på Sveriges landsbygd under den agrara revolutionen,* 331–44. Lund: Bo Cavefors Bokförlag.

———. 1978. "Population Growth and Proletarianization." In *Chance and Change: Social and Economic Studies in Historical Demography in the Baltic Area,* ed. Sune Åkerman, Hans Chr. Johansen, and David Gaunt, 170–84. Odense: Odense University Press.

———. 1985. "English Summary." *Grenverket. Studier rörande jord, släktskapssystem och ståndsprivilegier,* 231–43. Stockholm: A.-B. Nordiska Bokhandeln.

Wolfe, Martin. 1972. *The Fiscal System of Renaissance France.* New Haven: Yale University Press.

Wordie, J. R. 1983. "The Chronology of English Enclosure, 1500–1914." *Economic History Review,* 2d ser. 36(4): 483–505.

Wrigley, E. A. 1985. "Urban Growth and Agricultural Change: England and the Continent in the Early Modern Period." *Journal of Interdisciplinary History* 15(4): 683–728.

———. 1988. *Continuity, Chance and Change.* Cambridge: Cambridge University Press.

Young, Arthur. 1794. *Travels in France during the Years 1787, 1788 and 1789.* Vol. 1, 2d ed. London: W. Richardson.

Young, Frank. 1994. "Durkheim and Development Theory." *Sociological Theory* 12(1): 73–82.

Yun, Bartolomé. 1994. "Economic Cycles and Structural Changes." In *Handbook of European History, 1400–1600,* ed. Thomas A. Brady Jr., Heiko A. Oberman, and James D. Tracy, 1:113–42. Leiden: Brill.

Zaret, David. 1985. *The Heavenly Contract.* Chicago: University of Chicago Press.

Zeller, Gaston. 1970. "Industry in France before Colbert." In *Essays in French Economic History,* ed. Rondo Cameron, 128–39. Homewood, IL: Irwin.

Żytkowicz, Leonid. 1985. "Trends of Agrarian Economy in Poland, Bohemia and Hungary from the Middle of the Fifteenth to the Middle of the Seventeenth Century." In *East-Central Europe in Transition: From the Fourteenth to the Seventeenth Century,* ed. Antoni Maczak, Henryk Samsonowicz, and Peter Burke, 59–83. Cambridge: Cambridge University Press.

Ziegler, Philip. 1969. *The Black Death.* New York: Harper and Row.

# Index

absolutist states: French, 124; Prussian, 193, 195; Swedish, 196, 209

agricultural productivity, 6, 13, 68–69, 82, 97, 103, 105, 111–12, 132–34, 138–39, 143–48, 169–72, 180, 185–88, 195, 198, 216–17, 221–22; labor productivity, 69, 78, 82, 147; land productivity, 68, 102, 105, 147; records of, 5, 12–13, 67, 205; yields, cereal, 13, 68, 82, 98, 100, 132–33, 138, 144, 146, 148, 172, 176, 180, 185, 210, 216–17, 218, 219

agricultural technology, 5–6, 82; convertible husbandry, 77–78, 98, 139, 175, 187; crop rotations, 16–17, 34, 68, 82, 98, 100, 103, 112, 130–31, 133, 170, 172, 187–88, 200, 205, 216; horses, use of, 6, 68, 75–76, 78, 103, 133, 170, 172, 210, 217; legumes and grasses, use of, 6, 68, 77, 98, 133, 148, 169, 175, 188; plows, 28–29, 78, 82, 98, 112, 210

agriculture: crops, 13, 17, 64, 77, 81, 92, 100, 103, 111, 127, 133–34, 138, 145, 169–71, 173, 188, 206, 210, 219, 222; industrial crops, 78, 101, 134–35, 170, 173; viticulture, 134–35, 138, 161, 170–71, 173, 176, 188

*Angerdorf,* 164

Black Death, 69, 100, 102, 110, 134, 172, 207

Bloch, Marc, 4, 5, 11, 15–16, 24, 28, 31, 49, 127, 140, 145, 230

*bocage,* 24, 44, 124, 131. *See also* field systems, classification of, enclosed field systems

*Bördsrätt,* 226, 233

Brenner, Robert, 233, 236

Burgundy, dukes of, 113–15

*Champagne,* 124. *See also* field systems, classification of, communal open field systems

class relations, 9, 25, 52, 65–66, 129, 131, 161–62, 165–69, 177–81, 203–4, 233. *See also* customary tenants; lords, feudal; serfs

cities. *See* urbanization

Coke of Norfolk, 86

common fields. *See* field systems, classification of, communal open field systems

commons, 20, 62, 164

communitarianism, 24, 50–51, 62, 130, 163

community organizations, 18–19, 26, 39, 50, 62, 163, 165–66

*constrainte solidaire,* 155

courts: hundred courts (Sweden), 225; Imperial (German lands), 189, 192; King's courts (England), 66, 84; manorial, 26, 50, 66, 85, 129, 162, 191; *Parlements* (France), 26, 119, 135, 145, 154; provincial courts (Netherlands), 118–19; Public Peace (German lands), 190; Royal courts (France), 129–30, 154; Vehmic courts (German lands), 190

culture, local, 24–25, 65, 130, 236. *See also* communitarianism; individualism

269

currency, 86, 117–18, 151, 189, 224, 227–29; copper standard (Sweden), 228; paper money, 86, 118, 228. *See also* institutions, financial
customary tenants, 26, 65, 85, 95, 129, 203. *See also* serfs

de Vries, Jan, 97
demography, 6, 29–30, 33–35, 54–55, 61, 75, 91–92, 102, 104, 106, 112, 126, 134, 144, 158–60, 172–73, 174–75, 194, 196, 199, 207, 209, 211, 218, 222–23, 234
deserted villages, 73, 100, 173, 207–8
Diets, Imperial (German lands), 191
Ditmarsch, 25, 179, 181

ecology, 5, 28, 29–30, 54–55, 59, 91, 125, 158, 198, 234
*élu,* 153
Empire, Holy Roman, 157, 189–93. *See also* German lands
enclosure, 13, 70–71, 78–79, 107, 139–41, 145, 183, 187, 220–21; parliamentary enclosures (England), 79
England, 58–89, 98; agrarian change (after sixteenth century), 77–82; agrarian change (late medieval and early modern), 66–81; the agricultural revolution, 82–83; ecology, population and markets, 59–61; field systems, 61–65; lack of warfare and maintenance of democracy, 87–88; legal and financial institutions, 83–87; multivariate analysis of regional differences in economic growth, 73–77; regional pattern of class relations, 65–66
estates. See *Estates-General* (France); Parliament (England); *Riksdag* (Sweden); States-General (United Provinces)
*Estates-General* (France), 150, 224
ethnic settlement, 31, 40, 42, 45

famines, 82, 139, 144, 156, 222

farms: consolidation of, 13, 70, 145, 187, 221; size of, 19, 69–70, 79–81, 106–7, 135–37, 146, 149, 156, 166–67, 181–83
field systems, classification of, 11, 15–16, 52; communal open field systems, 16–20, 49–51, 61–62, 75–76, 92, 127–30, 161–63, 199–200, 202; description, 2–3, 65; enclosed field systems, 22–24, 43–44, 51–52, 64, 131–32, 163–65, 204–5; field systems and transaction costs, 48–52; less-communal open field systems, 20–22, 44–45, 51–52, 62–65, 92–96, 130–32, 163–65, 203–5; origins of communal open field systems, 28–41; origins of enclosed field systems, 41–45; origins of less-communal open field systems, 41–45
fishing, 73, 101, 104, 105, 207
Flanders, 45, 91, 95, 97–98, 99, 100–101, 102–5, 112, 114, 115, 117, 118, 121, 125, 132, 135, 139, 143, 145, 148, 156, 167, 231; cloth industry, 108–10; farm sizes in, 106
France, 124–56; agrarian change (late medieval and early modern periods), 132–44; the agricultural revolution, 144–48; crown policy and the survival of communal agriculture, 154–55; ecology, population and markets, 125–27; field systems, 127–32; regional differences in enclosure, 139–41; regional differences in labor relations, 141–42; rise of royal bureaucracy, 153–54; rural industry, 142–44; state taxation and policies, 150–53; warfare, 148–50
freeholders, 27, 66, 85, 95–96, 132, 165–66, 180; *skattebönder* (Sweden), 203–5, 214, 221
Frisians, 25, 42–44, 108, 114

Gaunt, David, 217–18
German lands, 157–95; agrarian change (late medieval and early

modern periods), 169–86; comparative agrarian stagnation, 186–88; ecology, population, and markets, 158–60; enclosure, 183; field systems, 161–65; legal decentralization, 189–93; peasant freedom, 165–69; "refeudalization" of eastern Germany, 177–80; regional differences in farm sizes, 181–83; rural industry, 183–84; Thirty Years' War and seventeenth-century decline, 184–86; warfare, 193–94

Goubert, Pierre, 151

*Grundherrscaft,* 178, 215

Gustavus Vasa, 209, 211, 213, 225, 226

*Gutscherrschaft,* 178, 215

Habsburg, House of, 113, 115

*Hagenhufendorf,* 22, 164

Hagen, William W., 178–79

*Handfesten,* 164

Hanseatic League, 172–73, 199, 209

Heckscher, Eli, 121, 214, 239

hide, 19, 161

Homans, George, 4, 27, 42–43

*Hufe,* 19, 161, 164, 178, 181–82

individualism, 25, 65, 97, 131

industry, 11, 73, 79, 219, 235; metal, 73, 184, 220; textile, 11, 72, 75–76, 81, 99, 101, 106, 108–11, 142–43, 156, 174, 183–84, 219–20

inheritance customs, 38, 40, 62, 64, 70, 130, 162, 182–83, 204, 205

institutions, 8, 47–48; financial, 55, 86–87, 113, 117–21, 227–29 (*see also* currency); legal, 55–56, 83–85, 113, 118–19, 154, 163, 189–92, 225, 234 (*see also* courts); state, 9, 55–56, 87–88, 113–17, 124, 153–54, 191–92, 223–27 (*see also* absolutist states)

*intendants,* 154–55

Junkers, 178, 239

labor services (*corvée*), 66, 95, 108, 162, 177, 181, 193, 203

land division, customs of, 38, 49

Land Law (Sweden), 224

*Landtage* (German estates), 191

Le Roy Ladurie, Emmanuel, 124, 133, 138–39, 144

*locator* (*Lokatur*), 96, 163

lords, feudal, 37–39, 52–53, 65, 95, 129, 131, 161, 166, 177, 181. *See also* class relations

Low Countries. *See* Netherlands

*manse,* 19, 161

*mantal,* 202, 213, 218

markets, 6, 54–55, 61, 75–77, 92, 99, 100, 104, 121, 125, 160, 174, 199, 234

*Marschhufendorf,* 22, 96, 164

Marx, Karl, 3, 239

Meitzen, August, 3–4, 31, 40

modernization theories, 236–37

Netherlands, 90–123; agrarian change (late medieval and early modern), 97–108; the agricultural revolution, 111–13; change in farm sizes, 106–7; change in labor relations, 107–8; ecology, population, and markets, 91–92; field systems, 92–97; legal and financial institutions, 118–21; the marketplaces of Europe, 121; monetary policy, 117–18; political decentralization and democracy, 113–17; revolt against Spain, 105–6; textile industry, 108–11; trade and industry, 99

new institutional economic theory, 8–9, 46–52, 237–38

Norfolk, 59, 64, 70, 81, 83, 86, 89, 90; Norfolk fourcourse, 82, 89. *See also* agricultural technology, crop rotations

Normandy, 22, 25, 29, 30, 44, 133, 138–39, 141, 146, 149, 152, 156, 231

North, Douglass, 47–48, 55–56, 84, 86–87, 237–38

Parliament (England), 79, 86, 88, 224
pasture farming, 24, 62–64, 69, 71, 78, 103, 107, 133, 139, 146, 170, 175, 177, 185, 206–7, 210, 217, 222
*pays d'élection,* 153
population. *See* demography
prices, control of, 152
Provincial codes (Sweden), 200, 202

*reduktion,* 214–16, 225
refeudalization, 177–81, 182, 195
religious beliefs, 65, 116
revolts, 79, 97, 144
*Riksdag* (Sweden), 224–25
Rösener, Werner, 167
*Rundling,* 165
rural prosperity, 13, 69, 72–73, 74, 175–76, 217, 229

scattering, 32–33
serfs, 26, 65, 95–96, 100, 107, 129, 131, 177–78, 181
*solskifte,* 17, 29, 35, 202
States-General (United Provinces), 115–16
*Strassendorf,* 22, 164
Sweden, 196–229; agrarian change (late medieval and early modern periods), 205–21; the agricultural revolution, 221–23; coinage, 227–29; domestic industry, 219–20; ecology, population and markets, 198–99; field systems, 199–205; state institutions, 223–27. *See also* enclosure; *reduktion*

taxation, 53, 56, 87, 111, 114, 117, 137–39, 150–51, 211, 213, 223, 225, 235; *cadastres,* 137; *gabelle,* 135, 152; *taille,* 135, 150–51, 155; tolls, 152, 160, 212, 224
tenancy, nature of, 13, 66, 69, 72, 95, 107–8, 141–42, 175; copyhold (England), 72; sharecropping, 108, 141–42, 146
Teutonic knights, 171, 193
Thirsk, Joan, 20, 33–34
transaction costs, 8, 47–48, 52, 55, 85–86, 113, 142, 154, 192, 223, 237–38
Tudors, 86, 104

urbanization, 7, 92, 99, 103, 126, 135, 160, 188, 209

villeins. *See* serfs
voting rights, 96

*Waldhufendorf,* 22, 164
Wallerstein, Immanuel, 237
warfare, 56, 87–88, 102, 104, 105, 148, 193–94, 235; Frondes (France), 150; Hundred Years' War, 110, 149; Revolt against Spain, 105; Thirty Years' War, 150, 184–86, 192, 194, 212; Wars of Religion (France), 142, 149
water authorities (Netherlands), 97
*Weiler,* 165